"Humankind has not woven the web of life.
We are but one thread within it.
Whatever we do to the web, we do to ourselves.
All things are bound together.
All things connect."

- Chief Seattle

"Two are better than one;
because they have a good return for their work;
If one falls down, his friend can help him up.
But pity the man who falls
and has no one to help him up!
Also, if two lie down together, they will keep warm,
But how can one keep warm alone?
Though one may be overpowered,
two can defend themselves.
A cord of three strands
is not quickly broken."

- Ecclesiastes 4:9-12. (NIV)

Dedicated to

the millions of children
whose brain destiny
was determined
before they
took their very first breath.

BRAIDED CORD

Tough Times In and Out

By Liz Kulp

Better Endings New Beginnings

Minneapolis, Minnesota

Braided Cord

Tough Times In and Out

Published by:

Better Endings New Beginnings

www.betterendings.org

Printed in United States of America

ISBN 978-0-9842007-1-9

Library of Congress Control Number: 2010923349

ACKNOWLEDGEMENTS

My 12 Strand Cord Team

A SPECIAL THANK YOU TO MY CURRENT AND EVER CHANGING
BRAIDED CORD CREW and THOSE WHOSE STRAND
IN MY LIFE IS COMPLETE

FAMILY

My parents – Karl and Jodee Kulp, my extended family – Norman and Beverly Benson, Jill Behnke, Dana and Charlie Berg, and Dan and Carrie Benson. My birth parents who gave me life.

FRIENDS

Vicki and Jerry Ness, and Liv Horneland, my prayer warriors; Leslie and Donnie Samuels, my church leaders; Anna Watkins, sister of my heart; David Magnuson, brother of my heart; Ann Yurcek, mom when I need another; Kathy and Jeff Haley, my parent's support crew, AJ Jenkins, Trauma T & Regina, Dave Gonzales musicians who believed in me.

EDUCATORS

PEASE Academy – Mike Durschlag, Osseo Senior High School – Karen Gallagher, Osseo Secondary Transition Center – Deanna Berge.

JUDICIAL

Brooklyn Park Police, Brooklyn Center Police, New Hope Police, Minneapolis Police, Hennepin County Judges, Hennepin County Public Defenders,

HEALTH

Native American Community Clinic – Dr. Lori Banacek, Dr. Lydia Caros; University of Minnesota – Dr. Pinian Chang; Health Partners – Dr. Scott Oakman; Hennepin County Detox – Gary Wick; Vinland Center – Candy Dostal; and the staff at MeadowCreek, Hennepin County Detox, Hennepin County Medical Center, North Memorial Hospital, Southdale Fairview Hospital, Methodist Hospital, Merit Care Fargo Moohead,

SOCIAL SERVICES

Grandma's Place – Karen Johnson; Opportunity Partners – Billie Caldwell; Hennepin County Adoption – Cathy Bruer-Thompson; Hennepin County Mental Health

EMPLOYMENT

Osseo Secondary Transition Center – David Andell, Placement Partners – Ann Marie Ransom, Minnesota Workforce – Amy Veeches, Goodwill Industries – Trish, Alan and Jill and Rise – Peggy Kramer.

CRITTERS

Dogs – Abraham, Isak, Josef, Beki, Bonnie, Makone, Limey, Pinky, Lana, Mak II and the other five little puppies; Cats – LaKiesha; Birds – Sonny, Midnight, Limon, Secret, Tell, Precious, Cario I, Cario II; Guinea Pigs - Mo, Greedy I, Greedy II, Tiger

ABOUT
FASD
FETAL ALCOHOL SPECTRUM DISORDERS
chapter written by Anna Watkins (sister)

With unashamed honesty, Liz Kulp, once again opens the closed doors many families face daily loving human beings with complex neurological, emotional, cognitive, and behavioral damage. Beaten. Made fun of and shunned. Kicked and contained, Liz puts a face on fetal alcohol spectrum disorders (FASD) for the tens of thousands of US babies born each year.

I grew up with Liz, she is my heart sister and I lived in the Kulp house for almost five years. I was no easy teenager. And blend Liz and I together. World, you best just watch out. Karl's strength balances Jodee's nurturing. It is a healthy place to safely grow. They changed my future because of how they parented me and Liz changed me as a woman.

Liz adds reality to the adult lives of hundreds of thousands of adults who spend their lives in prisons, institutions or life on the street. She exposes what can happen once childhood is over.

Today, I am a personal care attendant for young children with FASD. When their mother 'warned me' about their behaviors and disability, I laughed. I told her that was no problem, my best friend of eleven years has FASD. But, the reality of friendship differs vastly from the caring for another human being with FASD. The struggle these tiny children face minute-by-minute and the dedication and stamina of their adoptive parents put forth in love, structure and research is to be commended. The rages of these little ones when life overwhelms and frustrates them is not a simple temper tantrum, they are brainstorms.

The responsibility of bearing a child is humongous.

Today, I carry a developing child under my heart. A study by Kaminski (1992) suggests that drinking one or more alcoholic beverages (1.5 oz. distilled spirits, 5 oz. wine or 12 oz. beer) per day was linked to increased risk of growth problems in infants.

How much alcohol really harms a baby?

When is alcohol the most harmful to a fetus?

These questions are still not answered and I "REFUSE" to take such a risk when valuable and precious cells are growing each second! I really don't have the capability to know which ones I can kill. My child's father is already protecting me and our tiny growing daughter.

We are committed to give our child a life of quality.

Preparing for this new human being is exciting. We have

changed our lifestyle to eating well, limiting my stress and gentle loving. Our adventure together to "celebrate a sober pregnancy" began because of my sister, Liz, who stands in her sobriety with us.

Friends call me to party, I decline the invitation. Radio advertisements offer club excitement with free ladies drink nights. I avoid them along with holiday drink recipes filled with alcohol. Dustin stood for "our sobriety" even on New Years Eve!

Our child will have the best start.

It is our job to provide that.

I dare you.

I double dare you to

"Raise the Standard"

in Building Better Baby Brains.

FASD is a life-long, 100% preventable birth defect.

Each and every baby deserves to be kindled in a womb that is alcohol and chemical free.

Who is willing to stand alongside pregnant women in celebration of sobriety?

If we can do it, so can you!

Liz's forever sister

Anna Watkins-Homsey

PRE
FAS

This chapter written by Jodee and Karl Kulp
(Liz's adoptive parents)

ver thirty years ago Karl and I met over a discussion of fishing. While it didn't take long to discover we both sought challenges and adventures, we soon realized that two very independent people were going to have two very different opinions. We agreed to disagree. Often our understanding, or more to the point, misunderstandings were due to our strong differences. Yet, it was in these differences that balance became our stronghold. We kept our individual personalities, ideals and opinions on each bank as we clasped hands over the tumultuous waters of the children under our care by building a bridge. We knelt together clearing a storm's debris and stood side-by-side to fix the damage. Our patience was seasoned in wisdom as those we cared for fell prey to life and nature. Respect expanded to hold the diversity of little stomping feet as they crossed into adulthood.

We believe children are worthy of being loved and it is when you feel loved you have the power to grow by the ignition of trust. It is trust that blazes healthy change. We thank these children, birthed to others, who strengthened us, teaching us that love does not always heal the one being loved.

Before we shared children, we shared the depths of the seas, the dance of the skies, and white water wilderness. When we chose to add children we joined the ranks of the many loving foster, adoptive and kinship families and learned quickly that loving other people's children was a team effort of respect for the whole; the child, their families and ourselves.

Choosing to love took us to places of deep understanding. We learneChoosing to love took us to places of deep understanding. We learned that love often makes a big mess and in the process of mistakes, hopefully, done in the right spirit we gain wisdom. For young people, adult transition is a growing process that each of us stumbles through.

In 1987, we adopted, our foster daughter, Liz, a colorful and dynamic little person filled with songs and dances and jabber, jabber, jabber. Unknown to the adoption agency or her new family, Liz had fetal alcohol spectrum disorders (FASD). It took until age 12.5 to receive a medical diagnosis of fetal alcohol FASD with hidden biochemical, neurological, and physical differences due to alcohol consumption during her development in the womb. We were told; this damage to our precious daughter was irreparable and we accepted our daughter's differences and the challenges they offered. We chose to love her unconditionally while she filled our lives with unexpected bursts of behavioral surprises

As we got to know Liz, we realized that though her intelligence and abilities differed from the other children we had guided in growing, her mind was alive and vibrant. Our daughter is a capable human being with significant life challenges, differently-abled and whole. misinterpreted. We chose to learn all we could about this disability.

Our daughter, Liz, fell in her beginning adulthood. She was hurt repeatedly. Her heart stopped and she was defibrated with her blood alcohol level at .48. Without the ability of understanding cause and effect and without the skills of generalization, she believed nothing was "her fault." In Liz's mind, life happens "to her" regardless if she triggers it with her actions. The acceptance of responsibility for the risk she put on her life was nill and we discovered saving her from her mistakes when she was no longer accepting our guidance or teaching prolonged everyone's agony. She learns on-the-spot over many repetitions and it is a very sticky process. Luckily, we had over twenty years of practice loving Liz, before she jumped us into her adult FASlane.

In the late 1980's, Michael Dorris released his book, "The Broken Cord", written about his experiences as an adoptive father with his son, Adam, who he discovered had fetal alcohol syndrome. His book introduced this 100% preventable disability to the general public. The book won 1989 National Book Critics Circle Award for General Nonfiction and helped provoke Congress to approve legislation to warn of the dangers of drinking alcohol during pregnancy. His "broken cord" term meant a lifetime of permanent brain differences. Some say, Liz began life with a "Broken Cord" as tens of thousands of babies do each year. But, we learned that even though one person's cord may be broken, the family and community cord does not need to break. But, we learned that even though one person's cord may be broken, the family and community cord does not need to break. Our cords can braid into Liz's life to smooth the chaotic, missing or fragmented parts and pieces.

During the summer of 1999, Teresa Kellerman, Brian Philcox and Bonnie Buxton offered us Fetal Alcohol Awareness Day on September 9 and tied a square knot with communities and families to help persons with FASD. As her parents, we tied and retied the "FAS square knot" to strengthen her with unconditional love, safety, healthy touch, nutrition and skill building. Her personhood was precious and her spirit was alive and strong. Her sense of humor sparkled and we honored her unique approach to life. We learned she was capable of most anything we set before her, tiny bit by tiny bit, experience by experience. We discovered, to our chagrin, our teaching methods were often the problem. In home schooling, we discovered Liz's mind is rich in perceptions and awareness, but filled with language, learning and communication differences. We learned to break down tasks and turn concepts into object lessons. We traveled, and cooked, and immersed ourselves in activities. We taught ourselves first, checked out the details and then shared by focusing on her interests and strengths. We back-changed to allow her the privilege of success.

By fifteen, we caught glimpses of the personhood amputated before her birth. However, the knot our family tied that held Liz safely in our home, as a child and an early teen, did not contain her once she was determined to fly from our nest. Liz used every tactic she had to untie our rope and she quickly ran off the pier to swim with sharks. For over twenty years, Karl and I have fought instinctively to help Liz. They say when you face your enemy you may find it to be you. We soon realized that if we continued to step in and save her we would prolong the agony – she would have to change or die. We waited it out, stopped rope tying and started braiding people with different disciplines and experiences into our lives. Our process of learning to braid was messy as we entwined friends, snared family and entangled professionals. Yet, together we entered into a common knowing that enhanced the whole. We learned, with baited breath, to step aside to allow for a new braid strand for Liz to grow. We had to learn to tolerate some behaviors to allow strength in other places. Sometimes we must see the truth before we can believe. Liz is simply one of many persons living with FASD biological and nuero-chemical differences. The words and truth you find within this book are hers sprinkled with words from Karl and I, professionals and friends who have walked beside us.

We share our "Braided Cord" in hopes that Liz's path and the knowledge we have gained will be entrusted to people wiser and more capable than we. Our 12-strand cord strategy, developed over those tumultuous years secured her – just as it does in mooring boats, holding parachutes, securing mountain climbers or pulling skiers up steep slopes. A 12-strand cord could be spliced and rebraided. Braiding could continue for a lifetime. It will take the thick wisdom of braided and compassionate people to build communities of liberty for our citizens with FASD. The process of producing Braided Cord, Tough Times In and Out has been a work in progress for Liz for over eight years. Reliving this through her words written in journals, poetry, rhymes and raps in addition to reviewing old medical files and correspondences has been very painful, but birth does not happen without pain. Her journey and the editing of this manuscript has touched me to the depths of my core self and brought me piercing heartache. No mother in the world who loves her child would ever want her or him to walk Liz's journey. And yet Liz's nightmare story is repeated family-to-family quietly hidden behind closed doors. Our family has chosen to reveal this pain to allow for new growth of programming and strategies to enhance the lives of our citizens with FASDs. We hope through our work as a family our actions speak, however messy, louder than our words. Her truth and experiences, whether we agree with how the reality played out, are hers without our filters.

Liz is now braiding the cord herself. This book, *Braided Cord - Tough Times In and Out,* is our daughter Liz's project. It is her wish to share her experiences and thoughts to help others and clear paths for persons with fetal alcohol spectrum disorders (FASD). Her voice is only one voice in this vast wilderness and the hundreds of written pages she handed me deserved publishing.

Karl and Jodee Kulp

Foreword
I March

was born an addict and ever since I was tiny I have over-
done, overlooked or overwhelmed myself. I was born
with fetal alcohol spectrum disorders, otherwise known as
FASD. That means my mom drank while I was trying to
grow in her stomach and because of her drinking some of
my parts got mixed up and didn't grow too well. My differences are hidden and that's a real pain, because it is easy to judge
a person by what you see.

The most difficult parts of my life are caused from my
brain which was probably the most affected. I have trouble
learning new things and I live in a world that is louder, softer,
harder, scratchier, noisier, shakier, slippery and more chaotic
than most of the people reading this. I want you to imagine
what it is like to feel the seams of your socks, the label on your
clothes, the flicker of fluorescent lights, the mumblings and
rumblings of every noise around you, and then try to learn

new things.

Overwhelming.

Yes, that is what it is often for me. In addition, I hear really well, but I am unable to always process what I hear. It is like the words gain a life of their own when they enter my brain. I am unable to sleep like other people and for my whole life, before medication, I rarely slept over three hours. Or eat like other people – I have always had a complicated and sensitive stomach.

My mom's drinking ripped away who I was to be and helped create who I am today and what I am able to be. If she had known how it would change my life I bet she would have made a different choice. But she didn't, and we can't change how things are. I am as I am. I can't even talk to her about it. She's dead. I was a foster baby and then adopted.

I am glad I was adopted. I ended up in a really good family. We did fun things. Mom and Dad gave up a lot to raise me. They tried to fix the damage done because of my birth mom's drinking. Some things worked and I am a better person because of it. But all the love and money couldn't fix my body and brain damage and the way I understand my world.

I know I was more than a handful.

I blew up their savings and lost them customers.

I stole their time and minds.

I stressed them into illnesses.

I used and abused their money and goodness.

I stole their hearts.

I love friends and people.

And in the beginning of my adult life I trusted everyone.

I trusted them almost to my death.

These were my tough times. I hope I am out. I am watchful.

Mom and Dad gave me a strong independent spirit that won't stop, won't drop even though I have been in really bad places and had really bad experiences. In my journey to become an adult I have been stabbed, sliced, raped, shot, beat, kicked and starved. I have been homeless, addicted and state committed. I have woken up on park benches, in strange places and in the ER room. I have had my life restarted by paramedics more than once. I don't quit. I believe I met my birth father in county detox.

At first, I thought it was cool to have the party house. People would come over to my apartment and never leave. I was put out of seven apartments in two years and by the time I was twenty I still did not understand how hard it would be when I once again became homeless. All the videos and movies I believed were real and the lyrics of songs I felt so strongly about eventually became nothing but cigarette butt ashes. When I had no place left to go, I was willing to live with strange men that were using and selling drugs. I've slept in living rooms, hallways, vacated apartments, and laundry rooms. I even slept in a black plastic bag to keep warm when it was freezing outside. And though the alcohol I drank kept me warm, it did not stop the blood flowing from my sleeve from the glass liquor bottle that had broken when my man pushed me to the ground. The ice in the snow drift scratched my cheek. The glass broke when I hit the curb. It was horrible and it was not the life I imagined. I didn't even have a piece of cardboard to cushion the cold.

I had to fail first in order to succeed.

And I failed over,

and over,

and over again.

I spun myself around in my chaos and at times I sucked social workers, doctors, police, counselors, teachers, treatment programs and hospitals into my tornado of a life.

My chaos always sucked in my Mom who stood faithful waiting ... praying ... for me to live through whatever craziness I created for myself.

Luckily for Mom, Dad hung onto her and they are still married! They needed each other during this time. I was a really hard case, as you will see.

If I could change anything about myself it would be nothing, because I have learned so many things at such a young age. It makes me smarter because I learn by experiences. Tough things teach me real good. I am more aware of people and the things that can get me into trouble. I am not mad that I have FASD. I am happy because I learned to work harder than other people do to accomplish even simple things and I do it just as well when I finally learn it and sometimes better than other people.

Mom tells people I am an accelerated normal, by that she means if someone does something a little – I over do. Normal is what you're born with, so I believe my normal is as normal as anyone else's. I hope I can help others with FASD know they are not dumb or alone. Being different is okay. I am who I am. If a baby is born blind, being blind is normal. If you are born deaf, being unable to hear is normal. I was born with brain damage so for me the way my body feels is normal and the way I react is normal and the way I think is normal for me!

My adopted parents gave me faith in God and myself. They held out hope when everything in my life looked hopeless. I think my Mom wore out her knees praying for me. She fought the heavens for my life and my parents braided me into their family cord. Many others joined this braid as doctors, friends, a producer, psychiatrist, job coaches, independent living skills workers, social workers, mental health professionals, judges, attorneys, police, paramedics, teachers, nurses, counselors and on, and on, and on, twisted and connected into my life. My braided cord is now a cruise ship thick rope to hold back my FASD.

When my adult journey began in 2004, my adoptive mom and I began writing back and forth like my mom had done with my teachers. We used it to talk. Sometimes it was on scraps of paper. Sometimes it was phone calls. Sometimes it was text messages and e-mail. She wrote and I wrote to help me figure out my mixed up life.

I am now in my twenties and my transition to an adult has been very difficult. I am a "survivor!"

Mom, Dad and many others have worked to help me. Many people with FASD are not so lucky - our population is very vulnerable and most of us look normal. People think we act weird, we don't get it, we make too many mistakes. Society's belief that you must fail first to get help costs lives and millions of dollars. In this decade, tens of thousands of babies are born each year in the United States, more are born in other countries. Alcohol and babies don't mix and hurt babies in all social classes. Live in my brain and body one day and you will soon discover it is hard. Really hard. Regardless of your color, age, sex or religion – you will be discriminated against. Discounted as incapable and misunderstood. Often!

In my journey, I have met many people with Fetal Alcohol Brain Injury - some were pawns in gangs, some modeled or serviced men or women for money, many went to jail or were committed for mental health, some called Detox heaven - many drank continuing their life of consuming alcohol beginning before their birth. Homeless, jobless, throwaways struggling to live. There will continue to be a lot of us who struggle in adulthood. Living in modern times with prenatal alcohol brain and body damage is almost impossible.

DON'T FOLLOW MY or THEIR PATH – It is TOO hard.

The message I give to teens and young adults living with FASD is just because things seem fun and exciting don't give in to it. It can destroy your hopes and dreams. You have parts of your life that are meant for giving. Life is so much more!!!!

My life was about to change drastically as I entered public high school. I had always been a challenge, but beginning my senior year there was no stopping me. Thank God my parents had an 800-Call-Home-FREE-Number – my journey took me to places that my was my only way home.

– Liz Kulp, 2010

Chapter 1
9.1.1
Toppled Towers

I woke to a knock at my front door and Beki, my dog was barking her head off. From 4:00 a.m. until 8:00 a.m. that day I was home alone, almost alone. It was just after 7:30 a.m. and it was the sheriff! Or at least someone who looked pretty official and arrived in a squad car. He asked about one of my friends – the one sleeping in my bed. She had knocked on my window at 5:00 a.m. to be let in and then curled up and we fell asleep. She didn't want to go to school that day and I had called the high school for her pretending to be her mother. I told the school, my daughter had meningitis and would be out for the day, but probably feel better by tomorrow. Laryngitis? Meningitis? I didn't have a clue. I also didn't think my parent's telephone ID would pop up at the attendance office.

The staff called her mother and her mom called the police for her to be picked up at my house.

Her mom had figured it out right.

Mom was speaking in Australia and had already been gone for a week. I had hoped to go with, but we didn't have the money. I even entered the Tiger Woods Start Something contest to win $10,000 to go, but the winning deadline had passed and we never heard anything before she left. I was disappointed and Mom explained that probably thousands of kids entered and even though my idea to share with people what it was like to live In my body with sensory issues, other people had good ideas too. She promised to take my ideas and share them with the people in Australia and I had helped her package sixty experience FASD kits.

Dad left that morning at 4:00 a.m. to catch a flight to shoot photos in Alaska. It had never been my parents' style to be gone at the same time, they always took turns or included me. I was homeschooled. Our family was together most of the time. Mom and Dad office in our home. Dad's employee was coming In at 8:00 a.m. and then our neighbor, who was my RN and nanny as a baby would arrive at 5:00 p.m. after her day job. So, that left opportunity between 4:00 a.m. and 8:00 a.m. for trouble. My girlfriend thought it was cool I didn't have to go to school and now she was sound asleep in my bed.

I didn't know about truancy since Mom home schooled me from ages ten to fifteen and I didn't have a choice to 'not' do schoolwork. My friends didn't know she made me work my butt off learning new things.

The police-looking person hauled her out to a lady who was screaming on our side street. I went back to bed without a clue that life was about to change big time!

They closed the schools and friends started coming over. Our house had always been the safe place for kids to come. And they came with booze, and weed, and condoms.

I didn't hear from Mom for five days.

I didn't hear from Dad for two days.

I felt very alone and so did my friends.

*

More than just the towers crashed that day. My life tumbled into a big mess.

After the Twin Towers fell in New York City and my life toppled out from under me I outgrew Mom's school program. I wanted friends, fun and things to do.

I tasted life and I wanted excitement. I wanted exciting friends and I wanted as much as I could get.

JODEE (Mother) - "Airplanes have crashed in New York City … thousands may be dead …" Time stood still as Australian's watched TV. "Pentagon. Pennsylvania." Silence. My co-presenter's son worked in the Pentagon, my brother-in-law and his family lived in Pennsylvania, all flights were stopped, telephone communication halted, not even e-mail. Silence. In the land down under we waited, inaccessible to the USA, in the gracious care of our hosts and continuing our presentations. Karl was in a similar situation in the State of Alaska. Flights were grounded. Communication stopped. Liz was alone.

A week later, I took the first flight back to the states. Carefree travel abandoned to M16s. The smell of stale beer and cigarettes greeted me as I entered my home.

I was glad Mom came home. I didn't know if she would ever get home and I knew I had been a bad girl. She looked in my room and saw the BIG mess. There were burn marks on the carpet and I was worried I was going to get into all kinds of trouble. The whole house smelled like a bar and Mom knew the minute she walked through our door.

She just put her arms around me and said, "I love you. I

am glad I am home." I took her by the hand to my room, "We can rip all this out and start again." She hugged me, then she said, "What color do you want to paint your room? I am home to keep you safe."

Mom couldn't keep me safe, just like she couldn't keep my exchange sister, Nina, safe. She died that summer in a train accident two weeks after she went back home to the Czech Republic. She had been my big sister for almost a year and I loved her. She was so beautiful. She showed me the beginnings of excitement and helped me understand things you can tell parents and things you can only talk about with friends like sex, drugs, drinking, shoplifting. These were the things parent's don't understand. My friends and I had a special church service for her, we danced and sang for her, but it didn't change anything to bring her back. She was gone forever.

Mom and I took all the furniture out and tore up all the carpet. And while we were tearing up the carpet, on September 18, the phone rang. It was the Tiger Woods Start Something program, "I won first place, Mom! I won the $10,000!"

Mom and I went out to get purple paint and purple carpet. Purple was Nina's favorite color. We got big purple flower trim and we scrubbed and worked together to clean up the big mess that was left in my room and our house.

Before my dad got home everything was beautiful again and I felt like I was not such a bad girl. I wanted so much to be like every other teen girl.

Since I was little I have always loved to do hair and make-up under the lights and the mirrors in the bathroom. It is a quiet fun place for me to be. This path I'm on probably started when I was eleven. I was a nerd. I wore clothes my mom liked. I did nothing with my hair. My friends helped me change all that and when I do something, I do it up BIG!

It began with the neighbor girls who told me that if I was going to be a cool girl and fit in 'all' I needed to do was wear make-up and have the right hair. They started putting their make-up on me using cover up, eyeliner and shadows. My mom had only let me use a little mascara on special holidays. When Dad saw me he made me wash my face. I hate washing my face, I really don't like water hitting my body, I prefer soaking in the tub. I was hurt and angry and decided Mom and Dad wanted me to be ugly and boring. My friends were looking out for me so my life could be fun and exciting.

I loved excitement.

They dyed my hair the 'right' color. It turned bright red like a Christmas ball. Then they covered the red with a really dark black brown. Mom wasn't happy, but the color was so dark there was nothing she could do about it and black it stayed for a long time.

They gave me all their extra makeup and told me to use it. It took a lot of work to use all of it. More of anything always seemed better.

Mom said I looked painted.

Do you remember that, Mom?

I thought I was pretty and your words hurt.

After Mom got back from Australia and we redid my room, one of the kids in the neighborhood moved in with us - with her mom's permission. She was at my house almost all the time anyway, and I finally had a little sister, Anna.

My little sister got a pair of jade contacts and they made her dark brown eyes look really cool. I got blue colored contacts. Actually the colored contacts made bright lights easier to see in. The sun didn't bother me as much or the flicker of lights so I made that my big excuse and decided my eye color was ugly. Soon I was hooked on colored contacts plus make up. I felt that to be beautiful I needed to be covered everyday, every minute.

I drove Mom crazy and I begged her for double pierced ear holes. She kept her 'no' so big I didn't dare cross it, but then her seventy-year-old aunt told me if she was my age she would have earrings along her whole ear. Mom let me do small doubles and like I said before - when I do I can over do. I doubled the holes until I had eighteen self-ear piercings. Each hole made Mom sad. They made me feel better because when she made me mad I just put another hole in my ear. I didn't even need a needle, I just punched any old earring right through and by fourteen - within a few months I had all the holes punched. Then she made me mad again and I pierced my nose. Luckily for me that was the ending. Mom said I had enough holes in my head, I had holes in my brain from FASD. She screamed and freaked! She showed me swiss cheese. And Mom cried when a few ripped out of my ears and left torn edges. The hole idea was sick, but I didn't know it then.

Once I set my mind to change, I change 100% for the good or the bad. I always think it is for the good until it's too late – fun, cool, friends, money, whatever my head is at the time. I hang onto my ideas like a monkey's hand in a cookie jar! Nothing can pull me loose unless I chose to let go or they take whatever it is totally out of my life.

I can go and often did go overboard with cool.

I tried really exotic hair styles.

People noticed.

I had color crayon red hair and black hair,
some days it was blue.

I spent hours making myself beautiful.

I glued rhinestones to my face and teeth.

People noticed.

I stood out in a crowd, on the bus, wherever I was. Often people called me by names of famous actresses, but I never needed to look like them. I am and was happy to be me.

People called me Sparkles.

I had no idea how much other people influenced my life and how my brain injury played me. Making myself beautiful was the first time I felt like I was in control of something. I knew I was cool. I felt like 'good for me!'

Make up did get me into some trouble though. I used too much. I used the wrong color and looked orange. I lost lipsticks and freaked out. I put make-up on light switches and door knobs and drove Dad crazy. I put make up on Mom's car and made her crazy. Make-up became it's own kind of addiction and from that point on I felt ugly unless I was covered in makeup. The problem came when it covered my hands and everywhere my hands went. I didn't understand why people got so mad when I left I mess. I thought I looked pretty and didn't see how those two pieces fit together.

*

I wrote my book when I was thirteen and Mom took the first copies off the press to Australia with her. My book is called – *The Best I Can Be: Living with Fetal Alcohol Syndrome or Effects*. Two reasons I did it – first I wanted to make money and second I wanted to help people know how I think to make MY life easier. I guess I did a little of both. I had no idea my book, *The Best I Can Be, Living with Fetal Alcohol Syndrome or Effects* would make a difference in my family's life. All I wanted to do was make money and help other kids with fetal alcohol. I figured if people knew what my life was like it would help others. When I wrote my first book, I sent a copy to the Tiger Woods Start Something Foundation to win $10,000 to start making a difference for persons with FASDs. I also put together a little kit to help other people know how I live in my world - there was a piece of scratchy twine to tie around your neck, a piece of tin foil to put on your head to change sounds, some beans in a plastic bag to change touch and a plan for creating chaos with lights and noise and a random spelling test.

There was no press or announcements for my winning first place in the Tiger Woods Start Something contest. The world was still spinning in the 911 disaster. They told me I had to complete my project before 2002. Mom said, I had to decide what to do with all that money. It was mine to make a difference in fetal alcohol spectrum disorder (FASD) awareness. I paid for a reprinting of my book and I chose to start a girl group we called the Mo'Angels with three of my friends. I bought my friends new matching clothes for the photo shoot of our CD cover and I used the rest to produce 11 songs.

There were four of us in the Mo'Angels. I first met Kat when we grew up in the same neighborhood. We started hanging together and went skating on Friday and Saturday nights. The next girl I met was Malica, I met her taking modeling classes. Not long after that on Christmas Eve 2000 I was visiting my friend and Anna came over. We became friends right away. Two years later she lived in our home and we put the group together. The first song we did was 'FAS Affects' to prevent moms from drinking alcohol when they are pregnant. We worked really hard on it and were lucky to get a producer and a studio to work with us.

Our goal was to have fun and we recorded songs to change kids' thinking. Maybe I could stop fetal alcohol! My friend's dad was a producer and he started to help us. We bought these cute little outfits that all matched and twice a week we worked on songs in his basement.

AJ and Dave really put out effort to help us. Especially AJ. He was always there for us, like a Dad to protect us. Eventually we were such brats that he quit helping us. Then Mom quit being our manager. Too bad, we had a lot happening, but we were really young and into ourselves. When I listen to our songs today I know I can do better, but I believe our singing and songs did make a difference in some lives.

What was I thinking? I was only fifteen! But somehow we pulled off things a lot of people with more brains and more money didn't. We were just four teen girls with a crazy mom and a dedicated dad who worked like crazy to help us have fun and stay out of trouble. I think they hung with us just to keep us out of trouble.

We did get the word out about FASD, at least a little. I got to go places with Mom and talk about FASD and how it affects my life. I like speaking with Mom and going places and being just with her. We mostly have fun together. I hope what I say has affected people. Some of the trips went really good and some were a disaster. There are people all over the USA who have experienced me - for the good or bad.

KARE 11 News came to my house to interview me and we were all on the 'Whatever Show," and then one day my Mom got an e-mail saying we want you and Liz to come on the Ricki Lake Show in New York to talk to pregnant young women. They were drinking with their babies in their stomachs! So my Mom, my brother David and I took an airplane to New York City and stayed in a fancy hotel and went shopping in the city. The next day we went to the 'Ricki Lake Show' and I talked to the women and just about all of them changed their minds on drinking. When the show was over we got paid $25.00 each and rode to the airport in a limousine. A few weeks later the show was aired and it was fun to see us. Some people even saw us in Australia.

After all of that we were invited to write and produce a song about Foster and Adoptive Care called "Searchin' for a Home" and perform it at the State Capitol. We had only thirty days to write it, learn new dances and perform. We did it, 'right in the Capitol Rotunda!' Then we performed it again on a cable TV show!

After September 2001, Mom quit home schooling and I got to go back to school with regular kids. PEASE Academy was a charter school for teens who had already been or were in treatment. It was small with only about fifty kids and eight teachers. Mom said that was good. I think she was worried because of the drinking I told her I did when she was in Australia. So Mom found a sobriety school. It was a place teens could get a sober safe education. Most of the teachers were awesome.

The next year life was busy with recording and hanging out with my girls in the group. My home girls and I stayed sober and drug free. Mom and AJ had some pretty strict rules on us and we mostly stayed under the radar and in line. We made up dances and lyrics. We spent long hours talking and practicing. We got the Prom gig at our school and we begged Mom to go to this music search and get this guy to listen to our stuff.

She did and once again we won. Mom said she was the only grey-haired lady in a room of 500 rappers! I think that's funny. The producer who listened to us, gave my mom the opportunity to bring us to Chicago for free auditions. All the moms and girls and AJ drove to Chicago.

My sixteenth summer was pretty fun, I had a little sister, we had the Mo'Angels and we were getting attention performing our music. We performed in most of the major diversity events in the Twin Cities - Juneteenth, Rondo Days and we even had a gig every other Wednesday night at a club for persons with special needs. We thought we were stars and I thought I could do just about everything. I believed I was almost grown. Me and a my little sister believed boys were the most exciting thing on the planet. We carried cards with our name and phone number and we handed them out to every cute boy we saw. We called them pimp cards. We eventually got into a lot of trouble because we had too many boyfriends. We bragged about being playa's.

We should have caught Mono or got sick or something because in the beginning of that summer we challenged each other to a kissing contest. It was always just kissing but we sure traded spit with a lot of guys. I beat her out by eight boyz and she scored seventeen! – Liz

JODEE (Mother) -
Oh Lizzie – How do I eva' stop you from such excitement!

Yo' I'm outta control. Love you – Liz

Mom and AJ worked really hard to help us, but eventually stopped working with us. Me and the girls were moving from working hard to hardly working and that stopped the shows. In addition, audiences can be really mean. We'd work so hard do our best. At one conference performance the adults talked through our whole performance. At another conference, one person said loudly to the whole world, "look at that tub of lard" and pointed to me. That one person's words changed my thinking about myself and how I looked. I began to hyper focus on getting a "really flat stomach" by doing 600 sit ups twice a day, push ups, presses and watching what I ate. I was not a "tub of lard!" but I sure felt like it after he said that.

> *Out of control, I'm doin' disaster to myself.*
> *I can't see it, but everybody can.*
> > *I'm damaging my health*
> *I say I don't need it.*
> *I don't want it.*
> > *But I need somebody's help.*

The Mo'Angels ended on St. Patrick's Day, 2003.

Chapter 2
Underestimated by FASD

People underestimate me. They believe I cannot do things and what they don't get is when I believe I can do whatever I need to. It is a matter of choice and focus. It is a matter of feeling safe and capable. Oh yeah, and hard, hard work.

JODEE (Mother) - Liz's missions to seek and destroy herself astound me. She is unable to see the end from the beginning and once an idea gets into her head, nothing stops her. Her antics are cataclysmic. I am again wading out of the swamp without sleep in dirty hair and snake filled waders. My mothering seismometer has been rattling and I cannot put my finger on when the next earth shaking event will reach climax. Sleuthing has turned up nothing. Something is about to happen. She seems to be trying so hard to break into independence.

I took driver's training and then I thought about myself and decided driving a car was not such a good idea. People get into accidents. Other people do stupid things. Sometimes I react too big and if I did that when I drive I could be trouble too. Someday I will have a car and drive, but not now. Not until I am better able to control myself. The world always gets in my way when and we don't think the same I get snagged.

My life is pretty much the same. I create my go to bed and get ready ritual and I separate myself from the ritual so I can focus. To get ready for school I don't let anything get in my way. I get up at 6:45 a.m. I don't get to school late.

This was the beginning of my first love. Finally, I met a guy and I just wanted him and only him. That was new for me, so we started a relationship. At first we never cheated on each other. We enjoyed the same things. We had fun and laughed a lot. We went to dances, skating, movies, played video games and cards. We even wrote music together. I never felt 'in love' with anything before, it was like an addiction. We were young and we both hurt each other with lies and games.

JODEE (Mother) - In the fifteen years, Liz has lived with us we have seen glimpses of attachment. She is still wary of family and I worry how quickly Liz becomes relationship dependent. In her first love her life is focused on pleasing her boyfriend. She is paranoid of making him mad. She left old friends to be near only him. He wants Liz to give him a baby when neither of them are ready to be parents. She blows out of control to family and other friends because she is frustrated with her relationship. He has begun degrading and treating her disrespectful in front of his friends. He gets angry when she won't buy him what he wants – candy, cigarettes, trinkets. She obliges and sacrifices herself.

For the first time in my life I finally felt love. He told me he loved me and wanted me to have his baby and get married one day. After seven months went by things started to go bad and he quit calling me and was never home when I called him. It took a week to find out he was using drugs. I was so hurt to be replaced by drugs. We called it quits and it was so hard. But it was the right thing to do. Dad had a meeting with him and told him drugs or the relationship. Dad even talked with my boyfriend's parents before he talked to my boyfriend. I hoped with all my heart he would choose me, but he didn't.

February 2003

Dad shared the positives — he even wrote it down for him to read later and show his parents — sensitive, kind and thoughtful. He is respectful to adults and good with his little brother. He is kind to small children, fun, helpful and willing to try new things. And Dad shared the stuff that was getting him in trouble — missing work, swears, skipping school, and using marijuana. Dad told him he needed anger management class and he expected him to treat me with respect and have a clean drug test for three months to see me again. We couldn't date again without his six months of sobriety.

JODEE (Mother) – Liz is being drawn into the masquerade of music videos, magazines and TV where the performers look stunning after hours of professional grooming. The call of Rap pulls her. She says angry lyrics soothe her. Her writings have become violent using the f-word, degrading herself and other women. She loves gangsta' style.

Dad made me write positives and negatives. Mom and I wrote the little workbook, *Broken Heart, dealing with feelings of loss and understanding grief.* Mom breaks things down so I can get my hands around things I cannot touch, or see, or play with. Grief is one of those things.

Mom wrote to me, "*A broken heart is the feeling we get when someone we love hurts our feelings really bad. The feelings we have are called grief. You may feel grief about the loss of a boyfriend or a girlfriend, a pet or a family member. You may also feel grief when you find out that you have a brain injury or brain damage, are moving to another place or have a hard time learning. People feel grief about different things. Grief is the way to heal an emotional hurt. Grief takes time just like healing a cut or a burn takes time."* The little book helped me understand, but it didn't take the pain away. I helped my mom write some pieces of it to help other kids going through this. I wrote this part.

I learn to cope

Sometimes the angry and sad feelings come over me like a giant ocean wave. Sometimes I just want to be alone. Sometimes I don't care about myself or anyone else. I know I have to keep myself safe. When I have a strong feeling I need to stop, calm down and think ... I learn to do things so I can cope with what is going on. I can eat healthy, exercise, get enough sleep and spend time with safe friends. I stay away from alcohol and drugs. I kept on keeping on.

*

Then I went boy crazy. I thought a million boys would heal my broken heart. But that didn't work. I got myself into BIG trouble. This time with my own drug use – smoking – cigs and blunts with friends. I met "new friends" in the high school sobriety program. How stupid am I?

*

I got a D- on my final science test. It was so unfair!

I told Mom I wanted to call an IEP meeting and let everyone know. So I did. There were seven people at the meeting and then me. I told the teacher it was his test, not me that caused the D-. He asked me to explain and I told him, I know about phenology, which is just a big word for plant and animal life cycles. I understand that and I can answer those questions, but when he asked me to 'pretend I lived on Mars and explain phenology to a human, my brain stayed on Mars and I did the whole test like that!' He said my test was creative and would have been better in English. My basic testing teacher asked me about passing the basic standards. I told her I would keep taking them until I passed. She offered me accommodations. I said, 'No, I am doing these tests for me, not for anyone else.' They don't get I will do the hard things.

*

JODEE (Mother) - Dear Liz - Broken hearts hurt really bad Liz. Time heals. I look at you and see a strong young woman getting ready to become an adult. There is so much I want you to know before you try this. It is a big world out there with many blessings and also much trouble. You have worked so hard to graduate. I am very proud of you. Soon you begin your adult life. Are you ready? Are you a little scared? I am! Love always – Mom

*

I quit going to church and teen Bible study.

I told my truth and found the things I said made fun of by some of the people in our group. They told my secrets and laughed. The things we shared was just for the group to know. The leader said we could share what we needed to work through and I tried. I thought it was a place to be safe with my thoughts and experiences. It was the last time I opened my mouth about what was going on in my life. I don't feel safe even there.

Friends said, "You drink on St. Patrick's Day." And on St. Patrick's Day 2003 my life changed again. I got kicked out of school — for drinking? I only drank one drink.

March 2003

JODEE (Mother) - Monday night Liz came home smelling of Brandy. Brandy and I have a long history. It is what my parent's drank when they tumbled into alcoholism. She tried to explain that she was kissing a boy who had been drinking and it must have gotten on her tongue and lips.

"Yep, yep, yep," she slurred. Her short walk to "be right back" had taken four hours.

I asked, "show me how big 'one drink' is."

She pulled a tall 16 oz. glass from the cupboard.

"And what did you add to it?"

"Nothing, I drank it like pop. It was warm."

She could barely stand so we journeyed to the hospital. She had eighteen months of sobriety since September 2001. This is a very unsafe and concerning use of alcohol.

I was so mad! What I didn't understand is that I told. That was the rule. If you relapse, you have to tell and I told about the alcohol. I got kicked out because of the marijuana.

I didn't relapse on marijuana.

I hadn't used it before!

JODEE (Mother) - How does Liz topple a world upside down and land on her feet? The next day, she went to school and because she is in a sobriety high school she got kicked out. Not just because of Monday night, but because she smoked marijuana on Saturday night and did not tell.

"Tell who?" She stated, "I didn't need to tell. It wasn't a relapse. It was a start." Liz told me a lot of things at the hospital. She had snuck over to her old (prohibited) boyfriend on Saturday and "Wasn't it cool that I filmed all my friends smoking marijuana. The smoke looks really cool, Mom."

We needed a new school and in one day there it is! She is enrolled in the High School of the Recording Arts. The school is like Liz dreamed it up...150 students, 90%+ mixed ethnicity, four sound studios, great teachers ... she will be starting in one week. She had just passed the states testing after her third try and took it again for the new school, passing. And a week off school, to boot! This is not fair! I wanted major consequences! They will not be performing the next Mo'Angel gig. I resign as their manager. I believe the words they sing must reflect their actions. I found the video camera and proceed to call mothers quite interested in viewing this movie. Liz, move over, I may not win every battle with you. I might not even choose to fight quite a number of them. But, I will win this war! Somehow you and I will get through this.

Mom let my little sister go to the new school with me. We were going to be cheerleaders, and rappers, and write and produce music. It was all very cool. Then, Mom shut it down and put me back to home school and put my little sister back into sobriety school. She said it didn't have enough controls. I spent the rest of the year reading books she thought were important, learning to cook, helping her clean the house and writing a 24 page report with drawings and graphs and charts and notes about HIV and AIDs.

I wanted to go to the club for my birthday. Other 17 year olds went to clubs for their birthdays and I thought that would be cool. Mom and Dad said a big, "No!" I packed all my clothes in a laundry basket, called a friend to pick me up and ran away. Mom took down the license plate numbers and called the police to go get me. The police carried my laundry basket into the house. What was I thinking?

Mom and Dad said if I do it again I will get in double trouble for running and being out after curfew. Mom talked to

Steve, an old guy with FASDs about what they should do to me.

I think I lucked out.

They didn't ground me for life.

Stephen Neafcy (50 year old adult with FASD and his wife Barb Neafcy - Jodee and Karl - My, oh my! Us FASD'ers sure know how to turn a person's hair gray, don't we! Liz is a high functioning FASD-Teenager. With prayers and support Liz will get through this. Now for you, Jodee, this is more of a challenge :o)

I believe this: Right now Liz is feeling embarrassed and that she really blew it with you, Liz wants to come home and apologize but feels running away and making a big issue of going to a club downtown by herself has damaged something very precious – your respect! I have been there and needed to be reassured that all will be alright. Not that you should let all this just pass on by. Have a family meeting. Discuss what each of you felt. What will happen in the future? Ask Liz what she feels she needs to do to makeup for this unacceptable behavior. Above all, unconditional Love is needed here!

Jodee you are such a fantastic parent and mom, Liz in her heart knows this and Loves you so much, I am praying! Barb is praying! Most of all God is with Liz right now! Let me know how I can help. When Liz comes home tell her that Barb and I Love her and we Love You too!

June 2003

After that I helped Mom a lot. I was pretty much glued to her and when I asked for a late birthday party and Mom said, "Yes, it would be my last teen birthday party."

I was so happy. Mom made me write my list of people I could invite. She only gave me 25 lines on that paper and only one sheet and then she checked them off like Santa Claus! Naughty or nice. I was afraid not enough people would come so I decided I needed to invite more.

I was answering phones and cleaning at a program for families with kids who have FASD and my boss said I could use his copier. I ran off hundreds of copies to pass out on the bus, at parks and in the high schools. I gave copies to my girlfriends and they ran off copies. We invited every boy that qualified as cute. Just in case not 'every' boy we invited came. I invited 25 girls. Years later I still run into people who talk about that party. I sure made a lot of new friends that night!

JODEE (Mother) - Dear Liz – How could I ever forget the biggest event in my half century. Thank God I got to invite 'my friends' after I found that little pile of left over 'new' invitations in the bathroom drawer. My friends, the police, were a nice touch. They asked me to stop the party, but with 250 invitations floating around the city, we decided it was impossible. I asked them to stop and check on things. They were friendly at 8:00 p.m. and 10:00 p.m.. I thought they did a good job saying hello just before midnight so no one missed curfew. It helped that God turned up the heat. 98 degrees was a perfect temp, and you asking me to make fry pizzas that then bake in a 400 degree oven. Brilliant. Too bad, we don't have air conditioning and we had to keep the windows closed to keep the noise inside. Aren't you glad I stayed busy painting the hallway steps, no one even tried to go upstairs. And talking to your friends with a wet paintbrush was a nice touch when things got a bit noisy. Everyone was so polite. Did you notice all the soda ran out at 11:00 p.m.?

Funny. – Liz

August 2003

JODEE (Mother) - Karl and I celebrated our 25th wedding anniversary by taking a cruise and left Liz with adults skilled in working with persons with FASD. Perhaps her shenanigans were a take off from the movie 'Home Again'. Karl and I realized quickly that once you change structure and control, all rules disappear. Liz put away a game we called Life and pulled out Trouble and Easy Money? She forgot Sorry. 'Somebody stop her!" I focus on the summer positives. She had a part-time job. She learned to ride the public transit. She quit bringing home drug dealers to meet me. She is learning to cook. Surrounding Liz with the right people will be very important if she is to do well in life. But who? I know I need to start handing Liz off to others, it is probably the most important piece to her development.

Fall 2003

My sister and I started a real public high school with 1,700 kids and it was like a dream. It was her eleventh school in ten years and she told Mom she wasn't a real kid. Mom asked her what her dream was. She wanted to be a cheerleader. Mom said, "Okay, then do it." She tried out and made the squad. Real high school was fun! Football games and hundreds of people rushing up and down halls who could become my friends. It had been a long time since I left a regular school. In cooking class I was bullied with comments about racial issues, sexuality and my disability. The boy hit all my pain buttons. He was not nice. I decided to stick up for myself. Watch out world, get me mad and you got your hands full. I saw the principal and counselor.

Nov. 19, 2003

It's hard to be a girl these days, it's overwhelming, not a phase. We put up an image cause we think we are not good enough and our minds are weak and not tough. Living behind it all, you trap yourself behind a wall. But only you can see behind that fake beneath your skin. You find yourself slipping over the edge. You're alive, but feel dead. Tired of the evil taking control through your pain. Overpowering your soul. You're gonna quit this shit and let it go. Gotz to take care of my health and get to know myself.

JODEE (Mother) - Thank you for the information regarding Liz's birth mother, it was the final piece we needed for her assessments. As expected with FASD her IQ score has decreased again. She is now at a 70 IQ with adaptive living skills at 55-65. The last drop was a full ten points. Liz remains in concrete operations. She qualifies for Developmental Services as she scores in less than 3% of the US population.

We have seen the disparity between Liz and her friends grow over the years. It is a sad thing. Perhaps this will open social service, job and academic opportunities for Liz's future ... looks like we may have a long twisting road ahead with this little tiger.

I went to church to gain strength after a really tough weekend and cried through the last 15 minutes. Karl was out of town. Life is harder without my partner.

A church member noticed "You look like you need a hug. Are you all right?" I was afraid to speak. Life overwhelmed me. Soon I was surrounded by people praying for me ... one ... "knows in his heart that Liz can control the wandering if only we would lay down the law with her" ...another... "You are broken now ... broken in just the right place so the healing can begin ... " I asked for prayer for my daughter ... they continued to pray for me ... "your house is in chaos" ... "if you were a better mother" ... "you must come under the authority of your husband" ... "you are rebelling against him and if you stop your daughter will be fine."

Do I join the 'wandering' crowd? Wondering what to do ... wondering if we are doing the right thing as we parent kids who wander off the path ... can't find a path. I add quietly, "I am dealing with a child with 70 IQ and FASD."

"That is the problem. You put your excuse in fetal alcohol. If you come under authority THAT will disappear." I shut my mouth ... "Lock your house tight" ... "do not let those children with issues in."

Where is the beating heart of the church? I love urban kids who call me for prayer... I drew in a deep breath to check what I was hearing. "Those children have issues?" My mind races through ... Poverty, dysfunctional families, homelessness, brain injury due to prenatal alcohol and chemical use. I remain silent, judged as making excuses.

I understand empathy is often impossible – even between families of children with FASD. None of us can walk in the other's shoes. We witness mere snapshots of another and pass judgment. Empathy without compassion or sent with self-interest causes pain. It silences my spirit. Where are the fruits in this rebuke? I discover that the word empathy was coined in 1904. I had hoped to teach Liz empathy. I will continue to teach kindness and compassion. We have no right to try to walk in another's shoes unless we can embrace each totality.

Parent of child with FASD - Empathy doesn't mean you have to have actually experience the same thing. That would not make sense. We could both be parents of children with FASD, but my experience of FASD would be different from yours. Empathy is the ability to see something from the other person's point of view. You don't need to have experienced something, but you need to be able to reflect on their point of view and see it as valid and relevant. It is like putting yourself WITHIN the other and viewing things from their position, improving understanding. On the other hand sympathy allows you to experience something WITH the person rather than from WITHIN the person. I think empathy is one of the most powerful communication tools there is.

Renae (Life Coach for adults with FASD) – You are right about not understanding empathy and about learning kindness. The young adult with FASD I have in my home at the moment is one of the most gentle and kind individuals I have ever known. I watch him feed clients in wheelchairs unable to assist themselves and it brings tears to my eyes.

Parent of child with FASD – We have been through similar circumstances ... people making 'heartless' comments about our children. It is out of ignorance for this debilitating, FASD 'invisible' disability. I share your pain. Perhaps the people in your church would like to know more about FASD, to 'support' you better when they know all the facts! Please discuss this matter with your minister—I hope you can find the 'strength & courage' to do this soon. Please don't suffer alone – people need to 'understand!

Teacher – Liz is doing a great job in my class! She has a great attitude and always works very hard. She has a big project due.

December 2003

I wish I could jump back in time.
I wish I could make my mind.
But the mistakes I made are already done,
> *now I am left with no one.*
> *No more love. No more drugs.*
What's left of me.
I have no more power except to kill my dreams.
Should I give up
> *or should I wait for a better day*
cause right now I'm not doing okay.
I'm on my way down an empty road
> *where there is no place to go.*
That's how my days feel, non-stop.
But I try to tell myself I be on top,
> *but it seems I just dropped.*
My heart is set on fire and ready to burn.

I tell myself, don't stop until it is my turn.
I want to get away from the life I live in.
I want to get away from giving and not receiving.
No love, what should I do to get some love from you.
I'm so lonely, why do I always end up with a phoney,
        cause a girl gets horny?
All I wanted was some sweet, tender love.
I needed you like I need a drug
        cause I can't handle this sitting here
        with reminisces of my first kiss, my first thug,
                my first love, my first dick.
Thinking about it now makes me sick.
        No lie.
                I think, I wanna cry.
                        And at times I wanna die
        cause living with this pain is no game,
        memories of the past
        I wish they could last,
    but then times are all gone away.
I'm livin' onto a new day.

JODEE (Mother) – Liz's abandonment issues are exploding. We walk in a mine field. We had hoped over all these years that Liz would attach to us, but that attachment is still insecure. At least we are a safe place for her venting. She stomps us and twists my words to fuel her anger to ignite rebellion. It seems to soften her confusion and heart break. I realize I miss the definition of her words. I can't be an ostrich in this. I need a ventilator to breathe. She sucks the air out of the room and so often her words leave me speechless. How will she ever survive the love conundrums of adulthood? I miss the definition of her understanding. I realize my world-view and hers are chasms apart.

Know what? I'm all alone, you are always gone, I'm trying and trying to reach you so I can teach you love with respect for each other. This love connection has caused a big effect on my life. I don't wanna live if I can't be your wife. I breathe, but I can't exhale. It feels like I am living in hell and I just wanna bail. Because livin' everyday with this pain is like a stain what won't get out. I just don't wanna live life not know'n what loves about. At night, fusing and turning my heart into flames. I am so fucking tired of your games. I ask God, please save my soul. So I can let go and take control.

JODEE (Mother) – Liz's is tenacious. Once her mind is set on something, she gives it her all. At the moment it is pulling good grades in her senior year in high school, but being in public high school as a person with FASD is also her downfall. She plans on getting an apartment as soon as she turns 18. We just learned she plans to graduate early, she has enough credits. Other students did that and are independent already. I can only imaging her life untangling. I see a future of swift destruction — diet management, idea for vengeance, need for beauty. How will she keep a job? How will she keep up an apartment? Karl and I explained it takes over a thousand dollars for the 1st month rent, last month rent and damage deposit.

I loved my senior year, I made a million friends and I learned a lot of things. When I like something or when I put my mind to it, I can do it real good. I got an A- in Economics and I debated changing the Constitution in Government to give rights to unborn babies. Everyone voted on my choice and that was cool.

I passed my pre-college entrance tests for business music school. Can you believe it?

JODEE (Mother) – We are mean, nasty parents. Tonight we intervene to stop Liz from self-destructing. I think we are in for a ride. Pray for us. How will she survive adulthood?

Then school set me up for my next step. I thought I would be done and adult, but no! – a transition program. It was the first time, I realized I was REALLY different. Mom made an appointment with Grandma's Place. It is an apartment with staff to learn to manage your life. I am interested in managing my life. I want to "live life!" I am almost eighteen! Adult! Free of parents!

JODEE (Mother)
I told Liz about Grandma's Place.
She asked "Can I smoke there?
I said, "yes."
"Can I have boys spend the night whenever I want?
I said, "I don't think so."
She replied, "that won't work then because I want boys over all night because when I am 18 I can do whatever I want."

I was not planning for a future – I was looking for fun. Adults told me – *"when you are eighteen you can do whatever you want."* I was counting the days!

JODEE (Mother) –I know Liz is just one of many in this country with FASD, but it surprised me to hear that for her to succeed at Grandma's Place she was going to have to spend a few years in major failure to rub down rough edges. I hoped between Grandma's Place and three years of a transition program by twenty-two she would be ready for some kind of healthy independence.

Regardless how much I want to slow the train to her adulthood, she will be legally an adult and my job is over. Without preparation for conservator or guardianship there is little I can do unless she wants help that we offer. I am glad we have this time at the transition center before graduation. I can't imagine her continuing schooling next year without this introductory experience. The music school accepted her in the lower level business program.

If what the professionals at Grandma's are saying is true, I wonder if she will ever attend.

Am I dreaming impossible dreams?

People who live different lives are different people and the space between my life and my friends going to college got wider. I know that the journey after 18 years would be harder than being a teen, child or baby. I gathered up a group of "friends" I liked who were exciting people with fun ideas. And they liked that I was exciting too.

Behind them I was followed and charted by doctors, therapists, emergency workers, police and even a couple fire trucks. The professionals and caregivers tried their best with their ideas, tactics and strategies to make a difference in my life. No one really knew what we needed to do to make a difference. I sure didn't. I was happy being me, and getting me to settle in one place of safety was slippery. Apartment managers shuddered about gang bangers and street workers and the excitement of my mission impossibles.

I met people with the same brain injury as I have and even though we were all different many of the things we lived through and the way we experience life was strangely the same. That was one of the cool things about meeting other people who have FASD. We understood each other. The stress of everyday melted away. When we were together we felt normal. But even in the beginning, I realized one thing, the kids whose parents treated them normal and didn't baby them learned to do tough things eventually. And those kids, didn't want to be protected. They wanted to live life.

I started to appreciate the hard work Mom and Dad made me do with my brain. But I didn't want to keep doing it. It seemed boring. I was full speed ahead!

School Counselor - Real life expects you to make the right choices or wrong choices then either reap the benefits or pay the price. When you don't see the consequences in real life until AFTER you mess up it makes life very difficult. Liz and reality are far apart on the scale. The best way is to stand firm (yes, you are right, everyone in the pool for this one) and tell her the truth (not what she wants either) and let her come to it. If she is lucky she will figure it out before something really bad happens. We can only hope. We can only do our best.

Teacher - If everything that she reported is accurate, I'm concerned that she gets both the medical attention and counseling to process this as she, at least in how she's telling this, just seems to have accepted that this is the way things are and it's not that big a deal. She talks so tough, yet is so vulnerable to victimization that I can't help but feel overly protective. She has an incredible heart and spirit. I don't want to see anything else chip away at that.

JODEE (Mother) - Liz usually does not lie unless she is scared of the truth. Her stories are the way she sees the world, when she does not see herself in an activity she really believes she is not a participant in the shenanigans. If a plan goes haywire, she is easily triggered and proceeds to do something horrific to make up for the loss of her plan. We will all have to work together. Her understanding of her truth is what we, adults, will have to wade through.

Today I'll be startin' ova
>*I'm gonna become sober*

Not once, but for all time
>*I won't let my goal fall*

Instead of giving in
>*I'm gonna over extend*

My grounds, where I stand neva' again

Will I give myself to please a man
>*Girls think that they need love*

>*So they go to thugs*

Or start abusin' them drugs
>*"No!" I said,*

>*"Don't let the devil over power you!"*

You're just slippin' into hell like he wants you to do
>*Forget them boys!*

>*They don't do nothin' for you*
>>*They cheat. They creep.*

>*They can't even support you.*

They use, abuse cause you pain
>*till you're emotionally insane*

And you're locked up in jail.
>*Cause you can't maintain*

That's such a shame
>*He's got yo' mind all twisted*

You can't leave him cause you'll miss it
>*So you keep comin' back*

>*Cause one day he'll change — Ha!*

>*And you'll get engaged — Ha!*

>*Just think you'll be a nice beautiful wife*

Then I realize this is my life — Ha!

And I don't know if I want to live anymore
I don't even know what I'm here for
My sweet, loving heart is tore
and should be locked away
Till I can wake up to a new day,
wait for a new life
That livin' in be a stronger woman
Where I don't need a man
til I see the ring on my hand
But till then
I don't trust no one or myself
I just wish I could get some help

I made a list of ten things to help me change my life.

1. Try to stay drug sober
2. Try not to have sex
3. Try not to throw up
4. Cook Christmas cookies
5. Cook a meal
6. Make up dances
7. Organize my room
8. Do my hair
9. Write poems
10. Write lyrics

Mom and my teachers think I should see a psychologist.

```
Meeting notes —
Concerns for
interview with
two psychologists.
1 Addictive
  behaviors
2 Eating Issues
3 Adoption
4 Male Dependency
5 Relationships
6 Racial Identity
7 Transition
8 Future Supports
```

I am not interested, but I will go with Mom.

Chapter 3
A New Year

January 1, 2004

Smoking weed and drinking became a quick fix addiction. I mean it only took a little bit of time to get hooked. I fell fast and hard. I'm not worried. I'm over it.

True, there are some things I miss – the feeling of NOT CARING, being happy without having a reason and the feeling that all my problems are solved. But on the other hand I'm happier. I've been easier to get along with. When I was using I set goals that I never got to. I seemed to be focused, but I never got anything done. I was truly lazy. I stopped caring about other people and only cared about myself. So I begin this New Year grounded.

Dad drew a long, long line on paper and he said, "Liz, you have a big life ahead of you. This is how much of your 80 years you have lived." He put that in red. "This is just the beginning, how are you going to live your life?"

Then he had me write on the line what goals I wanted to accomplish by the time I was 18, 20, 30 and 40 years old. At 40 only 1/2 my life was used up and he asked me to start with how I see my life when I am 40. I wrote I wanted to be a rapper, live in California, have a car and make about $19,000 a year. He looked at me strange and said, "Liz, I think we have some work to do." When he says that it always means trouble for me. The whole next week after school I had to break down in baby steps how people do things - from being a baby to being an adult. The list included - feeding, money, bills, manners, rules, advice, emotions, freedom, health, speech, dress, support, teaching, decisions. I'd bring him the list, and he'd give it back with a 'that look's better, but I need to see more steps'.

Sometimes he makes me SO mad!

Then when he finally accepted my papers he told me he wanted a list of 50 activities that were good for me.

I was grounded until I finished ALL THAT!

*

I know I need to work for school and grades – Good grades. I am happy to go to Music School next year. I can't believe I passed the college exam for music school. Mom said, "Do it for my birthday present."

So I did and I passed.

I can't believe I can go to a college.

I guess I have to choose better friends, but making friends is not a problem. It is easy to make friends. I stand out in a crowd so people's attention is drawn to me, which I love. I have many things I like to do in my spare time such as rapping, performing, dancing, clubbing, partying, doing hair, writing songs, and just kickin' back with my homies (friends).

I love a good time! Friends that can get you into a lot of trouble. Dad's friend says, "It's your friends, not your enemies that get you into trouble. You're enemies don't care."

JODEE (Mother) - I read what you wrote. Thank you. I hope you understand it in your heart. I wish I would have known you would meet your "best friends" in sobriety support – students using it as a front to deal. The place where the school and we felt you were safest was the most dangerous for you and gave you the quickest path to new drug using friends. I am sorry I did not understand. I like the new transition school. They have a great attitude and really provide opportunity to the students to grow in understanding and adapting to personal challenges.

Teacher - I appreciate your daughter in class and her fine attitude towards learning and her work. I wish her all success.

March 2004

Dear Mom – I am very happy that I'm graduating soon because I will be more on my own. This summer me and my home girls are getting a crib (apartment) together that will be a fun, but scary experience.

Moving out takes on a lot of responsibility. I need to pay bills on time and have a well paying job. Also, when I graduate I want to get some more studio time so I can make my own album.

– Love You Liz.

*

Third trimester and I have started in the transition program. They do cooking. Some of the kids go to college and work from school. Some of the kids have to deal with really hard things here like CP, Downs or Autism.

I am glad all I have is fetal alcohol to deal with. People can't see that I have that so they think I am normal. My FASD does not show itself out.

April 2004

I was so excited to go to Senior Prom and my girlfriend and I got tickets and invited some guys who cancelled on us AFTER we were dressed and ready to go. We had super glue rhinestones to our heads, had new dresses and looked great. We couldn't believe it, so we decided instead of wasting the tickets we would go together. Then we got a call that my friend's Mom died that morning. We were bummed cause our date canceled, but that's not as bad as your mom dying. He was all alone so I called him up and asked if he wanted to go to prom with my friend and I. He said he didn't have a suit, but my Mom had two men's wedding suits in her car and one fit perfect. It was kind of like Cindefella. We all looked great. We had a really good time. Plus my friend didn't have a suit for his mom's funeral and now he did.

We went back to my girlfriend's house to spend the night. Her parents were home so Mom felt it was safe. Little did she know the parents left right after we got there. Party time! And it was that night I met one of the people who would influence me over the next year in a really big way. This guy liked me and we hit if off. Then the worst thing in the world happened. My old boyfriend - my first love showed up - he was friends with our date! And he made out with my best friend.

The truth hurts, but not knowing if it's right or wrong it flashes in your face and blinds you from a love I was still on re-bound. Life is not fair. I put a smile on my face, but deep down in side I feel crappy. I pull on strength to keep on going, nothin' showing. I'm sick of time after time, you playing with my mind. I couldn't stand watching it and two days before I turned 18 I hooked up with a sexy, slick bad boy with the nicknames of Shishe and Satan. I thought that was cool. His nicknames should have been clues.

Duh ...

I was headed to independence and no one could stop me. When an idea gets into my head it sticks like glue!

*

Mom and I and my girlfriend, headed to Florida for speaking about FASD. Mom rented a car and got a place out in the country so we couldn't get into trouble at the conference. She was always in our space and watching us. Going to the bathroom offered freedom to meet people outside of the conference and when Mom was were speaking we met some cute guys who invited us to meet up after Mom was sleeping. They came and picked us up, but things didn't go the way we planned. They got pulled over and we got taken back to our condo by the police with a good long lecture.

We thought Mom was asleep and didn't know we went out or how we came in, but she was just pretending and we figured it out on the way to the conference when she said, "I woke up last night and no one was in your beds. I prayed so hard that the police would bring you home."

My mom is like that. Don't mess with her prayers!

Chapter 4
Allegators' Bite

KARL (father) -

When our kids are mad they will say anything to hurt the person offending them. The best offense to this child is a strong defense and they attack to protect the self and even the score. Many families experience this form of retaliation from these special kids. Families who isolate to protect their brain injured children are vulnerable to misinterpretation. The reality of an event can quickly blow out of proportion, leading to allegations and investigations. To complicate matters, a child with FASDs may believe their confabulations and administering a polygraph may not work because it IS their reality.

Our daughter learns by experience and her experiences in our family of structure, control and unconditional love held her back from her manufactured dream of freedom at age 18 when she could do whatever she wanted. Society told her. "You get to make your OWN decisions." We were told "she is an emerging adult, you need to let her go." When Liz called the police on Karl for abuse we drew a line.

We had parented her almost eighteen years, and we believed we did our best. Meanwhile media wooed her with sex and drugs and freedoms that in the end would almost kill her.

April 22, 2004

Dear Liz,

You have been having worse and worse behavior in

the last few months. Here is a brief list of your unacceptable behavior:

1) going out on school nights and staying after your 10:00 p.m. curfew.
2) loudly playing the RAP music with its filthy language to be heard throughout the house.
3) being completely disrespectful of both Jodee and I.
4) disregarding our authority over both you and our house.
5) being completely irresponsible about caring for our home by always having a filthy mess in the bathroom and both of the downstairs bedrooms.
6) not cleaning up your own dishes nor doing the evening dishes as we require.
7) not cleaning up after your guests.
8) not getting up in time to be ready to leave for school at 7:10 a.m.
9) calling late at night and expecting to be picked up, even though you were told to be home hours earlier or not to go out at all.

Finally, calling the police as a way to punish me for doing something that you didn't like is the last unacceptable offence and the issue which requires this action on my part. You need to know that I have the right to control who is in my house, and what they can do when they are there. I have the right to say, "You will not play music that contains filthy words in my house."

I have a right to require you to treat me and Jodee with respect. If I say "You are grounded", or "You are not permitted to do that", you must comply as long as you are under 18 and living in my house. You have always been allowed to question a decision that we make and ask for an explanation as long as you are respectful. If you question respectfully, then you can expect a respectful response. But we have the last say in all matters, even if you disagree with our decision.

Jodee and I both love you. I think we have demonstrated that this is true by the loving and very supportive way that we have treated you for the last 18 years, and by all of the things that we have done to help you to grow up happy and healthy, giving you the opportunity to be home schooled for years, and to go the best schools even if it required us to drive you there in the a.m. and p.m. But, because you do not comply with our house rules, and because of the behavior listed above, as of June 7, the day after your High School graduation day , you will no longer be allowed to live in my house. Please make your plans to find a place to live, to arrange your means of support, and to get your possessions ready to take with you. If you wish to leave things with us temporarily, then that will be fine as long as they are put into boxes so they can be stored for you.

You have a lot to do between now and June 7th. You need to begin working with your counselors to find a place to live and to find a job. I hope you will focus on getting your job at school done and preparing for the next stage of your life over the next month.

I do wish you happiness and success as you go on.

Love, Dad

JODEE (Mother) - Just before Liz's commencements I backed into sticky fly tape and spent the next 30 minutes with Goo Off trying to get it out of my hair. Life is getting very sticky in more ways than one.

RENAE SANFORD (Life Coach for adults with FASD) – Liz, It is so wonderful you are graduating high school and moving on to a new part of your life. I know your parents have worked very hard to get you there. I feel very proud of you, even though we have not met. Have a wonderful time at your graduation.

JODEE (Mother) - How do you communicate with someone who does not reason or put together the pieces in the way you understand?

We stepped out of the way of our wild thing. Holding her hostage to our controls and structure was becoming a pressure cooker. Too many families go bankrupt because of allegations. We had witnessed the carnage - loss of retirement, home, divorce, other children, professional licenses, and even incarceration.

We met with the social worker who left trying to determine DD (developmentally delayed), MH (mental health) or a combination of services. We have never had services with Liz so all of this is new, but we know we cannot work with, live with and love an adult Liz without supports. We were running out of time. The clock was ticking to graduation - we found an apartment across from Grandma's Place, thank God they have night staff. The area connects to four bus lines, it is walkable to stores she frequents.

At this point the money we saved for her schooling would fund the school of hard knocks. I went looking for a life coach to fill in the gap between our parenting handoff and approved supportive services. Liz wasn't listening to either her father or me. This whole process worries me, but I must let go. I guess one of two things could happen.

1. She will reach deep within herself and pull out the independent, stubborn kid we've always had and prove to us she is capable.

2. She will fail.

Either outcome will direct us to the next steps.

RENAE SANFORD (Life Coach for adults with FASD) – I am a community rehabilitation worker specializing in FASD although I am certified to work with all disabilities. One of the things I have found the most difficult when I train people is to teach them to set aside all their training and accept the idea of an external brain. Some skills are trainable and come about in time. In other areas the kindest thing we can do to support healthy growth is to manage them and accept that this is a part of forever life challenges. Each client will be different.

JODEE (Mother) - Liz has moved into her new apartment. She lives close enough to get to quickly and far enough away to not just "drop in." She is across the street from Grandma's Place where professionals understand this disability. We will take this a day at a time. I have found a supportive life coach to help her. She seems very competent and Liz likes her. Thursday is Mom day, we cut coupons, plan meals, write our grocery list, go shopping and then we cook. When she gets confronting, I offer, "If you are willing to act like an 'adult' I will choose to be an adult instead of a parent."

Educational report to Social Security

Teacher Special Education Social Worker - Liz wants to learn new things but struggles to grasp and retain them. In order to learn new material it must be introduced in vocabulary or with knowledge she already knows and then enhanced with the new vocabulary. It is difficult for her to retain learning and things she has already learned may be forgotten while she is adamant that no one taught her.

For example: she may be able to spell a word correctly and not read it. She may be able to read it and not spell it. Two hours later the roles will be switched. Abstract concepts are especially difficult. Learning in one area does not readily transfer to another area. She gets easily frustrated. Daily living skills may also pose a memory problem. She may have learned how to wash her hair and then forget how to do it. She may have learned how to boil an egg and then not remember how to boil water...

Bad decision-making. The two girls I was going to live with whose parents agreed backed out. So my boyfriend moved in with me the day I got my first apartment. It started out OK, and then he moved his friend, he called his cousin, in. And then things got messy. His friend moved his girlfriend in and his girlfriend moved her sister in. Then my guy went to jail! And I was stuck with all these people I barely knew and I kept trying to look cool so my parents didn't know.

For protection, I decided to invite all my so-called "best"

high school friends over and they never left either. So now I had a one-bedroom apartment filled with people. Mom had no clue who some of these people were and once when she came over she got so mad she held the biggest, tallest, baddest guy by the neck against the wall. She wouldn't let him go and I left cuz I didn't want to see her murdered. But she didn't die, she ended up talking to his father! After that every time he saw Mom he hid under his hoodie.

Things were crazy and I got kicked out of two apartments in the same complex!

JODEE (Mother) – The police have provided Liz a citation for immediate eviction. If the police have three citations in one unit in 90 days they loose the license to rent that apartment. I spoke with the police officer in charge regarding this. They feel bad for Liz being taken advantage of by "friends" but they cannot control it and they need to get the "hang out" OUT. She has made it very difficult for them. Her "guests" stay all night. They had an egg and grape fight in the apartment. Egg yolks are everywhere – walls, carpet, and window screens. Her dishes are broken and scattered. Not to mention the gang initiation of cracking a kid in the face with a metal chair, the indent of his nose screams. And the return of the rival gang with bat, sticks and guns.

Liz was found hiding under the bathroom sink.

How will I survive her?

How will she survive?

She refuses to return home.

Thank God we have Billie, her life coach. At least Liz listens to her. I know there is no sense in me getting all perked up over this. Worry on my part has never provided the impetus to change Liz. A true friend has offered her space in the basement with a mom on site – it looks like a possibility and it is 30 minutes away from her "new friends".

Then a "real" friend offered to let me move in with her family in their basement. Her mom's place was on the other side of the city and Mom had gotten me a Life Coach to help me make better decisions. I liked her. She was a good teacher and helped me learn new things. She talked sense into me when I was acting a fool.

Then my boyfriend got out of jail and moved with me! We lived with her mom for four months and then I made another "Bad decision".

I still had my life coach and she was great.

She didn't put up with anything, but she wasn't like my mom. She was a lot younger and she wasn't white so she understood things in a different way to help me understand. She got on me about keeping my stuff in order and having the right food and not wasting my money. She expected me to behave like an adult and work on my issues. After the summer craziness and being away from the neighbor'hood' I was ready to try life again.

Mom said I needed a job before I got my next apartment, so I got a pizza job and signed up for a new place the same day. All by myself, I didn't need help. One more time Mom and this time Dad helped me move to the next place. I was moving into the same complex where my parents had met each other. I was sober and my boyfriend was not playing with chemicals any longer. Things were actually going pretty well so I signed up for school at the transition center. I had started my adult life sober!

Mom and Dad were asked to take another exchange student, the little sister of another girl who had lived with our family. The first day she came she handed my boyfriend a hundred dollars for weed. He had been straight since June and that door opened right back up to his addiction. They smoked the whole thing together.

I had a job.

I was back in school.

I had my own place and I had a new really fun little sister. In order to get her needs met, he hooked back up with old friends and dealers in our apartment building. He'd send me to go pick up his stuff and once we were sitting on the dealer's waterbed and my friend put a cigarette through the plastic. We got out of there fast.

BILLIE CAULDWELL - Life Coach - Liz was very strong in her assertion that the purchase was absolutely necessary. I will definitely have to fortify my backbone when it comes to her wants. She asked me to call her today (for back up) because she is asking her extra house guest to leave. Yesterday I asked if it might be better to use her money for food rather than the cd's. She was not interested in this option. In the future I'm going to try and insist that food is purchased on Fridays and that she needs to plan ahead. I imagine it will be rather uncomfortable to experience her outbursts when this occurs. It's also interesting to hear that she did actually have food. She stated that everything was gone and that she would just starve. This enlightens me to the fact that it is often necessary to check her facts.

I will be turning in my Sept. billing at the end of this week. I will let you know where she stands. I asked her boyfriend about his intentions to pay for rent and food. He stated that he had to pay restitution before helping Liz. He also became angry w/Liz about the fact that I had asked the question. I know she doesn't want this, but it's obvious she doesn't truly realize where her finances stand. I will go over this with her next week to see what she thinks.

but she kept me and my boyfriend on a good track. When I met my new social worker and she decided I didn't need a Billie any more. I am an adult who can do my own life. And I agreed, I didn't think needed services either. I was staying sober and drug free even though people at my apartment who I called my friends were using everyday.

Then one day, my new sister and I went shopping and got roses for the apartment and a bottle to drink together on the bus. We drank the whole bottle on the bus ride home as we laughed and talked. We went back to my apartment drunk and my boyfriend had been using. He was so mad that I got drunk he beat me. It was the first time I had ever been beaten and I got this huge bump on my back. He was really mad.

JODEE (Mother) - I am disappointed the County does not see the need for some type of support. Billie was our life-line to sanity and structure for Liz. She was our buffer in a storm and we worked as a team. With Billie, Karl and I could communicate as concerned and loving parents, while we supported the structure Billie added to Liz's life. It has taken Liz months to develop this relationship of trust. A child with a insecure attachment is like a sailboat with a broken rudder.

What do I know? I am just the mom.

Dad found out he hurt me and called the police. Dad and the police came and got him out of there and I told them I would be safe. After that I started drinking to make my boyfriend mad when he made me mad. I quit taking all my vitamins so I could get my anger back up. He laughed and got turned on when I threw up and wanted me to do it for him.

I finally invited some gang guys over that called me their little sister to protect me. They loved drinking and it didn't take them long to find out I could drink them under the table. I could hold alcohol like a grown man and I was a tiny 5'1" female. I had broken up with my boyfriend and was under stress and soon discovered that drinking was the best I ever felt. I know it's crazy, but in one week I was totally taken in by the whole drinking thing. I didn't feel pain. I didn't feel scared. Nothing could over power me when I was drunk and cross me and I'd get back to the kind of mad anger I had overcome when I was a little kid. The difference is that Mom and Dad worked hard to help me maintain and settle me down. My new protectors liked watching me get revved up to fist flying full steam ahead Liz.

One time I got mad at my girlfriend over a stupid bag of chips and she flicked me off and I grabbed her hair and she grabbed my hair and ripped out my earrings and I ripped out hers. We kept at it and at it without knowing then the guys I called my protectors were video taping it thinking the whole thing was hilarious. I lost my apartment. I refused to stay at home, Mom and Dad sent my exchange sister back to her country. My boyfriend and I broke up. I drank to fall asleep. I drank to escape my problems.

Within a month I was seriously addicted and hiding it.

I probably couldn't have gotten away with this if I had Billie. Billie didn't play, she'd get in my face if I was acting bad. She talked to my boyfriend straight-up. We worked together on things to make our life better. I could call her when I needed something or had a question.

*

Mom came in to help me clean the apartment and get me out, acting like a church lady scrubbing the oven and cleaning stains, listening to my friends throw swears back and forth and lay on the floor instead of work.

I saw that look in Mom's eyes.

We all went out for a smoke.

She locked the door and we had to knock to get back in.

Mom was armed with brushes and sponges and a big smile. She "invited" each person in one at a time with a "F--" speech, "Since you can use the word "F--- for a noun, verb , adverb and adjective, welcome (friend's name) here's the f'n brush and here's the f'n soap, get the f' over in the f'n corner and scrub the f'n stain." Mom did that with each kid, all six of them and kept using the f-word for like twenty minutes. Then she got quiet and wiped her hands and said, "Good, I used them all up." No one said anything for a long, long time, until someone said the N-word and that look came back and we knew were in for a historic lecture.

*

Now I was alone and on the street and I was doing really stupid stuff. – ... *No one understands me, I was told I'll die like my mama. But I don't give a shit. Let me get hit! ... I'm prayin' for an angel to take me away to a betta day ... I cry hard tears ... It's like a stain, it won't get out! Misery no one knows about. Can I stay strong and let it go?* ... I would black out and then see tapes of what I had been doing. A black out was the same feeling I got when I had night terrors as a little kid. I would be busy talk-ing and moving and doing things and not have a clue later that I did them. ... *krazy lil' mama always in some drama* ... I would dance for hours or have conversations I didn't remember. ... *Sometimes I wonder why I'm so crazy. I guess Mama dat's what ya gave me...* I would catch the bus and get myself home and not know how I got back home. ... *refuse to lose, forgettin' about da wrongs in my life and I'm staying strong ... so I can live on ... tell me why, my mama died and no one got identified?*

I was banned from bussing in some areas. My loud behavior at the Mall of America gave me a one year no entry status so I did not go in the mall. I know how to obey rules – You can not go in the Mall! I was coming back home. My bus went through the mall where I needed to transfer. I was only sitting at the bus stop to transfer. I was told I was not allowed to be there since my year was not up. I was wrong thinking that and it cost me a $100 fine.

Bruce Ritchie, www.faslink.com - They can become the forgotten kids, the children that have nearly invisible disabilities. They have arms and legs, can see and hear, run, play, etc. ... They are the last children to be chosen for play and the first to be blamed. Their illness is not fatal, but a small part of their hearts and souls die with every rejection. Their behaviors may seem as odd and unpredictable to themselves as much as society.

I moved back with Mom and Dad and they let my girlfriend live with me. That really wasn't as good as it could have been. A boy had just taken huge advantage of her with date rape and she never told anyone but me. My friend felt really abandoned and ashamed and she hid it by hurting herself and her parents even more. Her parents didn't know what had happened to her and neither did mine. Mom and Dad tried to help, but we were too wild – we snuck out after they went to bed to find boys. We didn't come home at night and everyone worried. We slept at other guy's houses in the wrong part of the 'hood. We thought we were being cool. Our parents called us fools. They had no idea how foolish we were. My friend quit going to school and she was an 'A' student. The boys who hurt her kept going to school and people never figured out the really bad things that happen. My Mom tried to get her to school. Her parents did too. No one knew the truth. We just piled more bad behavior on top of her pain, somehow hurting ourselves was calming.

November 2004

JODEE (Mother) - I never expected to come to such a place of craziness. Even when I try my wait three days hoping life will change things seems to only get worse. I pour tears into Liz's old dog, Beki, age 13, and she is weary. She, like my daughter, could die any day. I need something to hang onto and bring joy back into my life. I would like to learn more dog training. I wonder, dare I say it, could a really smart dog help me understand Liz and FASD? What are the new methods for training furry kids? I feel strained with Liz's lifestyle.

I need a new puppy!

BONNIE BUXTON (Mom of adult with FASD) - I'm here for you. Been where you are. You're doing all the right stuff including keeping busy and continuing to build your own life. Please feel free to bounce things off me.

Mom bought a new little puppy and she is paying more attention to the puppy than us. At least she is not screaming at us about our crazy behavior. The puppy's name is Bonnie and she is really sweet, even my old dog Beki loves her. I pretty much gave up my dog Beki for boyz.

December 2004

JODEE (Mother) - Thank God for my huggable furball. As I work to train her, I realize how ridiculous it is for me to think the pup should have the my world view. How can I expect Liz, with a different brain structure to understand my reality? How can I expect my dog to understand? There are more people trying to train dogs, than people trying to help kids like the Liz's in the world. I wish I knew my daughter better and understood her mind. Bonnie is teaching me, in order to truly train, I must understand. But how?

I have found an organization called Dog Scouts I am thinking of attending. I can't imagine just me and my dog for a whole week away from the insanity of this life.

Christmas Eve 2004

JODEE (Mother) - Our children spent Christmas night together at our home laughing and telling stories of all the naughty things they did to us when they were growing up. Hearing their stories retold as young adults we wonder how we survived. I think back to my childhood and realize my daughter is addicted to alcohol. I know the pattern, I have lived it as a child. Knowing means it cannot be ignored.

BONNIE BUXTON (Mom of adult with FASD) - It's hard to come to grips with the fact that Liz is an addict. This is not her fault, she was programmed to be an addict. Often addicts need to go thru rehab dozens of times before something clicks. I can offer some degree of hope, our daughter is doing relatively well despite coming from multi generations of addicts on both sides, but there was a time when I thought she'd be dead of crack cocaine.

Chapter 5
Slippin' Back

Slipping back into the love-hate relationship
  Back to your old life
  Back to your first love
It's an addiction
You have like a drug
You try it once and its remains
  Drives you insane
  Bad memories fill your brain
  Can't keep your goals
    because your strictly out of control
With your heart on fire
It gives you the desire
To go back – there. I do.
Too confused
  I don't know what to do
Because my life was all about you
But once again you broke my heart
  Tore me apart
  Fucked my friend
Another lesson learned I have been burned
I learned I can have something better than you
  Love is hate. Hate is fear
– Fear is a lie about myself

January 2005

In less than a month, I got another apartment and I promised with my whole heart to really make this work. I got up every morning for school. I stayed sober – at least for a while and I kept my job. But then once again I began inviting the wrong people over.

In the beginning, I tried really hard to keep things clean and in order, work, go to school - - party. Then party took over. The movie the guys made over the big fight with my friend was hilarious to them and they decided to see how mad they could get me and tape it. They started telling me all this stuff this other girl was saying about me. I was pouring alcohol down my throat and getting really really angry. The angrier I got the more they pushed to amp me up.

Pushing. Laughing. Pushing. Laughing.

She said. She said. And she said.

I was beyond thinking. Mom and Dad always worked to bring me down and keep me out of rages. Rages that were for the survival of my emotions. My body tensed like a cat ready to pounce or a dog ready to bite.

Push. Push. Push.

Words ... And then she said ... Get her ...

She said about you ... Laughter.

Self protection ... saving face.

These were my protectors, the guys who made money doing things people don't want to know about. My behavior was hilarious to them.

Push ... push Liz's buttons.

The gun lay on the table and I picked it up to shut the girl up and all the things she was saying. Luckily a girlfriend followed me outside and talked me out of the gun. She told me she had an uncle she loved who was in jail for life doing something so stupid - I handed her the gun. You don't mess with this girl, she had lived through more garbage than you ever see on TV. I was so angry and in the mode for fighting, the combination of alcohol and anger mad me feel super strong and I pulled the stop sign out of the ground and smashed the other girl's windshield.

Today I wish I could take back things that happened back then that I was a part of. I wish I could say I am sorry. I really messed up. Everything was a BIG mess.

People who don't have a place to live or food to eat moved in. My floor was full of bodies and everyone was messy so I got messy.

No one cared about my things so I learned to hide what was important and knife the door. No one did the dishes and I quit eating with silverware. I made crazy meals no one would eat mixing things like marinara sauce spaghetti with tuna, or cereal with macaroni and cheese – anything to gross them out so I could eat my food and they'd leave me alone. I had to clean up after everyone and I gave up and became like them. Sticky fingerprints were on everything. And my friends sticky fingers were stealing and pawning my stuff. It made me crazy! Here I had finally gotten rid of my abusive boyfriend and I surrounded myself with abusive friends who did things I had never even seen on TV. They promised to have my back. Protect me. I shudder when I think back. The memories hurt.

JODEE (Mother) - Bonnie is a sanctuary when Liz falls into life's cracks. She licks my salty tears. She shows off to make me laugh. She is filled with dog antics to slow my heart. There is a sparkle in Beki's old dog eyes as she teaches house rules. I am observing this teaching. Beki watches closely to assess a situation, she stays calm and limits interaction to avoid confusion. If the pup is out of line, it is quickly and firmly handled. It appears she has a number of warnings to nudge the pup into proper behavior and thinking. From what I note it begins with getting attention and tongue flick signalling.

I had been working at my pizza job for five months and didn't want anyone to know I had a brain injury. I didn't want any special treatment or be put on front street with a job coach. I didn't need a sticky-note with "this girl is an alien" plastered on my head! When the management changed, the new manager kept grunting at me and giving me dirty looks. The old manager never did that, we had fun together at work and everyone worked hard. The new manager cut my hours from four days to three days and then to one day a week.

I had gone from twenty hours to three hours! One day the manager pulled on my clothes and called me a slob. She did it when I was on the phone talking to a customer. I got so confused I hung up the phone. That made her really mad. How can I wash my uniform more times without money when she cut me back to three hours a week?

She asked me to read the map and I told her I couldn't. She asked me if I was educated. How could I tell her, my eyes had trouble seeing and understanding maps? The lines and colors move. She thought I was stupid. I am educated.

My first manager told me I had to always leave by 8:00 p.m. and there was no overtime. When the new manager told me I had to work late I told her I couldn't' do that. I knew it was against the rules.

She told me "people like me shouldn't work with food. I said "Fuck you, I quit." You know what she did?

She smiled at me and said, "fine." She won!

JODEE (Mother) - Liz was proud she had a job ... management hoped she'd quit. She played right into their hands. With a job coach Liz could have navigated the management transition and remained a good employee.

Once I quit my job I didn't have a reason not to party and drink with everyone else. A guy who called me his "lil' sister' promised to protect me so I wouldn't get hurt. He paid me alcohol to be his look out when he went out to get his money. Sometimes he hit is big and gave me money plus alcohol. He'd make friends of rich girls and then visit their homes to get things for the pawn shops. It felt exciting to be the look out but it also made me feel bad. I never stole anything, but he used me like a dog to find stuff for him to take - in cookie jars, under toilet seat, behind picture frames. Sometimes I found drugs and he really liked that. A finder and a look out. Always being a look out. Life really got rough. Then a guy who sold ice cream cones at the mall moved in and became my bootleg. He was older and all I had to do was give him the money and he would bring me back alcohol.

I made big time friends with that bathroom. Once again the bathroom was a safe place for me – it was warm and small. The door locked. I could be alone. Usually there was a soft rug to lie on. In some of my apartments I would simply go in and curl up in a little ball and fall asleep. I felt safer in the bathroom. I hid my vodka in the toilet water holder where the flusher is. It was cold and safe. Life was getting scary and I was

getting small enough from upchucking all my meals to fit under the sink and shut the cabinet door with me inside wiggled
around the plumbing pipes.

> *Do I run the lie or does the lie run me?*
> *All I want is to be free,*
> > *but somehow that can't be.*
> > *I drink when I feign to take my pain*
> > *numbs me up like novocaine.*
> *Will I change or will I die?*
> > *As loved ones ask why?*
> *Why you always make them cry?*
> > *So I put my pros and cons together*
> > *I decide which one's better*
> *I pour the liquor out*
> > *To find out what my life's about*

Mom and Dad started stopping in to say hi and check
on me. My friends didn't appreciate that. Dad screwed the
sliding glass door shut. My friends really didn't appreciate that.
Now they couldn't climb up the back steps and jump out the
window to get on my balcony and get into the apartment. My
"new" friends made my apartment into a music studio. They
said I could be a rapper and they actually recorded. I thought it
was cool. It was so loud! That didn't last for long.

One night Mom and Dad dropped in really late – there
were fire trucks, police, ambulances and everyone was standing in the cold except me. It was really weird how they got
the feeling so late to stop in. I was lying on the floor hoping it
was a real fire and I would burn up because my "friend" pulled

the fire alarms, and took the fire extinguisher and sprayed it all over the building. Nice friend. Then when my Dad and the police kicked everyone out, "my friends" just moved into the laundry rooms and smoked there.

Finally, Mom and Dad took a week and went on a vacation. They probably needed a break from me! When my Mom came back she had a letter from the landlord that said "I had a violation for disturbing the peace - horn honking, loitering in the hall, smoking in entrances." I hadn't done any of those things, but my friends had. They also said failure to comply or remedy this situation is a breech of lease and my lease will be terminated sixty days from the notice of January 18 unless she chooses to FIX this!!!"

I had only had my apartment two weeks!

There were also voice mails to my mom from worried mothers who could not find their daughters, who had been busy at my place. I kept going to school like I promised and now even my teachers were getting worried about me because they can smell alcohol on my breath some mornings.

I went to a club with girl friends and they had a dance contest. I entered it and the waitresses brought me free Daiquiris that I thought tasted real good. I figured since I was underage I didn't get ones with alcohol. I must have had eight of them. I kept dancing and dancing. I won the dance contest. Then I went home with some guys on the other side of town and got scared when they got into a fight. Everyone went with the police and I was picked up for underage consumption. Mom had to come and get me and I was over an hour away. They gave me a ticket and I would have to go to court three times on the other side of town and I had to work community service at the thrift store to pay off the fine. All this legal stuff makes my head crazy. At least this crazy night didn't happen at my apartment!

Like since I am the person on the lease all the things that happened in my home were my responsibility. It didn't matter that they would break in by jumping through the fire window to my balcony. It was legally all my fault.

Even if I didn't do it!!!!! Yes, you're right, since I had no control over the people who said they were "my friends" I got put out again – but this time two of my "friends" started working my Mom and Dad to believe they were on the okey-doke. They told my parents, they would help keep me safe and healthy. It was just a front. They needed a place to stay and they didn't have money so they set me up in another apart-ment with them as my roommates and we were to share rent. She got the first month's rent and that was that. The rest of the sharing part never happened – they got a new place and our family got used again big time.

People survive somehow and lying got their needs met. Being sweet to your face and dirty behind closed doors works for a while. From secret to secret is how the lies began; from secret to secret you said you were my friend. Rent … tele-phone … cable …. cleaning … and one disaster after another … I lost my safe bathroom when I moved into the next apart-ment and the Chief of Police was the husband of my old Girl Scout leader. One of the first things that happened there is they pulled the bathroom door off so I couldn't lock it. Mom didn't really know what was going on, she helped her get a job and her car back. Then she got her kids back and they gave their kids my bedroom and let me live in the closet. They were doing drugs on the low, but I never let on to my parents. They would not have understood and would have just been all over my business. I didn't want that drama from my mama. Mom got into people's business. Now my teacher was getting into my business and so was the county social worker. I was still going to school, but now I was drinking more and my head was getting messed up.

A girl at the high school threatened me and I told the school I was going to go over to the high school and cut her hair off! They called THAT a terroristic threat and sent an ambulance to get me.

*

Addiction is blindin' my vision
    from the realization of no patience
    of my needing a fill a cavity.
Don't try to pick a battle with me
    or there could be tragedy.
I ain't trying to be dead with my head filled with lead
Or die like my mama lie sliced and diced
Mama you gotta get your pickin's out of my head
    our casket bed.

*

Reminded time after time, livin' hard, broken heart.
All da' mistakes I want to erase.
I get chills running up and down my spine
Everytime it runs through my mind.
It's not pretend, it needs to end, so I can breathe again.

*

My first ambulance ride took me to the hospital and it was lucky that it was 12 hours since I drank. I had only a

.15 BAC when I got to to ER. One of the guys working there thought I was cute and gave me money to get home and told me to drink a different kind of vodka that wouldn't smell. I heard later my social worker was really mad, because when she came to get me I was already gone. They said, I slipped through the cracks. At that time I thought it was funny. Since I didn't like my roommates' lifestyle I left my stuff at my apartment (that I was paying for) and left out of there. I stayed with a friend who loved to party all the time. At first I thought this friend was older but then I realized she was only thirteen. At least she lived with her mom and her mom was cool, so life seemed safer. I thought it was really good a thirteen-year-old could do what she wanted and weird my parents still worried about me at almost nineteen. That didn't make sense. We needed my 'bootleg' friend to buy the booze. One night at her house he threw a phone at me and hit me on the head. I fell into the closet crying. Her mother came and hit him upside the head with a fry pan and had the other boyz drag him outside. He hid in the laundry room and slept there to wait until I walked outside. This was the second time I had been hurt by a man and I didn't know that it was only the beginning.

Today when I think about it, I realize how mean everyone was to this poor girl's mother. I wasn't mean to her, but I did drink there because the mom let everyone drink, or smoke, or do drugs. The woman was obviously disabled and the boys who ran through my apartment and life were now running through her apartment and life.

What happened to the teen, with a solid dream?
Who won't stop for nothing
with a passion for flowin' dem rhymes?

Chapter 6
Speaking Out
Kentucky Blues

Mom is an advocate for FASD and she invited me to go to Kentucky to speak at a conference, if I stayed sober. I tried and even made it for a couple days before it was time to go. But when Dad came to pick me up for the airport I had slugged down a bottle of Tommy Hilfiger perfume, so I didn't smell like alcohol I drank the night before. It was 4:00 am when we left for the airport and I hadn't been to bed yet. We were at the airport so early hardly anyone was even there. They had just opened security and I saw the sign that said, "Do not carry lighters on board aircraft." I took my lighter out of my purse so I wasn't carrying it and put it into my sock. I thought it was kinda weird, but rules are rules.

I liked a lot of jewelry. I wore a cross, a crucifix, a star and moon, a six point star, and an angel necklace. I hated taking off all that jewelry and I always set off the buzzers so I just raise my hand and say, "Wand me!" and they do.

This time as we are walking to the gate, they call my name and ask me to come back to security. They ask me if I was carrying a lighter. I told them I wasn't. They asked me if I had a lighter in my sock. I told them the truth. I did. Lucky for us mom had a copy of my book, *The Best I Can Be, Living with Fetal Alcohol Syndrome or Effects* in her bag. She gave it to them and told them this was a sign problem and they would be better off putting an X through things they didn't want on airplanes. They still didn't let us go to the airplane. We missed our airplane because we had to talk to airport security, and Minneapolis security, and Minnesota homeland security. But when I came back home the airport had new signs with pictures and x's like Mom said.

Most of the people in Kentucky were nice but some didn't like me. They would point and talk. I wonder why people do that? Some people in an audience can ask you really rude questions and you have to suck up. One person asked, "How do you not get pregnant?" That was a pretty private question in front of hundreds of people, but I answered as polite as I could, "I said, I have an IUD. My mom and I decided it was the best idea for me."

After that I really didn't feel like answering more questions and I wondered "What if I asked you that question, lady? Would you answer it in front of all these people?"

Most of all I had a good time. I made a new friend and I did her hair. She found out she had FASD too and she is 23. Her mom doesn't hardly ever drink, but she drank on the one day in pregnancy a baby gets his or her face. Her face is a FAS face, but she is not as affected as me. Her mom was at a family wedding that week. Surprise, it can happen to anyone!

My friend is not mad at her mom.

She didn't do it on purpose.

I promised Mom I would quit drinking.

Parent of adult with FASD - How interesting …it is like Liz just "wrote" another chapter in her journey of life book. Thank you for letting me know and thanks for what you do for Liz…it is as if you are doing it for all of us who are struggling with this unique angle of parenting … your victories are our victories … we share your sorrows.

BONNIE BUXTON (Mom of adult with FASD) – I know how much you love this girl. It's impossible to predict the future. There was a long period when I feared for Colette – guess I always will, even though things are currently the best they have ever been. I truly believe that maturity can help a lot. Colette at 26 is quite different from Colette at 20. She's learned a lot of stuff the hard way and even people with FASD can learn some things the hard way. She's learned that there are basically only 4 people in the world who have her best interests at heart. Brian, me, one girl friend and her boyfriend of the past 2 years. He has a job and car and treats her well. She calls Brian and me about a dozen times day cause I think she's kind of lonely. We see her nearly every day.

I can't pretend to give you any advice that might possibly work. There was nothing much we could do to help Colette but be there for her when she needed us, and listen to her. I didn't give her any advice except when she asked me for it.

JODEE (Mother) - I hope the story of the lighter becomes one more example of how these kids try so hard to do right and are misjudged. I took the risk and went to KY with Liz … Liz has FASD and it is real and her situation is real. Not just for Liz but for many others - the untouchables and misjudged - the let's throw them away and look the other way humans. People society and social services give up on. Without a huge amount of tough love – which is not necessarily good for these kids of first learning – we don't get the paper trail to prove we need help. How I wish life could be more understanding for these kids.

Thanks for walking with me.

I know Mom hoped that by taking me to Kentucky, I sober up and she could knock some sense into me. I love presenting and I think I did a good job.

When I got home, Mom and Dad offered to let me move back into my old room. Dad said "my way or the highway." I picked "my way" and went to my friend's house without rules.

Then one night I got so drunk at her place I fell on the concrete and busted out my two front teeth, the girl stole all my money and jewelry and pawned it to get her boyfriend out of jail. I got rushed to the hospital and the doctor put me into County Detox. Then Mom and my teacher took me to court and committed me to a treatment program.

JODEE (Mother) - Dear Liz – I know this is painful for you. It is also painful for me. I did not send you to detox. Your drinking behavior put you there. I asked for the assessment. I agreed to help get you well. If a treatment program is what you need, I support that even if you don't want it. It may be a NEED not a want.

Only the person who loves you most will help you the most.

I love you enough to get you well.

Love always and forever and ever

They kept me in County Detox for twenty-eight days!

It was there – Surprise! I think I met my birth father. In an AA meeting introduction. Like father, like daughter. I was still going to school, but now I was drinking more and my head was getting messed up. If you put the lick before your life you won't succeed.

I don't think people realize that when you're living in my brain you're living in hell. Life is like a jail cell and you can't get out, no matter how much time you shout! You're outta luck and no one gives a f--. Ain't gonna post bail. Ain't gonna send no mail. I wish I could wake up to a new day and a new brain.

JODEE (Mother) - CAUGHT AGAIN ... This time her old friend called the police and turned her in. Just got a phone call and she is headed to the psych-ward at the hospital in an ambulance. She was hiding in a hotel room. I could ask WHEN WILL SHE LEARN ... I know the answer ... after many experiences.

Parent of adult with FASD - I AM SO GLAD THAT SHE IS SAFE AGAIN. The problem is that learning the lesson can be deadly. Tough Love is not for these kids. My son is capable when supports are in place - at home, at school and at work. Just because my son was not in withdrawal and never has been, does not mean that we have not experienced very terrifying events that continue with us today and will never go away. Each parent and each family copes the best they can at any given moment. I am somewhat concerned that some folks did not see the forest for the trees.

May 31, 2005

I'm still in Detox. One of the girls has been here for a week is in my room and we're real cool. I just found out we are going to the same treatment program.

The men in here are so horny they keep messin' with me. This one man just came in last night and though he is cute, he is nasty. This guy walked onto the woman's side and came into the bathroom with his pants down and all ready he asked me to have sex with him and I said no. He was so bold. I was learning this was a typical guy thing. It was so nasty. I told him I have a man and besides I don't know him like that. He said, it's been a long time and you know you need it. So come on baby. I still said, 'NO' and walked away.

I hope I don't stay here forever . . . they are waiting for a bed for me. I wonder what number I will be there?

At detox we are called by our bed numbers.

It is funny a person can become a bed.

JODEE (Mother) - Liz finally hit bottom and remains on hold in County Detox until they can find a suitable treatment center. Not the most ideal or pleasant of places, but at least better than the streets. Her birthday is tomorrow. Perhaps you could send some cards or e-mail. She could use an uplift. Everyone else has been released and some are already on their second stay.

Donna Bernier and Laura Nagle — KY Bluegrass Prevention Center
Dear FASD Forward Community,

We have been given some very meaningful insights from you over the past weeks, and we feel that it is important to share these insights with this community of people who care about FASD issues.

As always, hindsight has perfect vision. Looking back, we realize there were things we should've said and done to help the conference audience be better prepared for the reality of having young adults with FASD and their families sharing their lives and stories with us.

Here are some valuable comments that we've received in the days since the conference:

From a service provider: "The panel made it so real for me. Karli was so sweet, and Rob and Erica spoke so well. I thought Liz was a brat, though. I don't think her mom should've been shown as an example of a good parent. She has obviously just raised a spoiled kid that doesn't know how to behave."

From a parent: "Thank God Jodee and Liz were there. My daughter is only 10, but she's just like Liz. I'm glad so many professionals were there to see them so they'll finally understand that I'm not a bad parent."

From a service provider: "The young people on the panel gave me hope, except for Liz. The others were examples of what a difference good parenting makes. Liz's mom let her do whatever she wanted. No wonder she's having so many problems."

From a parent: "If Liz and her mom hadn't been at the conference, I finally would've believed everyone who's ever told me I'm a bad parent. Those young people who were so friendly and compliant are nothing like my two kids with FAS. My children would've been overwhelmed, and would've acted just like Liz."

The young adults on the panel truly represented the spectrum of this disability: different ages (with Rob in his mid-thirties as the oldest and Liz, 19, as the youngest), diagnosis occurring at different stages in life (some very early, some as late as teenage years), different school experiences, and different life experiences. Every single person with FASD is an individual with a unique personality, temperament, body chemistry and environment. We regret not making these differences a part of the discussion.

However, we are thankful that these comments have been shared with us so that we can begin an open and honest conversation about our different lines of vision into this issue. We have to honor and respect each other, recognizing that we are all motivated by love and compassion. We have to talk and listen to each other. We have to begin to recognize our own judgments, our own assumptions.

It's easy to say "FASD is often an invisible disability that shows itself through behavior" – something that we say all the time. In the real world, though, we know that it's not that tidy. With Liz, her appearance and her demeanor distracted us. From the outside, she appeared to have a bad attitude and a lack of social skills. Who knows if this is a reality or a judgment? We don't have any idea if she has a bad attitude and a lack of social skills – all we saw is a snapshot of two days of her life. Often, that's all we get with each other.

What we do know is that Liz and Jodee, her mom, are doing the best they can.

Service providers are doing the best they can. Families are doing the best they can.

It's easy to look at someone else – a parent, a teacher, a counselor, a social worker – and think, "I could do better than that." We've all experienced that kind of criticism against ourselves, and we're all guilty of having that thought about others. If we want to create a community of support, we all must commit to recognizing the judgments we make, and begin working instead to contribute love, light and hope.

We honor the spirit of families living with FASD, who have been told that their child's behavior is the result of bad parenting.

We honor the spirit of service providers, who are given a short period of time and are expected to understand the whole child.

We honor the spirit of families living with FASD, who have made a lifetime commitment to a child.

We honor the spirit of service providers, who have made a lifetime commitment to serving and supporting children and families.

Please continue to share your thoughts, feelings and insights. Honest communication moves us all forward. Thank you so much for the work that you do, and thank you for your willingness to be a part of this process.

With deep respect,
Donna Bernier and Laura Nagle
Bluegrass Prevention Center

JODEE (Mother) -
Donna and Laura
Looks like Liz stirred the pot. As I said that was the hardest presentation I have ever done and I knew there were a lot of strong opinions. I had already heard rumblings. Liz is the truth for many young people with FASD. A reality that opened my eyes to issues I could not

imagine and took me places I never thought I would be. I am sure that this is just the beginning. Some families give up and let go. Others hide while going through tough times. Without Laura's tender and gentle pressure I would have taken the easy route and left her home. Liz is having trouble now. But what is the reality? There is no pat answer to help these kids, but we are making progress.

Liz looked forward to coming; it pulled her off the streets and made a positive impact for her. She went through her first major withdrawal from alcohol. She had been drinking a liter a day of Vodka for the last month - Kentucky was an initial detox for her.

Liz was able to see others with FASD who are going to college and succeeding happily in their own ways. She was able to laugh at the funny issues surrounding FASD thinking. She was able to look at herself without judgment and without being surrounded by street friends. She began to heal from the alcoholism that captured her in November after being in a violent relationship with a dating partner. She was honest with me. For those things I thank the Kentucky group for encouraging us to come regardless of our present situation. My story without Liz there would have been more revealing and both sides would have understood. But under the circumstances I deferred to respect her in a beginning healing process.

When we returned home Liz had 110 hours of sobriety and our family offered to let her stay with us if she did not take one drink and come again under our standard house rules and structure. In return, we would provide safety, love and support. That lasted one night. The reality of this disability is that as Dr. Riley, said 'out of 1,000 people with FASD, 771 repeat the process.' Will Liz become one of those to repeat the process? Hopefully she will not bear the next generation of FASD.

Liz learns by concrete experience - two days later she was found in a puddle with .342 (BAC) alcohol, her teeth knocked out on the sidewalk, her face submerged. That was the beginning of real help. We had attempted seven interventions between school, police and family. We finally had enough paper trail. Since May 18 she has been in

County Detox. She will be going to a treatment center that specializes in persons with neuro differences. They are few and far between. It is court ordered.

Liz and I have discovered barriers of adult transition I had scoffed at. Families that I had misjudged as "bad parents" or "unusual parents" I no longer judge. It is not my right to cast stones. The path she has walked is not easy. It is mind bending and heart breaking to be her parents. She now has 13 days or 312 hours or 18,729 minutes or over 1 million seconds of new sobriety. Alcoholism is a hard battle for many. It is a harder battle when you are born with it.

She told me – 'It tastes familiar. I like it.'

Liz was given a complex birth package - alcoholism with a schizophrenic mother who kindly pumped breast milk for the foster home complete with alcohol, incessant crying and four out-of-home placements in four months, failure to thrive, SI (sensory integration) issues. Her mother's homicide remains unsolved (an area a drunken Liz frequents), abandonment issues from a birth father, misdiagnosis of her disability for 12.5 years, food allergies, learning disabilities, and not having the look of fetal alcohol. Liz has a lot of issue she needs to deal with. Kentucky was pivotal in addressing issues a therapist has never been able to reach, but a bottle did. Issues the love of her parents could never provide, but the lust of a boy broke right through.

Liz is not a silent partner in this pioneering journey. She is a human being with her own life, a life I used to be a very big "external brain" to. I still find it difficult to not direct and control. I keep looking for people to help me. Perhaps in the next generation those pieces will be in place. I was told to let go and to give her space. I listened to professionals who knew more than I. Liz has lived through beatings, rape, knifings, theft, muggings and alcoholism to finally open the county services that would have prevented these issues in the first place. For Liz, her new orange clothes are a breakthrough. The last six months have hardened and softened her.

It took her ten days before clearer thinking begin to emerge.

While in detox she has written sixty new pages of her viewpoint of the last year. I know she wants it published. It will not happen soon. It is a long journey. It can only be published when the viewpoints of all the people who walked with her on this journey are included - police, case managers, social workers, metro transit, teachers, therapist, doctor, county and public attorney, paramedics, friends and family. It means all of our "best efforts" of success or failure need to be exposed, to allow for new thought to help other families. It means we cannot just read papers and listen to words from podiums. It means we will all get a bit mussed up, our thinking and hearts shaken.

Then and only then will we get a realistic understanding of this population and their families who are so often misunderstood.

Liz is one, but she is one of many.

Thank you for letting us be a part of this discussion.

LAURA NAGLE (FASD Conference Coordinator) - Jodee – You're right. Liz stirred the pot, and really brought a lot to the surface for a lot of people. Service providers feel threatened by their sudden intense feelings of "what do I do now!" and parents feel validated and hopeful that the service providers will finally "get it". I am so grateful that we are finally able to begin this real conversation in Kentucky – people are finally starting to be honest about their own assumptions and biases. Thank God! We can't talk about true support and true need until we recognize the filter through which we see the world. You and Liz brought us something amazing – an opportunity to start a dialogue that is essential to any movement forward.

I hope you don't feel hurt or "kicked" by any of the comments shared. Unfortunately, I'm sure it's nothing new to you ... I'm just so thankful that people are sharing these "insights" with me so I can use them to help create the community where I want to live. Really, Jodee, thank you for your courage. If you and Liz hadn't been at our conference, it would've been the "same old, same old." That is certainly not what we're all about here. We want to do this right.

Liz is a beautiful young woman. I love her smile. She has touched my heart, and reminded me about what's important. I work with lots of kids and families living with FASD, and I've seen very few kids with a spirit as untouched as Liz's. She's having a hard time right now, and I pray she lives through it ... but Jodee — her spirit is huge! She's not squashed or afraid of her own power – which is a secondary disability that no one talks about. Liz has avoided that one – thanks to her fierce and wild-hearted Mama! You and Liz are miracles – thank you so much for being a part of the work that we are beginning to do here. You and Liz are in my thoughts and prayers every day ... and if you ever need anything, your Kentucky friends are right here!!!

Lots of love to you, Laura

JODEE (Mother) - Laura – Please feel free to pass my letter on to the professionals. Believe me, with a kid like Liz I have been kicked before. The issue is to come under the will of God and not break the spirit. That is my prayer for Liz, then she can truly be used. Hugs

RENAE SANFORD (Life Coach for adults with FASD) - Jodee — I know you and Karl have done everything possible to the best of your ability to prevent secondary disabilities with Liz. And yet here they are. I say this to alleviate the guilt so many parents feel when their child with FASD start exhibiting these secondary disabilities. I am beginning to think of them as primary in order to better help these young people. Just issues that crop up later down the road. Very few families make it without something. I've come to wonder, if these secondary disabilities are more prevalent for the higher functioning, look normal, have a normal IQ, but struggle. These kids integrate into the community more and struggle to find a place among peers where they are accepted and feel like they belong. In the traumatic brain injury (TBI) world families taking loved ones home are warned to be aware of emerging violent outbursts or mental illness to prepare the family. This prepares the caregivers to help loved ones instead of being surprised, blaming, or grieving if and when these issues arise. In the FASD world we still call secondary disabilities avoidable.

Over the years I have seen, even with the best of intentions and interventions, families reduce, but not necessarily avoid these disorders. Even if we could reduce the numbers by a third, sixty percent of these kids would experience some type of mental health issue. Accepting the reality, preparing for it and learning how to cope with it without self blame would do far more for parents than the naive hope it can be prevented.

LAURA NAGLE (FASD Conference Coordinator) - Jodee – I forwarded your letter on to everyone on our conference list. Thanks for letting me do that. I'm leaving in the morning, so I'm sure I'll have a dump-truck load of messages waiting for me when I get back. I'll let you know if anything interesting comes of this... Hope Liz has a good birthday tomorrow... Take care

RENAE SANFORD (Life Coach for adults with FASD) – Jodee – Mental health services are lacking throughout the world and the programs and services that should have followed deinstitutionalization never appeared. Too many families struggle to do their best. I would like to see serious work done in the area of secondary disabilities and the prevention or preparation for them.

Chapter 7
DUMP TRUCK
Dialogues

Residential treatment professional - Hi Laura, Wow, what an interesting response to Liz! In 10+ years of residential treatment, I have seen many "Liz-es" in treatment – kids that run into the same brick walls over and over again and simply seem to just not get it. Our answer for so many of these kids has been that they needed a higher level of care or detention to get the message because they are just too stubborn to change. Those who are willing to write it off as "bad parenting" or Liz being "a brat" missed one of the biggest points that this conference was trying to communicate – that kids with FASD are wired very differently than we assume they should be. They may look "normal" on the outside, but their thought processes are not.

In trying to understand the vast amount of conference information, I have to confess, I have thought "well, why don't they just get it? And if they don't, how do we make them get it?" It's taught me a lesson about the assumptions we make in treatment that our version of a magic pill to make everyone we treat better just doesn't cut it, especially if we don't try to understand ever aspect of why these kids act the way they do. We were in the midst of program revisions, but in light of this conference, have had to rethink many of our details.

Juvenile Services Specialist, Department of Juvenile Justice Hi Laura, I just wanted to express my gratitude to Jodee and Liz for attending your FASD conference. Liz was probably one of the best examples of an

FASD individual that we as professionals are likely to work with. One without the obvious structural abnormalities and with the extreme mal-adaptive behavior that these individuals quite often exhibit. As sweet and compliant as many of the other panel members were, they do not represent the average client we as court specialist, caseworkers, law enforcement individuals, etc. are likely to encounter.

Once again, please forward my gratitude to Jodee, Liz and all the other panel members for participating in this conference. It is proba-bly one of the best trainings I have attended in my 26 years as a service provider.

Maria, Child Care teacher, proud to call Liz a friend. Laura, I am ex-tremely thankful to God that I was able to attend the conference that the Village Project team put on. Countless times my mother has come home from work telling me bits and pieces about her days and things that are happening good and bad within the project. I think that I had heard about FAS maybe once in my lifetime before my Mom landed where she did, and now it's all I can think about. Though she did well giving me the pieces, I wasn't able to visualize all of the issue. I went into the conference thinking that I would get a little more information on what to look for, and came out wanting to ask you for a job so I could get things done regarding this issue. The conference was extremely informative and the information was presented in the real way that it is imperative. I get so sick of the broken record crap I hear stating what the problem is, but going nowhere about a solution.

The wide spectrum was well presented by showing the full prob-lem and showing the full solution. While this is not to say that FAS is an easy thing to deal with problem/solution wise, the conference made the issue tangible. Please do not get the impression that I am saying all of this because my mother was there.

I just want you to know that the conference had a profound af-fect on me. I had meant to e-mail you, but life got in the way. I forgot all about e-mailing. That is, until I heard and saw the comments about Liz.

The second I saw there was a negative response regarding Liz, I made up my mind to prove the comments wrong. While I've written to you my impression of the conference, I have to say that my real eye opening experience lies outside of the conference. Liz and Jodee had no immediate plans (except for Liz's nails) Saturday evening so my mother and I tagged along and spent quite a bit of time with Liz and her mother. Liz really wanted her nails airbrushed and my mother was able to transport. When my mother asked if I'd be OK hanging out with Liz, I wasn't sure how comfortable I'd be. Mom introduced me to Liz at some point during the conference and if Liz was considered a "brat" I wanna know where these people are getting there definitions. Seeing Liz during breaks, I thought she was just someone milling around the Civic Center. My definition of "brat" is throwing temper tantrums, screaming and kicking on the floor, right in front of everybody. Which conference did the service providers go to?

OK, regaining composure ... I was fine with spending time with anyone especially knowing my mom would be there. It also helped that Jodee was so receiving of "Karen's Daughter." Liz wasn't going to have anything if she didn't get her nails airbrushed right away. She had found out that a place at the mall would do her nails and insisted on going. That's typical of anyone her age. When we want something, we want it. FAS doesn't allow her to step back and see that getting her nails done isn't instantly possible. That's the part I think others missed.

Liz was the youngest, the one who was still in the process. The rest of them were older example success stories. I will admit that my very first impression of Liz could have been like the providers. Howev my experience with Liz was for 5-10 minutes waiting in the hotel lobb for Jodee and my mom to pick us up. Jodee had said that I was welcome to ask Liz anything and I hadn't a clue what to say. Then I real ized the simplest thing would be to get the facts straight. I proceede to get the answers about when she had been diagnosed, how it mo her feel, and general stuff like that. She was so willing to answer a test out my friendship. I honestly wasn't expecting her to want to ar

and talk to me. But she was and she answered so clearly and respect-fully. The slight discomfort I may have felt disappeared right then and the rest of the night was a blast. I wouldn't trade it for all the tea in china. Jodee bought me dippin' Dots, which I love. Mom gave Liz a compli-ment about her hair and that sparked the idea for Liz to do my hair. We went to Target to get a camera for Liz and gel to keep my hair in place. Liz let me have some of her hair bands and went to work when we got back to the hotel. She did a beautiful job. Liz is very talented.

After they left I missed them greatly though I had just met them. Liz had a spice to her that showed itself through her insistence on com-mon sense. It was fun to listen to her interact with her Mom when Jodee would say something that may have not made total sense. This is not what I would have expected to see from an FAS kid but it just goes to show what is good when given the chance to be. Maybe the solution is to reiterate the spectrum part to the service providers. I think it was made quite clear at the conference, which is why I wonder which one they were at?

Proud Parent of 8 daughters, 3 w/ FASD - Laura, Jodee should be praised for not turning her back on Liz. Too often, parents find it easier to "disrupt", to walk away, from these wonderful children. I too know the heartbreak of dealing with a child so much like Liz (add Bi-polar, refus-ing meds) that I need people like Jodee to give me some hope. I can only pray that someday my daughter will ask for help or at least see the need to change the path that she is on. I hope that Jodee and Liz real-ize that some of us, if not all of us, needed to hear just what they had to say! Thank you for one of the best "trainings" that I have ever attended.

Attendee - Laura, Thank you for sharing these follow-ups. I have placed this correspondence and yesterday's input from you in my FASD binder from the conference. What a horrendous exclamation point to your efforts to educate us about FASD and the personal, familial, social, legal, educational etc. effects.

I hope we all finally get the point after walking a little farther in Liz's shoes. She and her family are in my prayer.

Attendee - Laura, Thanks for sharing the input from conference attendees and especially the letter from Jodee. Her honest and open response provided even greater insight for those just beginning to learn about that many aspects of FASD.

Attendee - Laura, Thanks so much for sharing this e-mail and your previous one–very powerful. The first one illustrated how strong our prejudices are and the second one presents us with the raw soul and experience of an adult with FASD ... and yet there is always hope. What a learning experience!!

Pediatric RN, adoptive mother – Laura and Donna, I find most interesting, is the attitude of the service providers. Hopefully, some of them will wake up and realize that they have not walked in Liz and Jodee's shoes and their judgmental attitude does not make them a service provider, but a service hindrance. As a parent, I find the isolation of living with these children to be hard to bear ... but the most difficult thing is to trust those who think they are service providers, but have no clue. They make my child's life and mine a living hell. Referrals that result in threats and demeaning statements are not worth the effort.
Providers need to take notice!!

PhD, adoptive mom – Hello Laura, I appreciate your sharing the letters about Jodee Kulp's presentation with her daughter. It took a lot of courage to share those difficult facts. As a provider I am appalled at the description of her daughter as a "brat." Let that person walk a few hundred miles in Jodee's shoes and see how she feels about it. We cannot control the actions and paths of others, no matter how much we wish or try. Have they ever tried to make a horse drink water, an addict stop using, a smoker stop smoking or an obese person lose weight? It has to come from the individual's desire and purpose and most of all their will.

On a more personal note, our adult son is mentally retarded and has many of the characteristics of a child with FASD. Born in Colombia and malnourished as an infant, we will probably never know the cause of his particular cognitive problems. A brain aneurysm at age 15 did not help his brain either. Because he has been labelled MR and because he has a particularly engaging personality (never met a stranger) he has been able to obtain support, work, and housing. Even with those good supports in place, he has not been free of distressing and frustrating behaviors ... like letting a friend who was AWOL from the army live with him, or giving a signed blank check to his "friend" to buy dinner, and on and on. When I took a moment to speak to Jodee, she was ready to drop everything and talk to me. It speaks of her commitment and caring for the cause of FASD children and adults. Please pass this on to her and know that I am extremely grateful for her writing and speaking as well as for your taking the time and effort to educate people about FASD and its far-reaching effects on our world.

Service Provider - Laura, The comment made by the service provider (that you cited) is a typical reaction to children behaving badly. I would hope that Jodee's response will help all of us to have better insight into the challenges of living with FASD and to be more tolerant and less judgmental of others, thus, enabling us to be more effective service providers. Thanks for sharing.

Chemical Dependency Professional - Dear Laura, Just a line to say that I gained great insight into FASD and I loved the conference! Excellent job! I am however, distressed at the comments made about Jodee and Liz. Jodee's not a bad mother, she's the mother of an alcoholic grasping onto to anything she can to keep her daughter safe. She has gone through sick extremes to do this, but this is the nature of HER untreated disease: Co-Dependency.

On Liz's behalf, she was at a conference without her best friend-
-the bottle. She was feeling very insecure, irritable, restless and dis-
contented, not to mention physical withdrawals which concerned me.
Every nerve in her body was on edge. Alcohol requires medical detox
and if not treated properly can lead to death. We were watching her
closely. This is a family disease and it affects the ENTIRE family.

Liz—a brat? Sure she is, but first and foremost she is an alco-
holic/addict. It took a lot for her to even attend the conference. Please
pass this on to others. I was delighted to hear that she is seeking help.

I encourage Jodee and her husband to seek help through Al-
Anon. I'm sure this has affected their marriage. There is hope and help;
I ask that if we have any prayer warriors out there that you add this
family to your list; they're on mine. These are wonderful people with a
bad problem. God bless you all for the work you do.

Director of the Inclusive Education Committee – Laura, The judgmental comments have unfortunately become a normal part of our society,
oh how I wish it weren't so. As a special education teacher, with
siblings in medical fields, I believe observations about behavioral/self
control issues drag up that old nature vs nurture argument for causes of
behavior and personality; both of course have a major influence. But
your awesome FASD conference shed so much light on this issue for
me. There are very real prenatal, natal, and postnatal issues – and this
function of the human being can be damaged causing dysfunctional
performance. Why would we expect behavioral function to be exempt
from permanent damage and dysfunction?

Another problem complicates the issue as I see it. We have
culture that is nurturing its babies, children, adults, and seniors on sar-
casm and judgment through television, music, and the movie industry.

Think about how young children are learning about their world,
communication and intimacy through adult programming such as soap
operas, comedy shows, reality TV, the evening news, and situation
comedies. I betcha FASD kids really intensively learn lessons from TV

much more quickly than we realize ... and imitate much of what they see and hear in an attempt to be "normal". Most TV behavior they would learn is pretty much "in your face". It would make an interesting research project.

Even those with minimal impairments, and those who believe they have no impairment at all, are being programmed to recognize weaknesses in others and demean others in the name of comedy. All you have to say after a good insult is "Just kidding," right?

I was amazed that Liz's mom was so able to focus on the positives, the strengths. Her dedication shows in Liz, and yet, Liz is her own person, obviously still struggling with pervasive behavior issues on a continual basis.

I think every presenter did a good job. These folks need to be teaching the teachers. Their input is desperately needed in special education teacher training programs. We need to return the educational focus to the children and their needs. We need to put the educational theories in proper historical and educational perspective.

We need to include parents in the process at every turn. We are all and should be proud to say that we are both students and teachers. Parents are the first teachers of the children, thus they are the natural teachers who can provide on site training to the certified teachers who are working with their children as students. And the certified teachers in turn, have a wealth of strategies to suggest to parents who may be overwhelmed and need theoretical information about strategies and implementation.

Working together, corroboratively, with realistic goals and positive attitudes seems the best approach to me.

Keep the faith.

The conference was the 2nd best I've ever attended (in 32 years of professional experience and 21 years of parenting), but these moms ... such awesome women, have inspired me and inspire me still.

JODEE (Mother) - Is there any chance we could have an instant replay of all or parts of the FASD conference. Over the years, it seems we have experienced the most judgment from persons highly educated. Perhaps they are sheltered from the reality of day-to-day living. An hour of therapy never exposes a whole life.

LAURA NAGLE (FASD Conference Coordinator) - Jodee – I would love to send video, but none of it worked.

LCSW, Clinical Services Manager - As a service provider, I was engaged and moved by the amount of reality that was injected into not only the panel, but the discussions throughout the conference. It put a real spin (as well as face) on individuals and families living with FASD. Sometimes as providers we get accustomed to putting people into categories and looking for a specific set of characteristics. This conference reminded me that there is no such thing as a "classic presentation" when it comes to FASD.

Just Another Mom - I just realized I didn't comment on my reaction to your part about Liz being a "brat" and you being "inept". It is funny ... My daughter reacted so strongly against the idea of Liz as brat....and MY reaction was strongly against you being "inept". Good grief...the parenting I witnessed in the time I was with you was remarkable...and what you have shared with me since is to me, anything but "inept". Your depth of love for your daughter and the incredible way you are using your knowledge (in spite of what must be extremely painful to be near) is a parenting most of us strive for, but have great difficulty actually doing in such times as you are facing.

You know...it just goes to show my mother's kitchen plaque I saw daily growing up is absolutely so ... "Lord, grant that I may not judge my neighbor until I have walked a mile in his moccasins." The critics are not mean or unfeeling ... just haven't walked in these moccasins, so probably shouldn't have an opinion. Yet I am glad they did, cause it gave reason to respond to it and now there is our opportunity to educate and reform thinking. We are really blessed, aren't we?

There you are again, running away from your problems, too scared to solve them. Just sit down and think, get your mind in sync. But no, you don't wanna face that shit, it's too dam deep and legit. So go on. Run away. Afraid to let go of your emotions so you keep it all inside. Day after day, it will stay and not go away.

Face reality? Afraid I'd lash out with a tragedy and jail time. A broken heart with nothing left using and abusing to pass the time. I have cried past my tears. Dressing for attention but no protection. Crushed. Alone. Raped. Robbed. Nowhere to go. Memories you can't counterfeit to deal with the pain. Can't think cuz my brains not in sync and my eyes are blind by my love for a thug. I look in the mirror and can't even see me. I lived my life for him. I love him so much I hate him. It was ova. Out'a control. I was wrong. All my flash is off. Everything is gone except myself. And myself needs me to be the person I can be and see through that door.

*

Have to work through hard situations with motivation, no matter what the differences, I'll be the remembrance to the game for people with pain. I'll be the Novocain for those needing to know they're not alone yet have something to condone. I have problems I could not run. I was young got loaded like a gun. Sometimes I wonder why my mama died and no one got identified for the crime. First off, left four kids. Second off, she was poor. Keep my head held high, cuz ain't nobody gonna make my dreams die.

Chapter 8
HAPPY BARF-DAY

June 1, 2005

don't know what to write right now. All I can think of is getting out of where I am. I just want to go home. It is my birthday and it has been the worst birthday of my life. I am trying to make the best of it here but it is really hard. I am learning a lot about myself. The people here use this place for a shower, bed and food.

I just want to go home. My teeth hurt. I can't believe I busted out my two front teeth. Pray for me. I am done with drinking and all this stuff. I am going to be way bigger than these people here who keep coming back.

– Liz

Happy Birthday to me.

Detox! What a place to spend a birthday.

Mom came today and brought a big cake. Some of the people here had never even had a birthday cake.

The cake said

get money when you didn't have any. I didn't have a job and I was broke.

JODEE (Mother) -What position do you take, when your heart loves someone despite their behaviors? The nitty-gritty of life is so much more than an hour of therapy. The execution of a concept is so much harder than prescribing a solution. Karl and I headed to an exchange brothers wedding leaving Liz and her shenanigans behind and hands more capable then our own. Three weeks of sanity with family and friends

> I did what I knew how to do best.
> I drank. And drank.
> And then I drank some more.

House and Pet Sitter - I am training Becky, Bonnie and Liz on self control and self sufficiency. I will tell you more when you arrive back at home. They are behaving in a much more calm, mature and co-operative manner.

I do not even try to be strong ... there are simply certain things that work best in a society (both humans to humans and canines to humans). It takes vigilance and consistant behavior on my part, but it is worth it in the end. No accidents or trash can tipping in the house for dogs and advance planning / communications and mature self sufficiency for 19 year old ladies.

I will not accept less when it is possible to have more. With all of my disabilities I would have long ago succumbed and been in a nursing home or dead. Determination and just plain common sense work for me. I will try to get the info on Narconon for Liz. I described the program to her and the benefits that I have witnessed and she is interested.

September 3, 2005

I still had my apartment and my two not paying room-mates and I'd hooked up with this homeless guy who gave me an ice cream cone at the mall. I invited him to live at my last apartment and then he followed me to the next, and the next, and the next place, and we'd drink together and pass out and drink some more. He got me alcohol whenever he wanted it or whenever I needed it. Mom and Dad hated him for the longest time, and I didn't get why. It just seemed they were being mean and unfriendly.

The one thing I thought would never happen to me is that I finally fall in love with someone not for his looks. I decide I love him for the person he is and the way he treats me and how he cares about me. He keeps my money, and my phone, and my keys. He says so I don't lose them. I want to marry him someday. I have never seen any other boy care so much about me in my life. He cares about things other people didn't care at all about. I believe this is the man God has chosen for me. I pray. God you know I love him and I want to be with him for the rest of my life. Can you please let him know it's real and not to mess up ever and that's for me in Jesus name. Amen.

Revenge doesn't pay well.

It hurts like hell again
    and again we hurt each other
You messed with two girls,
    hollered at many, fingered a few
when you said you were true
So I ... Messed back

> *with wild talk on the phone –*
> *collected numbers and showed you*
> *By jacking off one*
> > *I knew I showed you but I didn't have sex*
> *By jacking off one*
> > *I knew I lost myself when I was beaten by you.*

Finally, I am sober for a night, but my boyfriend was so drunk he got in a big fight with my roommates. Then my boyfriend went to jail and I ended up getting plastered after he left. My roommates locked me outside and told me I could throw up. I passed out. I was so drunk that the ambulance guys had to restart my heart.

When I was in treatment I was dedicated to stay sober and I got through the first two steps but I also still had a boyfriend. I really believed his promises to go sober and I attended the AA about 5-6 times. He came with to make sure no men looked at me on the street or on the bus. If they did he would beat them up. He is older than me and I thought he was my protector. He began drinking in the mornings and used drugs or drank all day. He actually drank more once I was out then I realized he did before. Maybe when I was using too I didn't notice it so much.

What I learned after I was sober and no longer in treatment was that he was not my protector. He controlled me in ways I did not like, he hurt me including knocking out my tooth when he was he was mad at me. He told me it was my fault because I ran into his fist. Every time I tried to get away from him he would grab my arm or leg. I always had bruises from him.

He told everyone we were soul mates and I was his

fiance. He told me if I left him, he would be long gone and I would be dead. All my friends told me to get away from him. My mother yelled at him. My dad actually kicked him with his foot out of our yard. He was not allowed on or near my parents property and he would not allow me to sleep anywhere without him even though my parents offered to let me move home for a couple months to make sure I was stable. If I tried to call the police to get help he would stop me and hurt me because he was so much bigger than me. Once I went to the hospital to find a place to sleep because he wanted to sleep in the park with the other people who had no place else to go. I couldn't go anywhere without him.

He took my cell phone, then my mom's cell phone, my apartment key. He always held on to something of mine I thought was important so I would come back to get it and then I couldn't get away again. He gave me hickeys all over so other men know I belong to him. A couple times they started bleeding and puffing up with blue blood. He was always begging for money and if he bought cigarettes for me he would also buy marijuana or alcohol.

I couldn't talk to my mom and dad. He told me they worked for the devil and they were stealing all my money.

I realize I need to learn to be strong for me and not with a man or chemicals. I need to move on.

I blackout and then wake up. The blackouts feel like my night terrors as a little girl. I talk and don' remember talking. I go places and don't remember being there.

I worry.

I worry, he is the only thing I have left. I am freaking about people knowing.

I don't want to go back to treatment.

I don't want to go back to detox.

*

It hurts to breathe; my chest is heavy like a person is stepping on me. My body runs on alcohol. I don't eat. I fill myself with liquid calories. I don't want to live like this anymore. It hurts to breathe; my chest is heavy like a person is stepping on me. If I don't drink, I shake. If I run out of money, I'll do almost anything to get scummy – lie, steal, cheat are the rules of my liquid hell. Imagine everyday your whole body shaking because you need a lick. Waking up shaking begging' to get lit, holding back till the next attack, being glued to alcohol. By six at night if anyone tried to take my bottle, they were bound to get hit.

My body runs on alcohol. I don't eat. I fill myself with liquid calories. I don't want to live like this anymore. When you're addicted, you think you need it so you can relieve yourself of the things you have locked up in your head and heart about your life. You suck alcohol or whatever you do so you don't have to face the truth. I'm outta control, losing my mind, if you think you can change me you're wastin' your time.

*

I wish I was working with Billie. She gave me ideas but wasn't always in my face. She was tough, but nice. She helped me run my life, but still live my life.

I never disrespect people who respect me. She did.

September 9, 2005

JODEE (Mother) - Dear Liz – Six years ago that you and I spoke at the Federal Court House with the governor and his wife. It was 9.9.99 at 9:09 am and it was the beginning of the ringing of the bells around the world to let people know about Fetal Alcohol. You were 13 years old. It was six months after we found out you had a brain injury because your mother drank alcohol when she was pregnant. It was before Mo'Angels. It was when you still had dreams and wanted help to reach those dreams. We joined together to work hard to help you be the best you could be. We believed in each other. We trusted each other. Together we discovered paths to walk on while you grew stronger. You were a pioneer in those discoveries. I and the other children in the world are grateful.

In the last two years you have become a lost little girl in the big world. Our hearts have been shattered. Sometimes I wonder if I have any heart left to fight this big battle of FASD. My sweet daughter, now a young woman, today my heart breaks again. My dreams, our dreams are not realized. The dream of many other children and adults of FASD. The dream of a HAPPY and SAFE ADULT LIFE for you.

You no longer want to hold my hand or listen to my wisdom. Your disability holds you back from your happiness and safety because you choose not to accept it. Today begin to Make Your Difference one tiny step at a time.

1. Find safe places to have fun.
2. Make friends that won't hurt you.
3. Ask for help from people you can trust.
4. Keep your life simple.

My love and prayers will always be with you.

Chapter 10
I died!

My blood alcohol was .438!
At the hospital they IV me to the bed and
drugged me until I got sober and bought me a
cab to get home. I was scared to sleep in my
own apartment. The apartment that I was paying
for, because once when I passed out they had beat me with a
belt buckle and I woke up with buckle shaped bruises and red
stripes that scabbed over. Another time I woke up and I knew I
had been raped. They had laughed and said it was just a joke.
They thought it was funny! Those weren't jokes, the marks
on my body, and spirit, and soul were real. I was falling fast.
Because I was on a stay of commitment eventually the sheriff
came with a warrant to take me away.

He had come by looking for me a number of times, but I
was hardly ever there because of my roommates. It was unusual, but it just so happened that night I was sober. It was back
to the detox center for me. They delivered me to Detox and I
wasn't drunk! Because I was not intoxicated it took a while to
get admitted. I had to stay in detox until a bed opened at the
treatment center. This time for sixty days and I lost another
apartment.

My landlord had enough of me and my "friends."

Mom shut down my apartment. This time she put my stuff in a storage locker.

September 25, 2005

Guess what?

I am back in Detox.

I violated my commitment so I am going back to treatment for 60 days. That's a lot. I hope I can be strong this time and not drink when I get out. I hope I meet lots of new friends I enjoy hanging with so I have some sober friends.

The little star in mine
The little star that shines.
Now that things start to come together
When the season changes to different weather
My life starts to become a whole lot better
My health increasing
My heart still beating
And my path is now leading to a reason for being
In this world
And be happy without a substitute
Cause I've already faced my conscious
As I face myself with truth
I start to speak to youth
On hard decisions
And life's ambitions
I realize that I'm a star
That shines up high and
No I am happy I did not die.

Being an alcoholic is so hard.

I want to stop, but just don't know how.

There is something always inside me that wants to drink. How come can't I get it? Over and over, I tell myself a safe place is not a party place.

I make up reasons for my drinking
– Me and my boyfriend have a problem
– We are celebrating
– I am sad
– I am happy
– I feel sick
– I feel good
– Someone makes me mad
– I think something got stolen from me.

Whatever the reason, I know it's not right to do it. I need to occupy my time better and stop hanging with the wrong people. One of my problems is not listening to advice when I have an idea in my head. Even if it is a bad idea I will accomplish it no matter what it takes and no one can stop me. People try to tell me it's a bad choice or they tell me that it is going to get me into trouble, but I pay them no mind and go about my business.

I learn the hard way.

Always join the wrong game.

When it comes to people trying to tell me what's right or wrong in my mind, at that time, I tell me myself 'I am right. I can do it. I must do it.' Then I discover myself in a bad situation and I can't get out. I never learn the easy way because I can be very hard headed.

I thought everyone respected me when I had an apartment. But I learned when I don't have my place most of them act different. They used me. They look for another place, another person. I didn't really matter to them. Even my sister – my little sister – the one I called true friend – dissed me in the end game. That hurt more than life.

I do believe the right people won't disrespect your house, steal from you or talk about you behind your back.

Someday. Someday I will find those kinds of friends.

God, do they exist? Are people like that still alive?

October 2005

I am back in treatment. This time for sixty days. I'm writing again. How come I have to be put up or locked up to find the time to write? Will this time be different or will I fall again like Alice in the rabbit hole going round and round?

Who are you kidding,
you're never close to winning
Whose story ya buyin',
am I tryin' or dyin' — Cryin'
I was torn since the day I was born
Plus I had alcohol deform
Livin' life with a defect
Lost peoples respect
At times I've lost my breath
Almost kept death it's hard to forget
What's wrong or right
Only at night with no light just flowing
Back in my Mama's footsteps make me so confused
So gets me to beginnin' to start to use – and abuse
Difficult situations make me impatient

Slow down girl yer movin' too fast like yo on speed
Yo' need to get on yo knees
Before ya catch a disease that will never go away
Death – that's the price you'll pay
Not a road you should cross
You'll loose – no gain, cause yourself nothing but pain!

In order to have a relationship with someone else I have to learn to have a good relationship with myself. I have learned that I can be a manipulator and I have to be more independent when it comes to material items – begging and pleading.

I know that writing helps me with my problems. When I write it down I can go back and read again and think about what I wrote. When I write it down, it gives me time to stay out of trouble.

October 23, 2005

I went by Pizza Shop today and saw a girl who used to work there. She said the old manager is gone. And I can have my job back.

I don't get how I can do so good with one manager and then turn into a stupid, dirty ass bitch for the next one?

October 24, 2005

Today I met my case manager and we discussed some opportunities for my future if I want. I can't live with Mom and Dad. I don't want that control – still want my own place, want to be with my boyfriend and go home. I guess the meeting went OK. People always in my business because I do such stupid things – ova and ova – ya think I can learn this? The longer I do without alcohol, the more I realize I can live my life without it.

October 25, 2005

Today staff pissed me off because he said I had a funky attitude with the nurse. God I pray to you. Can you help me please help me cope with my anger more maturely.

Rosa Parks died yesterday she was 92.

She took a stand.

I hope I can too.

October 26, 2005

I applied to get my job back. I am not good at reading people. I am not good with time. I am not good with taking care of myself. I am still a good person

October 31, 2005

Can't believe he did me so wrong,

got drunk, called up, caught up.

And I'm in treatment!

locked down, upside down   clown.

Constant pain got me goin' insane

With nothin to lose

But nothing to gain

Physically and mentally torn apart

I'm stuck in the dark

Cuz ya broke my heart.

Six months and fifteen days

Maybe it was just a phase

That had me dazed

Cause I was blind
I thought your were kind
> *But I guess that was stuck in my mind*
> *I wish I could press rewind STOP*
> *To where we never met*
> *Cuz meeting you I do regret*
Through all the abuse
> *To amuse – you and cause a sin*
> *It has to stop but could have been worse*
> *So I am going to end this curse*
> *Maybe you'll be rollin' down the street*
> > *In a big black hearse*

November 1, 2005

KAREN JOHNSON, Grandma's Place - Jodee - it sounds like Liz is doing well, we need to get her into an aftercare home where this can continue. I am now managing adults with mental illness, needless to say, a lot have undiagnosed FASD. I don't want Liz to fall apart again. Let me know if I can help.

November 2, 2005

RENAE SANFORD (Life Coach for adults with FASD) – Jodee - Yes, persons with FASD can work together for a time, but working with someone and living with someone are two different things as families who raise children with FASD will also tell us. They need a place to go and escape the stimulation of the outside world. They tend to be right in the middle of all the happenings going on. Having worked more than once in situations where young people with FASD were housed together, I can tell you it can be a recipe for disaster for the client and/or staff. There is never enough staff to handle all the situations that arise when one goes off the deep end. It is very different from working with other developmental disabilities when crisis happens. We must always plan for worst case and be prepared. Staff burnout is high. Still I am looking at housing two people with FASD, I still believe something can be done.

November 4, 2005

Today, I read my dialogue on the seductive part of me. I really liked this topic. Until this time, I never really thought about my behavior or it's affect on others. Seduction is power.

November 10, 2005

My man is back in jail.
Now I slip into the mind of two
One minute I love you and
The next minute I try to get rid of you
What's da deal
Life is so real.
Pump yer brakes,
slow yer roll
Hozstyle gonna take control
Don't try my gangsta
I got the power to make yer brain pop out.
Cause a young tragedy
Won't wear out like a battery
Got beef with your bad self
I'm gonna be bad for your health.
Little fast, trailer trash
Loud mouth laughin' sound
When I'm lit don't give a shit
Drunk azz, keep my balance
Now I hit the ground
Don't want to be around.

November 15, 2005

My man is still in jail.

we've been together seven months

Look inside to find out why

Look inside and start to cry

Look inside and find the truth

Look inside and teach the youth

Change can't happen til we know the game

Change won't happen til' we release the pain

Change won't happen til we turn inside out

Change hate back to fear is what I'm talkin' about

Face a demon — With the holy ghost

Face your yourself — who ya love the most

God help me. Jesus be there with me. This life is crap!

November 16, 2005

Went to check out my next placement –

PS It's bad.

November 17, 2005

Today is my 60 days of sobriety.

My boyfriend is still in jail.

I don't' know when he will get out

and I am still in treatment.

I hate you I love you

> *Boo this is true.*

I really loved you
But my eyes is learnin'
> *My heart is burnin'*
Without being able to determine
That fact ....Wait hold on.
> *Before I catch a heart attack*
Back up
Jump back to rewind
> *Back to the time we met*
> *Was that connection a big regret*
> *The worst affect*
> *On my life yet*
> *That I remember*
I wanted to be your wife
Life with you in my life
Have a couple of kids
> *What's with this?*
> *Why you go*
> *Mess with my kin on the low low*
Hozstyle straight locking
Low if ya gotta go
The block is froze
And no one knows
Da fine zero is tryin; to get the load
Keep on the hush lip
To dem that will give yo' clips
Got what ya want
Got what ya need
Get money serving teens
Makin' sure no one spills the beans

Through the wire we got the fire
Here's a tip
Think before –
don't open dose lips

November 22, 2005

Today I shared what I was grateful for.
I am thankful for my talent,
     being able to rap
and I am good
     when it comes to writing lyrics.
I am thankful for having the people helping me.
     Reach my rapping goals.
I know that if I keep this addiction
     who I'll be kiddin' is myself.
     AND I'LL BE put on a shelf!
When I have a world to give insight and
     to make noise to.

   *

My Goals

1. Get a new place
2. Sell my harp to pay for my next placement
3. Get a job
4. Get studio time

VICKI - Parent of 7 children with FASD - Jodee – I think the kid God gave you needs multiple archangels to hang onto her. She is not one that can be watched over by angels in training. Did you ever think you would have the opportunity to know reality so deeply? You know I was relieved when I first met her, "YOU" had to take her home. I have seven with FASD and combined they may equal one Liz. Each of mine have bits and pieces of her behaviors, but not all in one package. I do believe one of mine maybe a Liz in training. Everyday this kid wears the bracelets Liz gave her. She doesn't take them off and I can hear her clanging and know where she is. You don't now how valuable it is that Liz is walking the path with a lantern to give me light. – Vicki

JODEE (Mother) -Vicki – So now you know why I didn't mind all the jewelry. Bells ring out warnings.

VICKI (Parent of 7 children with FASD) - Jodee – Everyday I pray over each of my children, that God will give them a loving heart and the mind of Christ. That God will filter out the confusion in their brains. That He will put the things in that they can learn and that they will have a purpose and joy in life. I ask God to help them learn to be a good friend. Before school I ask God to bless them. In the evening we pray for healing of their teeth. What is it about teeth? We have no money for braces - even the ones that came in crooked are straightening. Their baby teeth that were rotted and little nubs are beginning to come in as beautiful adult teeth. They are white and pretty and not discolored from the drugs taken by their birth parents. Keep the faith!

November 23, 2005

I am leaving tomorrow.

I graduated in group today.

Mom and Dad offered to let me move home with THEIR rules. I might fail again.

I am afraid to leave. I feel safe. Grandma's Place is better than those rules.

Their letter said -

JODEE (Mother) - Liz, We welcome you home under the following conditions.

YOU CANNOT:

1. Drink anything with alcohol in it or use any type of drugs - You will be sent to detox.
2. Have contact with your boyfriend - this means no touching, no talking, no seeing, no hearing, no tasting – You will be returned to treatment.
3. Hang with drug dealers - You will be returned to treatment.
4. Smoke in our house. This includes in the greenhouse, garage and your room there is NO SMOKING.
5. Have friends call after 10:00 p.m.
6. Have guests without prior approval. You cannot ask if THEY can come in when they are already standing in our hallway.

YOU CAN:

1. Schedule studio recording time with ...name
2. Spend time with ...names
3. Join a health club and work out
4. Go to the hip hop church
5. Go to AA meetings

YOU MUST:

1. Complete all your community service hours
2. Look for a job
3. Look into school

YOU WILL:

1. Keep your room clean
2. Keep your bathroom clean.
3. Clean up after yourself.
4. Be pleasant to family (people and pets)
5. Contribute to family by helping.
6. Curfew on weeknights 10:00 p.m.
7. Weekend clearance: where you are going, phone number and when you will be home.

WE WILL PROVIDE YOU
1. Temporary housing and food

How could I do all that!

I give it a try, Dad wants evenings after work quiet. I am noisy. Instead of asking me about my day he tells me everything I have done wrong. I attack back. Mom tries to tickle me, I scratch her and call her an abuser. They won't let me have a key to the house. They want me home by 10:00 p.m. They don't want anything to do with my old boyfriend. I go to a movie and don't come back, I call Mom to get me. I am on the street with another stupid decision. Mom and Dad fight. Dad yelling and calling Mom names he never did that before. He tells Mom she ruined me. I plan to run away to Miami, but Mom finds out. There is no money for Grandma's Place and I am getting suffocated at home. I have been on my own for over a year. I don't like this and they know it. Mom sold my harp to pay for a one month placement at Grandma's Place – $3000 gone! I think it is weird that they call it a placement. Placement is what you do with dishes and sounds like you are placing people away or down.

JODEE (Mother) - Liz functions well with supports. She completed 28 days of chemical dependency program. The kid can drink 30 shots of vodka a day. We are hoping for waivered services and aftercare. Why did she do well in treatment? For the same reason she did well in home school. There were rules, structure and expectations she had to meet. They challenged her to be better and she rose to the occasion. She enjoys that but rebels against the safety net. We pay the first month for person centered structure in Grandma's Place and hope for funding.

Good news – The next step is at least closer to home. The new apartment is nice. The staff is nice.

Bad news – I am afraid this place is not right for me. I am used to being free to come and go when I want, they have pretty strict rules.

Bigger bad news – My boyfriend is homeless and no one knows. He is begging to be a part of this new plan. I am worried.

November 26, 2005

Now, I know this new place it not the place for me. All I do is yell at Mom and tell her this is not the right place. I scream and act crazy and it is more complicated than anyone understands. My boyfriend was homeless. He is good at getting into places. He is sneaky when he needs to be and he broke the screen to climb in and out without anyone knowing. Now he is now living in my closet. Staff don't even know. Mom don't know. I even have a roommate and she doesn't know he is hiding in my closet. This is nuts. Back to living a lie.

I had permission to go out on weekends and my boyfriend bought me alcohol so we could drink together in the closet. I ended up getting really paranoid we'd get caught. No one knew how come I was acting so badly, I think they thought I was just a bad kid. Eventually I acted so bad I had to run and I went to my girlfriends an hour away. I split! I had to get out before they found out I had my boyfriend living in my closet

It was better to go homeless with my boyfriend than get found out, but it was January and below zero. Mom and Dad wouldn't take me in. I had no money because two weeks cost me all my harp money. Two weeks for $3,000!

We rode the bus to stay warm. We found laundry rooms to sleep in. Once he talked me into calling an ambulance to go to the hospital so we could be warm. Then we found an empty apartment and we snuck into it to sleep.

A friend offered me, but not my boyfriend a place to stay. He stole from her, so she put him out and I followed him back to the streets. By this time I was drinking again, had no money and no place to stay.

Then my boyfriend went to jail because we rented a hotel with another couple. This couple fought really bad, the dude punched her in the face and swung her around by her hair. But they didn't go to jail! My man did! Off he went. He had a warrant and the noise of the other couple tipped them off. They just smiled happy they didn't go to jail too. We got put out of the hotel. Most of this Mom and Dad didn't know because I was keeping it on the low.

Mom and Dad refused to help me. If I got stuck some place, no one came to get me out of my messes even if I called and called. Mom and Dad turned off their phones at 10:00 p.m. and I was out of luck. If I called before 10:00 p.m. they'd say, "Oh, so what are you going to do about that? You know you can come home, 'alone', if you play by our rules."

Alone is what I didn't want. Their rules - sleep at a decent hour, no calls after 10:00 p.m., no drinking, no smoking in the house, no friends in the house, eat meals with the family seemed unfair. It was so cold outside.

I finally gave up and I did try to live with Mom and Dad 'alone' and during that time sobered up enough to want independence again.

*

I found a quiet furnished studio apartment I could rent week to week and I moved back in with my boyfriend as soon as he was out of jail. This place was away from everyone I knew and it took five busses to get home to Mom and Dad. We lived there for six months and things went pretty well most of the time. The manager was an AA counselor and she was there for us and supported us and helped us stay sober. She was tough. I started DBT (anger classes) and Mom was willing to drive for those, but only take me, not my boyfriend.

It was Easter, and Mom invited me to my Aunts but I had to call her and tell her I had a headache. I did have a headache - a big headache because my man had hit me upside the head with the fry pan and I had three big Easter Eggs. He held my mouth shut while he hit me so I couldn't scream, I thought I was going to pass out from not breathing. When someone is hitting you like that all you can think of is surviving. Later I was so angry. So I wouldn't tell my parents, or the police, or the social workers, he said I could punch him in the eye the number of years he was. I punched him twenty-eight times.

At least he didn't bite me that time. They make me bleed. People called us the vampire couple because my boyfriend didn't have his front teeth from getting pistol whipped when he was drunk.

Then I invited my friend over for protection, and she invited her abusive boyfriend over, and then they both moved into our 'studio' apartment. The manager was terminated and we were on our own.

My cat moved in and we started drinking big time again.

Then my friend with the boyfriend who had violent fights came to visit again and, yes … moved in …

and yes ... with her boyfriend ... she'd scream, they'd hit, we'd drink and ... Yes, once again I was looking for a new place to live. When would I learn that these people I called friends and alcohol were costing all my money and I was going nowhere?

*

My boyfriend got his teeth fixed. I went back to school. Mom helped him get a job. Mom figured out he had a TBI and changed how she treated him. She made him tell her what happen in his life. He was in a car accident and a coma.

JODEE (Mother) -Yesterday I brain coached a young adult male with a TBI who has never "really" had a job ... He's 28 years old. He feared employment because each time he tried he failed. (lacking job coach). Brain coaching and walking alongside "Abled" (not enabled) him to take the step to Voc Rehab. He viewed the presentation. Then I joined him with the counselor for paperwork. It took me one year to get him to this place. He tried to help himself, falling back to sleep on the street or hook onto a female caregiver. He has now been drug free for 15 months I decided to reach out.

His barriers include:

• If he did understand what the counselor was saying, he forgot when he changed environments (generalization).

• He couldn't fill out the paperwork and if he managed to he forgot to turn it in. (sequencing)

• He was given so much information, he only remembered the last thing said or maybe his brain never heard it at all because it was overloaded or could not receive it. (memory/retention/auditory processing)

• Interview training Getting the interview - getting the job ... appearance ... speaking ... walking ... more than just talking!

We found a little place in a quiet neighborhood away from old friends, my boyfriend had a job and we did pretty well as long as we didn't drink. We never drink when he has to go to work. It was good for him to work and once he even bought me dinner for $12.00. It was our first real date!

Mom started getting into my life again and invited me to speak with her in Florida. We worked on a presentation on early transition with FASD and we were going to talk to the professionals. Just before we had to speak I went to the bathroom. When I came out, there was this great plant I took a picture of. Then I saw another and I kept taking pictures until I was lost and could not find the hotel. Mom had turned her phone off so I prayed for God to help me and I called Dad in Minnesota.

Dad was in his office and he had me find the sun and read the street signs. He told me he Google Mapped me and if I just followed his instructions he would get me back to Mom. He told me he could see where I was. My job was walking straight and reading the street signs. He would say, the next sign will say, "this street name" and he was right. Thank God for Dad. He helped me get back to the presentation that Mom was in the middle of.

*

My boyfriend hoped to get into warehouse work instead of hot dog making and it started to bug him that he couldn't get a better job. Then he'd drink. And so would I. When we did drink stupid stuff happened. He'd kick me, or pick me up by the neck and shake me. What I didn't realize is what I thought was love was control. I believed he showed his love by keeping my money, wallet, ID and cell phone so I wouldn't loose it. He said he wanted to keep me safe because I am not smart. He says he needs to help me. Little did I know?

Sometimes he was nice. We drank away that truth. He head butted me and then he was sweet. He rebroke my teeth and followed me to the dentist to make sure the dentist fixed them right – to make sure I never told.

It hurts like hell again and again we hurt each other trying to get back on track, but can't. He scares me to death, but I can't leave. I am afraid of being lonely. That I will never find another man. He says if I leave he will be states away when they find me dead. I believe him. I make sure to keep his whiskers in my room and put them under my finger nails before I go to sleep.

We sleep in different rooms, on different sofas. I put a knife in my door jam. I drink til' I black out so when he comes on top of me it doesn't hurt so bad. I can't tell Mom and Dad. They will turn their backs again. He is kind after. I have fallen in love with him. What else can I do?

I got slapped and punched. I was always covered in bruises I'd wake up with cigarette burns on my body, that he said I did to myself. If you pass out you don't know what happens. I increase my throwing up, it was hard to keep food down and my stomach was tied in knots. I took the bus and got lost so I called the ambulance to get me to the hospital. I knew how to get home from there.

I was scared.

I drank more.

We drank more. I couldn't stand being without him and I couldn't stand being with him. I increased my drinking. It is just he and I now. I went right back to party life and did it again.

I told my parents we were doing really good and I tried to hide all of this from my family. I didn't see them that often and we made it six months.

Summer 2006

JODEE (Mother) - Liz has been participating in the Minnesota Organization on Fetal Alcohol Syndrome (MOFAS) Teen transition program and enjoying it. The goal is to prepare teens for transition and try to eliminate some of the secondary disabilities. The young people study learning styles and skills, job interests, and future plans. There is an interactive art piece for the teens and a dialogue session for parents. Everyone seems to be having a good time and learning. We work on building a circle of friends and developing safety plans. Hopefully this is a beginning of effective new programming.

Finally, I told my Mom, and she told the landlady who had also almost been killed by an old boyfriend and once again I was back on the street. Mom marched him over to his mother and confronted him in front of her.

Now there were two mothers involved!

Mom took me to a doctor to get medicine to help me sleep and with my mood changes. I have never played with pills and I was scared to take them, so the first time I got meds to help me I flushed them down the toilet. Mom was mad because they cost her $75.00. I told her, "You don't get it, Liz don't do drugs!"

Then I moved into an apartment with my girlfriend. I thought that would work, but once again I moved my boyfriend in, and she moved her boyfriend in, and then another friend moved in. And pretty soon I moved out because I couldn't handle the chaos, even though it was my apartment. So once again my 'friends' had my apartment and I lost it.

Let's see that is one

... two ... three ... four ... five ... six ... seven

... eight ... nine apartments!

I am a hard learner!

Finally, I let go of every friend, except my boyfriend, my family and his family who was now involved too.

BILLIE CAULDWELL - (Life Coach) - Jodee – I wanted to check in with you to see how Liz is doing these days. I know it's been touch and go for quite some time. Her life situation is definitely one of the more complicated I've encountered. I also wanted to let you know that I'm going to officially close her case out with us. I had informally placed her on hold and left her file in our system. If/when a funding source comes through (assuming our program can provide enough supports) it is easy enough to revisit her case. I look forward to hearing from you.

October 12, 2006

JODEE (Mother) - Beki, our sixteen year old dog died and Bonnie has not eaten. Her bones protrude. Her bounce is fading. I understand. She came to stop those feelings within me, now I must help her. We had learned to enjoy life together on this crazy journey. Bonnie plays the piano with her nose. Liz rides the metro without getting lost or picking up a "friend" needing a place to stay. Bonnie greets strangers politely. Liz keeps her home a precious refuge. All the love and work Karl and I had done, including a five year brain training program didn't stop Liz from exploration of the world. I had come to terms with that. Her need for self-experience in understanding the limits her brain injury placed on her was a journey she had to make without the controls and structure and safety we had provided. Bonnie helped me survive and remain loving. She deserves a precious dog gift for her hard work!

October 17, 2006

JODEE (Mother) - Sir Makone of Knarlwoods joined our home this past week, all fifty empty-brained pounds packed into still to grow folded skin. He is already two-year-old Bonnie size. A brainless nine-month wild guy who is peacefully sleeping by my feet who is afraid of the wooden steps to the kennel and the steps to the car, the carpeted steps to the studio and the white steps to the basement.

The dog is afraid of every simple step. In one day, he taught Karl and I a very important lesson – even though he looks grown he is a baby, and babies need oodles of love and guidance to grow.

Our big new dog taught us each step is a new learning experience because each step is different. It is in a different place, even if it is on the same stairwell. He reminded us that even though he wanted to do each step his mind didn't know how. He came to show us that some steps he could go up and some steps he could go down, but some steps he isn't yet ready to touch. Maybe someday, maybe someday when he is a big dog. We expect accidents and piddles along the way as he plods with curiosity and innocence into life experiences. Bonnie loves him and sneezes in dog laughter as Mak backs up and spreads his gangly feet to protect himself from a houseful of simple steps.

Liz, in her own way, does the same. She loves and hates learning. Mak reminds us to support the management of the journey through kindness, compassion, clear simple direction – and only one step at a time. For a while we will keep Mak leashed to our side because he does not have the skills to be independent and unknowingly could be injured or killed. We keep Liz tethered to us with the line of love.

Liz has learned much in her two-year college of hard knocks.

Mak's seven-step process to teach Liz new skills.

1. REVIEW – We review the options of how to teach so we have a backup plan. We make the initial calls, visit the site and discover the details.

2. WATCH – We tell Liz what she is going to learn and take her through the process to accomplish the task. In this first step she is the observant participant with us – we do not require learning.
3. WATCH – EXPERIENCE We repeat the experience with her contributing pieces of the learned task.
4. EXPERIENCE – WATCH We repeat the experience with her contributing more pieces of the learned task and we begin to step away.
5. EXPERIENCE – SHOW – She tells me what to do and I laugh and become a partner in "her" learning.
6. SHOW – LET GO – She shows me as I watch and then let go.
7. I CAN – She skillfully and a bit fearfully completes the process, while I sit in a parking lot waiting or stay close to the phone to guide. 'I Can', can take a while and when learning is mastered we move on to the Next Step in our adult journey.

Mak reminded us that just as we had taught Liz in our home, we needed to move to teaching her out-of-our home with the same love, compassion and expectations – step by tiny step – gradually handing over controls without judging to become her controls.

November 11, 2006

Toni Hager, my brain coach, came back and did all those tests again. She said, I have work to do. My digit spans have lost a couple of points. She said, my memory is working like a four to five year old. She said, if I work hard I can get my numbers higher again. If I do my life will be easier. Maybe I should. She said I need to eat right. I need to lower my stresses.

My boyfriend and I moved into a small apartment in a nice area. It cost more, but the people who took advantage of me didn't know where I was. I lived there almost two years with no complaints. I was always friendly with the staff. I even baked cookies for the landlord. There were times our life was very good. There were times it wasn't, but I never told.

November 2006

JODEE (Mother) - Liz invited us to a homemade turkey dinner, with gravy and mashed potatoes, stuffing and corn bread. I stopped by to demonstrate getting the neck out of the turkey and putting the big bird in the oven. I left her to peeling potatoes and cutting celery. I came back and chopped the onions and read her the stuffing recipe as she prepared it. I demonstrated cooking the giblets. I went home while she set her table.

When Karl and I arrived her Christmas tree twinkled in an organized living room. It had been a long journey to get to this place and the journey will continue. Today there is a lull in our storm.

I lived in nine apartments. I lost nine apartments.
I thought I had friends. I didn't lose them.
They were never real.
I am scared of death, bugs, boys, sickness, weapons
        and myself.
*

Happy 50th Birthday Mom
Mom 50 years you have over come
Moments you thought you couldn't make it through.
Marriage rough, because of what I put you through.
Making a difference in the world.
Mind over matter, no matter how it is
        I will always be your kid.
                Love Liz

JODEE (Mother) - I confronted Liz with her purging. She was not happy, but I guess no one is when you have others face your truth. I told her to make an appointment with a doctor if she can't get over it. She promised to work on her eating issues.

I know if I do much more than offer to transport to an appointment, she will not take responsibility.

I continued to work on dog training my new wild canine. I work on brain based education strategies to help Liz gain living skills. Liz gets a job in an elementary school kitchen. She loves working. Life settles down. Liz loves my big wild boy and takes him to obedience school. Bonnie loves Mak. They are a beautiful breeding pair for puppies hopefully next year.

When Mom goes out of town life usually happens in a big way and this time Bonnie and Mak got stuck and made nine really cute puppies. I loved those little puppies and spent time holding and feeding and napping with them after work. I know Mom was worried about my weight. I finally got an appointment with the Doctor who told me straight up if I didn't admit myself, she would have to commit me to their hospital eating program. I had tried to gain weight, but I couldn't. I was 84 pounds and I thought I looked good. Crazy huh? All I could see was how cool it was to get into clothes for a junior high girl. They were cheaper!

April 2007

JODEE (Mother) - Liz is being very logical and brave about this - it takes a lot of courage after trying to battle something to go and seek help on your own. She made the appointment six weeks ago and this was the earliest she could be seen. She did make some progress since Feb, but she admitted 'herself' into the Eating Disorder Program yesterday. Her weight was seriously low and the doctor was concerned about making it into the next day. She handled the issue with new medical professionals and is working hard to do what they say even though it hurts and is very difficult. We do not know how long she will have to remain inpatient. Her dream is to get her hurting body stabilized and then work on a longer term outpatient program. She seems dedicated to beating this.

I remember holding this tiny spindly dying baby who was unable to keep food down. Were her baby issues of projectile vomiting and gastrointestinal distress returning as an adult? Were her infant eating disorders tied to her issues during transition? Was it sensory?

Meanwhile I have nine new puppies to keep Karl and I busy.

May 2007

I graduated from the Eating Disorder hospital program and the adult school transition program. I began taking care of my body again, it is the only one I will every get.

I worked as a personal care attendant (PCA) for five little girls with fetal alcohol spectrum disorders; we did crafts and went on field trips. I also worked as a kitchen aid in the elementary school and I really liked the students. My boyfriend also got a job and when he works he is very kind to me. I think he likes working.

I believe we can make it together. I have a job coach now who also helps me with living skills. Her name is Ann Marie and she understands life. She is helping me look for a new job close to home. I hope it is a pizza job.

Some of the pups already have new families. Mom took Mak and Bonnie to Dog Scout Camp and I guess they had a good time. Mak came back certified, but he is still a crazy dog. He is a really good daddy to his puppies. My man and I spend time at Mom and Dad's playing with the puppies. They are so cute. I like the little wild puppy named Lana. I buy her a dog license. I hope she can become my service dog.

CASE NOTES - When Liz becomes hungry, tired, stressed or is handling multiple changes in her life she may not act in a calm manner. Job Coach/ILS staff will observe for any of these emotional signs and behaviors and if necessary give Liz time for herself and/or reschedule meeting time. Liz may become agitated while engaging in conversations with others and this may escalate to appear aggressive towards them. Staff will assist Liz in coping strategies to help her "cool down"

Liz is able to use public transportation, but is not as able to take bus routes that require long distance and/or complete numerous transfers. Staff will search for employment close to home.

Liz states that she is able to defend herself against self-abuse, but may have difficulty when the individual is much larger than she. Staff will monitor for sign and symptoms and seek medical and/or legal assistance if necessary

Liz does not "do drugs" including those prescribed by doctors. Staff will monitor if this becomes a health issue.

Liz does have a history of alcohol abuse, but has abstained from use. If staff feels that Liz's well-being is in danger, they will notify appropriate family members and/or medical professional.

*

I mentored a group of teen girls with FASDs. Life got better. I did a video on Women and Alcohol for high schoolers.

Mom and Dad are being nice to 'both' of us after two long years! I have a precious apartment with my birds! Mom let's my cat come to visit. It took a long time to understand what it means to keep an apartment. I finally have a cool job coach and a Pizza job.

I think we'll make it!

I love my man!

Mom was really busy setting up a camp for teens and adults with FASD. It was a real big deal to her. And now I was working at a Pizza Shop. I even did the work better than most of the other workers. I answered the phones, cleaned and prepared pizzas. I was the only one there who came to work sober and not stoned.

They offer me drugs, I say, "I don't do drugs."

Life for me is finally getting better.

I begin to believe in me and us.

July 7, 2007

ANN MARIE (Job Coach) - Update Liz is doing excellent. She is starting out answering phones. After speaking to the Manager, he stated that the training processing is not flexible. Each individual has to complete the same steps and process, as it would not be fair if some were exempt from this. Liz was very nervous, but decided she still wanted to "try" the job out. After 30 minutes of her first shift, she was already more relaxed and comfortable. She jumped right in asking questions and being very honest about her thoughts and feelings ... Initially, her scheduled changed several times, but she will be working a stable schedule each week of 4 days, 4 hours each.

Then one day, we got really busy and I took an order and the manager gave me his pass code, so I used it. Thirty minutes later, I was fired!

I was mad. I want to scream at him. You did not tell me the pass code was a secret. You were busy and you told me so I could type it in. I memorized the pass code to help you. You were frustrated each time I asked. Now you tell me it is a secret? I am not to know it? You were the one who told it to me!. I don't understand why I am fired. I used the pass code you gave me to help you out. I wanted to cuss him out, but instead I called my job coach and told her.

August 2007

ANN MARIE (Job Coach) - Update Staff discussed Liz's work performance with her supervisor at Pizza Shop on thirteen occasions. Her supervisor responded positively on twelve of these thirteen (92%). However, the one incident of negative feedback, was because Liz used her Manager's pass code without permission and resulted in termination.

Her job duties consisted of answering phones, taking orders, computer entry and making various food items. Each time staff completed job monitoring and spoke with her supervisor, he stated she was doing great.

The hardest thing about losing the job was the phone calls from the other people I used to work with telling me what the supervisor was saying about me, and how funny he thought it was that he fired "That stupid retard girl."

Chapter 11
Life in the FASlane Camp
Building a Voice for the Voiceless

August 3-6, 2007 - Camp Reflections

JODEE (Mother) Ann Yurcek (another mother of four adults with FASD)-
What we learned through this camp and previous camps is that when
everyone in the community understood the brain injury and language
of the culture of fetal alcohol, situations were handled safely and ap-
propriately in subtle ways. There was a natural order of support that
emerged. Young people prompted or redirected other young people.
Support people taught other support people. Everyone encouraged
each other. A compassionate camaraderie of respect with responsibility
became a reality. We discovered the exact opposite of the warnings of
the dramatic, violent and dangerous behaviors of persons with FASDs.
The off site quiet room we had available was never needed. The on-site
neutral support person remained available and alert, ready to work tri-
age if the opportunity arose. Though young people made random visits
to pet the service dogs and chat, no more direction than that to regain
composure and return to activities was needed.

For years, keeping our children safe from their FASDs, meant
parents were forced to harbor their children. Without protection families
watched beloved young people repeatedly fail or become another sta-
tistic. Building on the parent advocacy and growing public awareness,
we are hopeful that the new generation of young people will be able to

enjoy the interdependence they need for full and meaningful lives.

Hopefully effective healthy supports are emerging beyond families to promote safety for young people. We are in the infancy of developing multi-faceted intra-collaboratives of life models with interdependent person centered planning. We must understand the responsibility of adulthood comes in small steps when we adjust learning to a person's strengths that may not portray the common accepted verbal, visual, auditory and kinesthetic language of their culture - but instead values the beauty of what they say, who they are and how they understand. Their lives are a gift we can no longer waste.

We must honor our young adults as people first while being aware of FASDs. We cannot continue to throw FASD in their face. Instead of saying "Ah you just had another FASD moment" we need to model and show them in clear steps how to manage stage one behavior and become aware of it so they do not reach meltdown or put themselves in harm's way. It is what all successful people do. Our young adults can be successful.

A major issue in fetal alcohol is that most research and programming is geared for prevention, clinical practice, and programming intervention at younger ages. The time of youth is short and the damage alcohol does to these young people is life long. We need funding and realistic research to develop best practices for development of community embraced interdependence of our young people. We need funding to establish community-based test pilots with multi-layered transitional opportunities within healthy educated communities. If research believes it takes ten individuals to support one adult with FASDs then the logical next step is to develop communities where some of the best ten individuals are and develop a model that can be duplicated by eventually dispersing the original ten professionals to build new teams. We need a collaborative effort between private industry, public funding and families. There is too much work to be done to waste time and money - in jails, hospitals, schools, and the heartache of families and young people they affect.

We can no longer transition our young people whose loved ones have brought them so far into the statistics of FASDs.

I went to camp and tried to participate, but I had already gone back to drinking and I kept thinking about my old friend alcohol. Nothing was really fun for me at the time except drinking and parties and hanging with using friends. At that time I had a really negative outlook on everything unless I was tipsy.

I was surprised I did have fun and I learned some things. I think some of the things I said made a difference. I stood up for the people being treated wrong. The camp was actually pretty good, except in the beginning they treated us like babies. Mom called the people with FASD the experts. So a group of us got together and said our mind and Mom just said, "fine, fix it the way you want and tell me tomorrow." So we did.

My guy was acting all cool with the staff and coming on to one of the girls behind everyone's back. People told me and I thought they were just hating on me for having such a cool guy. One of my girls caught him kissing another girl and years later I learned he threatened her to not tell and script flipped.

Then another friend, from back home, who he was hustling on the side, called offering us an early ride home plus alcohol so we left. I didn't go to the dance. Mom's final report is available at www.betterendings.org. Here are some of the highlighted comments from experts, friends and staff.

FROM MORE FASD EXPERTS
(persons with FASD - typeface kept with Liz's as peers)

– I learned that other people have disabilities and you are not the only one that struggles with the same thing. I can now keep my head up and remember that I am strong. Our struggle makes us a stronger people, so now I see it as a good thing instead of a bad thing. We are special people and to keep trying and never give up.

– By seeing the whole spectrum I learned I was a piece of it but not the whole. I am a person, a normal person with a very complicated disability and now that I know the disability is not me I can get on with my life in a more healthy way. I am not a BAD person or a STUPID person. I am a person with gifts, strengths, and some pretty hard challenges.

– We are not FASDers or FASD kids. We are people. People with an FASD. People like you! I don't need glasses to see better. I need someone to help me think things through sometimes – but NOT THINK FOR ME!

– I really liked how one camper stood up for me. That was really nice. I can stand up for people too. I can stand up for myself. When it was girl's nights I felt really uncomfortable and the rules for me were to stay where I was told. Now I know that I can leave and get a staff person to help me and I don't have to stay when I am feeling unsafe.

– One often misunderstood young woman gave people a lot of support and I was impressed – I've seen how she has grown. She has a limit and when she is done she is done. When you need to get out you need to get out. Either you are going to be a distraction or drive yourself crazy. I understand how she feels when things get too stimulating, I am gone too. I can completely understand it – sometimes I wanted to get up and tell everyone to sit down and shut up too.

– If you stick with someone and have support in public people can't take advantage of you.

– I'd rather have a support person than

– Be in jail or in the hospital

– Be in a mental institution

– Be hurt or in danger or be dead!

FROM SUPPORTIVE FRIENDS

– Our challenge is to learn to speak clearly and simply enough without demeaning their personality and lives. If we talk down to them we feed into the difference and ruin their self esteem.

– We need to speak age appropriate even it they are cognitively different.

– Concrete thinking? – Perhaps. Usually they hear EXACTLY WHAT IS SAID and that is what gets them into trouble or misunderstood. They usually say exactly what they mean and people take offense because their words are not clouded in nice. Is that abstract?

– Something interesting I noted was the huge spectrum of FASD displayed in the variety of people. Some individuals were much more affected than others. Some individuals I would never have thought they had this disability at all! I can see the challenges in designing a camp that is intended to target the entire spectrum. It seems nearly impossible to keep everyone entertained in one large group. I thought it was a positive thing for individuals to see the spectrum for themselves, but I also understand their need for some separation between higher and lower functioning individuals. The activities for these two groups need to be different in order to apply to each person.

– There must be a way to accommodate the range of differences. It is important for us to understand the full spectrum and that was shown by allowing all levels to attend. I loved the boy in the wheelchair who struggled so hard but was happy and did his best in everything. His mom was great. They jumped in and participated in everything they could. On the other hand you have people who were able to be presenters, mentors and support. In the end I think the young man with the most complications spoke volumes without making many statements. Thank you for letting that family come.

– This camp changed my life.

I had no clue and I grew up with these kids. I never understood what my sister went through raising her kids. I get it.

– I learned that the person I accompanied to camp has a lot of
potential, which made me hopeful. I wish she got as much out of the
camp as I did.

– The achievements reached this year by both campers with
FASD and parents or supporters was a learning experience for all that
attended. As a group these adults & young teens taught us to listen,
and realize that they have a voice that needs to be heard. To make
this a place they'll want to come back to socialize with other young
adults struggling everyday with a FAS disability and achieving goals
that they have set for themselves thru trial & error. We need to all realize these young people have to work harder, be stronger than many of
us ever have to begin to try to be. All humans need skills to learn and
grow. The camp is a natural way to accomplish this.

– We need to keep this energy going – we need to develop a
place where the kids can have normal lives and be their best

FROM A CAMP PRESENTER (Greg Olson, Critters & Company) We need
to discover how to be a team player with these young people early in
their lives. Every child and young adult is different and what works for
one does not work for another. If parents and supporters are trained to
make observations early you minimize damage and the ultimate cost
to society and the young person. We need to provide training for care
givers and professionals in early development so that the adult and
teen battle is not so difficult. When you are in the midst of it you are
vested emotionally and the focus is on the immediate need rather than
the umbrella impact."

The disability of FASDs offers limited ability to tolerate differences in others and maintain attitudes conducive to society's norms of care,
respect, courtesy and responsibility. Society doesn't do it for them.
Our young people with FASDs must work ten times as hard to maintain

status quo.

We need to build attitudes that make a difference for all parties. A bad attitude can ruin success and destroy the lives of those surrounding them. We were only there two hours and there were only 32 known persons with FASDs. All the social issues that we deal with in every kid in America popped up at the camp in the main dining hall. When bad things happen we need to know how to keep it simple and not destroy what has been built in a relationship, self-esteem, trust, and knowledge. Intense personalities can come out in disabilities, but it is not our right to kill the spirit. We must learn to direct it.

I have not seen a good study of how each inherited personality impacts that disability to develop strategies for success. We tend to use a cookie cutter approach to mental illness and disabilities in living, recreation and employment. It is complex because the chronological age varies from the normal developmental process. Personality, brain injury, physical age and developmental age factor into the outcome of success.

Whereas the average population copies successful behaviors from others to build a quality adult life, the person with FASDs will take on any behavior because it appeals to them at that moment. How can we avoid this?

We saw the audience come in and the balance is really different from what common people understand. People greeted each other. People were encouraging others to sit down next to them. Some families controlled their camper so that the person is responding on a robot pattern. Yet for this specific person it may be perfect care to avoid issues. On the other hand, we saw Campers bully others controlling them to get out of their seats. We watch carefully for such instances in our violence prevention efforts and it seemed the Campers had set up hierarchy prior and the underlings jumped when they were looked at. The bullies were impatient when things went wrong and did not understand their behavior gave an instant reward but would damage them in the end and could undermine their camping experience.

Clear direction is vital. I saw a group of individuals that have trouble with simple social cues. I saw support people step in to clarify or help people calm down. And make their journey viable. Some did the opposite of what was said. Trying to be cool.

I saw young people given instructions who went forward doing anything they could do to help but the instructions were not clear so they could not alter what they we doing. They simply followed the directions given. I saw other Campers patiently waiting for clarification of instruction to know what they were doing next. I also saw people who had unclear instructions who were short circuited.

Campers were either really controlled to maintain themselves, on the edge of falling into the abyss or lacking boundaries. We observed that the everyday normal human behaviors, actions and statements were random instead of the norm. Caregivers continually dealt with complex and overwhelming issues that could change at the blink of an eye. Some behaviors are extremely out of whack from the norm but with this population it seems normal.

You cannot find answers without asking the questions. In a normal situation audience we would have stepped in and dealt with the behaviors and processed them. We strive to pay attention and reevaluate behaviors – ours, others and how our behavior impacts the whole. It is easy to destroy the network surrounding them. From our experience, with this population when they are challenged for their rude behavior from someone responsible they look at the imperfect response of the caregiver or professional versus their behavior so they miss the opportunity to grow.

FROM FASD EXPERTS (Persons with FASD)

I learned in the young women's group we were able to say we had an FASD. Finally we could say this is what I have and I want to work on a, b, and c. I was able to admit my disability and then identify what my needs were so I could take care of them. It was the most valuable thing at the whole camp. I got the most out of this experience. I am not the only girl that feels this way. We are all looking for support – not counselors and therapist, but people who are in our daily life experience life similar to us. The group of girls that met in the evening (sic) the whole point that was to open up to things we didn't think we could talk about and a lot of us opened up about things we didn't think we could talk about. It was a good thing to get out saying it. We need to do this again in future camps – it is so so valuable.

– I don't want my support person following me everyplace I go, I am not doing anything wrong.

FROM A CAMP STAFF – Sydney Sauber – One of the things I noticed in the first camp was that the young people were afraid to share their ideas or think. I wanted them to know they had good ideas and were capable in spite of having a brain injury. I wanted them to believe they were truly as amazing as I thought they were and that they could learn about their disability and work with it instead of against it. They could put security measures into their lives to live sober, healthy, and safely. I wanted them to know that taking medication if you needed it was a proper thing to become the best they could be.

I think this camp was a natural progression and this time the young adults had an opportunity to claim their voice and share their opinions. Not only did the adults in charge listen to them, but the staff worked diligently to accommodate their requests in an honorable fashion. Before camp I had lunch with a couple of the Experts with FASDs and we discussed life issues and expectations. Once the camp got started a number of the more vocal campers voiced their opinions of malcontent with me and I said "Well you can either keep on listing every negative thing on the planet or you can work to change it, and I can help show you how." With the approval of the staff in charge we selected three people to hold a private meeting with the more independent and older Experts.

It was clear a lot of the campers were not thrilled and the negative energy was being spread with "It sucks and if it doesn't change I am going home tomorrow," "This camp is lame," etc., etc. Once we met with the group we used it as an advocacy tool to help the young adults understand that their needs are important and they can work honorably to get them met.

These young people need to talk to someone who will be real with them about what men and women need and want in relationships. There is a group of girls who think they should be MTV women. They don't talk to their parents or support people about what being a real woman is. On the other hand the guys can't live up to this MTV Hollywood male image and have no idea what girls want or don't want. We need to up the learning and learn things relevant to our lives such as:

- Learn how my brain learns so I can work
  with it instead of it working against me.
- Creative expression of our life experiences and feelings
- Theatrics and dramatics - how to do spoken word -
  stand up comedy - caricature - poetry - turning pain
  into plays, turning their horror into humor.
- Fine art skills instead of sand candles
- Life skills done in a fun way
- Interviewing skills - Looking in the want ads
  - Filling out job applications
- Rap sessions for males and females needing advice
  or to share life, sexual, chemical and drug experience.
- They wanted a dance or a party! Away from support people.
  They were okay with selected chaperones. It was really low
  key in atmosphere – but pivotal in development
  of a national voice.

In the Rap Sessions, one young man took responsibility for his sexuality and made sure to get a checkup. In another case one young woman learned how when you drink or drug you kill the cells and connections you have worked so hard to build and then you need to start over to rewire them. Her eyes lit up and she understood and proceeded to get into a treatment program. Another wants to start a college class. She will cost the tax payers less money if she isn't in the City hospital ER room, in and out of jail, living off SSDI, living in a halfway house, and sucking up judicial, mental health, and medical subsidies. There was a lot of work behind the scene with many young people. One young independent thinking expert distanced herself from her support person and spent the hour in understanding her brain with one of the staff. All of us were very very busy.

I have a tender place in my heart for the lower functioning kids, but their potential is not withered away by the services they are provided or not provided. Their disability is more visible and it is more common for them to have appropriate services. I don't see that same dynamic with the less affected young people. For them I want to reach out to help them reach new potentials. One young woman wants to go to college but is afraid, so is another young man.

I know I am an outsider and not part of this small inner community of FASDs, but I think I have something to offer. As a young person I was underestimated and people took me for not smart. I had to learn on my own. I know ADHD is a different neurological issue, but there are some similarities. I am willing to do my best to bridge society and these young adults.

I never expected to stomp on as many land mines so ceremoniously as I did. Lois Bickford was very helpful and informative. She was instrumental in my work with the ropes course groups and helped me understand more about FASD, the politics, the community dynamics, the kids, and my role in the community. She explained to me in an incredible generous and compassionate way the historical significance of concrete and Swiss Cheese and I chose to use this as a teachable moment for our young adults. I wanted to show them that an adult can stand up and apologize publicly. I wanted them to see that an adult can have humility and make mistakes and go on. If I make a mistake it always matters to me to apologize.

Sue and I would have liked to do a closure ceremony for the young women and their support people who participated in the rap sessions. We wanted to have the young people lead their support person blindfolded to the ropes course and guide them through an exercise so the young person could experience what it is like to be responsible for a person's well being and provide an inkling of what caregivers really go through. We also wanted the caregivers to understand what it is like to not know what is going on around you, easily make mistakes that can hurt you and how annoying it is to not be able to take off the blindfold and walk away from the problem to do something about it. After that exercise we wanted the team to go off to a quiet place and the caregiver share a time when they had made a mistake and there was no happy ending. Perhaps we can program that into the next camp.

It took me a week to refocus and return to my work because my brain was so tied into the camp and its participants. One participant called to tell me she wanted to ask her parents to help her get into a treatment program, another young man helped me edit a chapter of my new book. I answered e-mail. I took calls. I know what it is like to be low balled all the time. I listened, I shared and I talked with each EXPERT with FASDs who reached out. I sat on my boat and played "I Am Amazing" and I burst into tears.

I took away feeling this incredible sense of responsibility. I thought I'd feel flattered that I finally nailed the song or accomplished seven presentations and eight facilitation groups in four days. I haven't even watched the videos yet. I walked away with gratitude. "Thank God I opened myself to preparing in a way that worked as well as it could." Overall I was able to somehow reach people and put the bar higher. I pushed harder in the small groups building on the large first presentation. I stopped people when things were hard and encouraged them – explaining how things got easier as you practiced. Things worked better when you got three pieces of information. I wanted to make them aware of the electricity running through each brain.

I felt grateful and insignificant as one little drop in this huge bucket. Jails and homelessness and early deaths are not correct outcomes. These people are amazing!

FROM A CAMP STAFF – Deb Evensen – This camp, built on the firm foundation of Barb and Ted Wybrecht's two previous camps in Michigan, bravely tried taking the next step: treating young adults with FASD like "adults". The mix of appropriate support and safety for the experts while offering them choices was tricky, and I worried a lot. In fact I barely slept each night and jumped up whenever I heard a sound.

I finally relaxed during the dance on the last evening as I watched the experts laugh, talk, cry, and simply act like young adults.

I truly believe we can do this!

I want to be part of continuing the tradition of a yearly camp and am willing to help figure out how to provide silent, but omnipresent support for these young people we all love.

Chapter 12
My Alcohol Dance

After all that we started looking for a different job. But with no success. I had been sober when I worked ... but ... I tried not to look at my 'happy friend' alcohol - him. I try to control myself. I am careful now. I do not want to be committed or in Detox again so I limit what I eat, where I go, who I am with. I even limit the amount of alcohol, my man and I are both drinking again. It was months. It went on and on. At first I tried and then things kept falling apart. Everyone said no or didn't call me back. Life is really hard sometimes!

Having a job was an important part of my life.

How could I lose it?

I was being kind to you. I tried hard?

I was proud of my job. I made pizzas and I topped them to look good. I liked my job. I wanted to do life in my way on my own. But then I entered the pass code. And on my own was what got me in trouble one more time

You don't drink when you work. That's the rule.

I filled out applications. I delivered job applications.

No. No jobs.

Ten applications.

Ten. No jobs.

Twenty applications. No jobs.

My friend alcohol came back. He stood waiting for me to return. He walked by me always -- my happy friend.

September 2007

I drink to numb my stupidness – a twenty ounce water bottle is now only half full of vodka. My man divides up what we buy so I don't drink too much. I got really bored and I started drinking more and more and more. Way more heavily and now I am in a facility with lots more rules and no freedom.

I never want this to happen again.

I really do want to be a role model for people with FASD.

It's half empty.
I used to drink the whole bottle -
    but not any more.
    I am doing well, so well -
only trouble is
I need it more often now,
    now that I don't have a real job.
I can drink now where I want,
    and when I want
        whenever I want.

I try hard to stay sober, I don't want Mom or Dad to know I am drinking again. I don't want my job coach to know, but I think she does.

I found a job where I can be a dancer for an agency. We go to parties to dance. It is such fun and very easy work. I found this job on my own to pay my bills without a job coach! Free drinks! My best friend's sister got me this job – a good paying job for dancing. I can drink while I work. Yes, they let me drink - I am adult - I am, see I can prove it too you. I mean I cannot prove it – my wallet was stolen at the party – my ID and my social security card. I kept my social security card when I got my job – This time I am an adult so I didn't give it back to Mom. I am 21... You know, I don't even like the taste of vodka.

Did I say best friend ... well maybe not anymore. I drank my first drink at her house from alcohol we stole from her parents. Her sister helped me get some money - dancing - dancing - it was fun. I want to go home – alone – now I have no boyfriend - we had been together for other two years - he is my best friend's lover. I hate him.

I would have had money – all the money I ever needed but Mom locked down the check book I took from her office. It has my name on it. How can I take my money? It was mine. She said it was ours. I bought nice things with the checks - things I wanted - or thought I needed. It didn't take long to spend a lot of money. It didn't matter to me there was only $15.00 in the balance.

What is a balance? The bank has lots of money.

My bruises - well – I have not been eating well - I have been drinking too much - I have not taken care of my birds - don't worry it was better when I was working - when I had to be someplace on the same days at the same time sober and looking healthy. Do I care? No. Yes, I mean no.

I dunno ...   I dunno ...   I dunno.

He grabs me. I run. I run out and down, and down and

out, and around. I am missing some of my clothes and I run to the police station two miles away where I know I will be safe. "Oh God, let Officer --- be there. Please." The lady at the desk calls, "I will be right there." He leaves what he is doing to see me. He cares. He has known me when I was a little girl. He knows my parents. His wife is Mom's friend. He takes me home. He is sad. He tells me if I keep up with my man, he is going to end up murdering me. He drops me at my apartment. I am alone and I know what he said is true, I could get killed. He picks my man up for a hold. Press charges? I can't, I've seen what happens to people who do – vandalized family members, sneaky stuff, nasty evil wicked revenge. I say no and my man is free.

*

The little neighbor boy ran down the stairs and out the door and Mak and the puppies followed him. All the fences and protection Dad put up to keep him safe didn't work when he ran out the wrong door and into the street. Dad said people chased him and he thought it was a game as he ran into a truck he didn't see. He was just having fun. Mom and I lifted him into the car and brought him to the vet.

He was already dead. Mom said, "Dead like you will be if you don't change your ways."

*

My head hurt so I took a pill I thought was an aspirin just before Mom had invited me to dinner. We talked that day and laughed. The pill was not an aspirin, I didn't know I had drugs in my house. I don't do drugs. I don't want to die I want to live. At the restaurant in front of my family - I slipped inside out. They thought I was drunk. I was not drunk - I didn't drink. They asked it I was drinking and I said, "NO!" I did not lie. I was not drinking right that minute, I had not drank that day. It was the little pill. Smell my breath! I tried to act grown. They were angry. THEY said there would be no more dining in public with them.

I spun out, I felt abandoned.

Then I drank and the more I drank, the more I drank.

*

Are you happy that I am torn apart?

> *Are you happy you stepped on my heart?*

My feelings are for real. Do you feel my pain?

Brought me so low. You took my soul to a point where I am lost and I don't know where to go. Are you happy?

We're back ... around the tree again.

> *My "friends" dropped me off*
>> *at Mom and Dad*
>>> *but they weren't home*
> *and I was cold*
> *and wrapped up in a table cloth*
> *she had on her stoop.*
>> *Stoop too low sometimes don't I?*

Shoulda Woulda Coulda

JODEE (Mother) - If only it shoulda woulda coulda been different. Not that I really want everything different, but one thing. If only my daughter's mother would have abstained from drinking - at least for a moment - at least for enough time to allow this beautiful child to be born whole. I can't put back what she was never given. Some gifts are only given once.

In essence I have done my job, done it the best I could. Laid my life down so to say, as have so many of us. So very many. My daughter has the best laugh in the world – a laugh that can burst a rainbow out of a thunderstorm. Too many thunderstorms, today I have no laughter.

Enough! Enough: Enough. I shout to the heavens, because the world is not hearing. Every night another mom shares a bottle with her unborn baby - somewhere   - someplace   - sometime … in celebration, in pain, in joy, in sorrow. There is always a reason.

Alcohol has lots of friends.

I want to run away. I want to grab myself a box of Oreos or chocolates or Boston Cream Pie, but instead I take vitamins knowing that is what I truly need - to pass another day - another test - of who I am - what I am capable of giving and forgiving - not what I want.

I want to drink a whole pot of coffee - so I pour myself a cup of chamomile tea. Perhaps that will ease the pain of another derailment - another collapsed bridge - another Twin Towers. For you or me, life is so simple because we can see the complex and imagine what could be around the next bend. But what if you couldn't, didn't, can't.

I want to grab my own bottle or chemical and numb myself from the pain - the chaos, - the confusion of consequences of her trail of tears. I sip my tea and instead weave a word tapestry for others to understand the pain and nonsense of FASDs.

My daughter walks on a very narrow line to maintain a piece of normalcy. A push or shove, however slight, can tip her over.

Balance for her is still in full pendulum swing - back and forth - back and forth - back and forth.

I want to cry, but I know if I begin I may never stop. I have held and counseled so many other parents, and friends and families as they reach out for support to fit pieces of a puzzle that don't exist because they were never created. I stay strong to learn and understand. And like Alice in the rabbit hole I fall into my daughter's madness where she needs a crew to clean up her demolition. In a whirlpool she is sucked into the unfathomable. Please child reach out so I can direct you.

I leave groceries at the front door, with her and 'a safe friend' to clean and repair and help her get back onto the ridge. I let go of the doing so she can become. Walking on a ridge is always hard - dips and turns, stones and crevasses. Those of us who raise children with FASDs understand all too well the death toll of Liberty Ridge. It is a hard climb and even with the most experienced climbers working together - few make it.

I stand on the other side of this new crevasse - looking for the next piece of gear to help her. It has been an arduous climb and I am weary. Like so many of us parents, no matter how well I care for my-self – I need rest. I need strength and fresh water. I didn't go to a FASD celebration yesterday. I couldn't, wouldn't, shouldn't.

Yesterday I had nothing to celebrate.

Happy International FASD Day

– 9/9/2007

Wednesday, September 12, 2007

JODEE (Mother) - Liz called, she is back in County Detox. It has been almost 18 months.

When she stumbles — she falls. Here we go again.

ANN MARIE (Job Coach) - Staff called Pizza Shop and Manager stated he had to let her go because she used his passcodes without permission. Staff called Regional Manager and discussed concerns. He agreed to place Liz on "rehirable" status. He set up interview to discuss this with Liz. Staff called to cancel interview and reschedule as Liz is now in Detox.

PREVIOUS TREATMENT COUNSELOR - It was good to talk to Liz again. I hope we can get this all worked out. I told her that the fact she called me for support was showing some maturity on her part.

I gave us each a task - she is to call the number on the back of her medical card and get numbers of therapists in their network. She then needs to make an appointment. She said they ask dumb questions and I explained that sometimes we have to ask what appear to be dumb questions in order to get some history of the situation. She seemed to understand that. My task is to talk to our independent living facilitator and get some resources of things Liz can get involved in where she can make sober friends and have things to do. – Previous treatment counselor

JODEE (Mother) - **Fly Away Dear Mother**

(Written by Jodee after a phone conversation for Liz)

Good morning dear Mother - I am safe. I did not die. I almost wanted to, hoped to and almost tried. But I stopped myself because you taught me how important living is. And I want to live.

And not be bound by all the trappings of my mind that spirals down into abyss twirling and swirling and spinning until I am small so very small and alone and only alcohol takes away the pain - like when I began in a liquored sea under my mother's heart.

I stopped myself mother because you took me from a place of empty arms into your home and into your heart and you poured everything you had to give into me - to help me and now I want to change and grow again to get up from where I have fallen back and back and down.

Pray for me mom - that I find another man. I cannot be alone at night for I am scared - so scared to be alone and so I go alone to where a friend stays and never leaves - an old friend I met not long ago but for always - my bottle friend - who comes when I am in pain - to relieve my mind of the twisting and turning and twirling. It does not let go because I come back to open the cap, and drink the drink, and feel the forgetfulness, I seem to need when nothing matters anymore and I cannot go on, but then I must. I must wake up. I want to live and not continue in such a way as I have done once again - once again I fell so hard but this time I saved myself. Not you Mom! Not you chasing me - finding me - picking me up from places you have never been. Perfect you would never go there because of who you are. But you went because of me. Because you loved me. You came to find me when I was hurt and alone.

So mom I called you this morning because I know that you're love is real and you do not forget the little girl who did work a job and did graduate from high school and did learn to do so many things others said I could not do. But I could. And I can do them again - I can you will see.

I will try to fly again. Perhaps there is another way.

This place is safe Mom - you put me here to keep me safe when I was just a beginning adult - a child still - now I know. I am 21 and wiser - perhaps. Perhaps not. I dunno.

I asked for help to come where I knew I would be kept safe and warm and cared about. A place where, people like me, with no one, come, when they are scared and alone. Those who come regularly call this place heaven.

Those who live on the street and under bridges and sleep with plastic bags for quilts. Once again, I see my dad, the man who gave me life - yellow and withered - here in the place he told me was heaven - county detox - his life so hard. The man I believe is my father is over 50 and he still cannot read! And I cannot call it heaven mom for I have a home and an apartment. I have a family and 13 birds that call me mother - birds of every color of the rainbow that sing me to sleep and wake me in the morning with songs.

Will you come and care for them and keep them safe and warm while I am here? Becoming once again the me I lost - the me lost to the bottle before I was even born. I want to fly mom. I want to fly away and be safe.

Life is so hard ... but I won't quit.

KAREN (Director Grandma's Place) - Hey Jodee - Tell Liz orange clothes don't work for her and that there is more to life then getting crazy drunk. Although you and I know, Jodee, that our kids and hello ... 'adults' learn by experience. Since this is my day-to-day life now with many undiagnosed FASD folks, we need to make sure those of us who understand FASD diagnosed or otherwise provide a safe place for them to learn in. My hands keep being tied to develop services for the Liz's of the world. No funding, no time becomes a costly conundrum.

My heart's goal is to let them know there are people out there that are good and bad. I keep using all the mental and emotional bandages I have to stop the bleeding.

JODEE (Mother) - I have to remember to keep hugging my hubby. We need to let go of my little girl in a woman's body. We need boundaries for each other from her life. I especially need that. It is so hard to be the mom. This path is isolating. I feel lonely. I have to let go of parenting. I have to come to terms she may die, or grow, or stay the same and it is not in my power to choose her decision.

September 12, 2007

How could you, with my best friend?
Sex – I caught you in bed. Her bed.
My friend since I was seven,
> *who I had gone to help,*
> *and invited you to come along*

*

Mom picks me up and the first thing she says is, "You

have over 800 text messages on your phone. That's $375!" She is shouting! What? I hate when she shouts. I can't hear when she shouts. It does no good to listen; her words roll in my head like a bowling ball along with the fact that my man is having a text message affair when I am at work! My words collide with her words, my words are screaming inside my head at my supposed man and the sneaky stuff I thought my mind was playing now makes sense. Oh, God, he is such an ass.

"You tried to control me," my mind shouts. "You watched so no men looked at me and while you watched you text!" my mind shouts louder. I think Mom might be trying to talk to me. I AM not LISTENING to her! "Her! My little girl friend!" my heart is screaming too. "You are so evil," my spirit is stomping up and down and down and up! "And I have forgiven you over, and over, and over, and over, and over again, for hurting my body, but now my mind and heart are gone too," my soul feels dead. I will live as proof ... "Fuck you bitch!" I shout at Mom and get out of the car. I wasn't even talking to her, too bad she always seems to get my crap slid on her lap.

I ended up at Game Works - got drunk to take away the burn from you, I put myself in Detox because I was afraid I would do something stupid and end up in jail instead. Detox? Jail? Detox? Got myself locked up in COUNTY DETOX to keep me safe from hurting you.

I get out at 2:00 today. What will I do without you?

What will be my life without you?

Can I do it without you?

You make me feel unable? You are full of lies. You want to change me, but you won't change yourself.

Dear Mom and Dad
Thank you for adopting me, so I have a family.
I think I would already be dead
if I wasn't adopted by you and Dad
Liz

ANN MARIE (Job Coach) – Staff called General Manager to reschedule interview and was advised she was "unhirable" because she "walked out" when she was previously employed in 2005. Liz agreed to look elsewhere

My dumb self now has five phones. My friend and I went shopping at the mall and the phone guy said my credit was perfect so I qualified for FREE phones. I got one for my girlfriend and a new one for myself. I could add her to my account for only $9.99 a month. I thought that was cool and my friend said, she'd pay me $100 a month to have the phone. The people at Grandma's Place made her give me the phone back, she was not allowed to have the phone. They think I set her up for the $100 deal, but she offered.

My man is back and we made up!

My friend who helped me clean disappeared from my life. My man said she was a bad influence, a thief and she stole my mop. I shouldn't trust someone who takes things. I miss her, but I can't trust "the snake in the grass" as he calls her. I am left with my man who is kissing up for his bad behavior. Then the comfort zone hit. Hit me, because another's guys number popped up on my phone.

October 23, 2007

JODEE (Mother) - Karen - Until today, the stint in detox stabilized

Liz. Then her 'girlfriend' dropped off 'her man' because she was sick of him. Liz and he have made up. I guess he needed a place to crash. I am not used to red flag men who abuse and threaten and cheat on women. Liz is going to be Liz regardless what we do. She can not see the heartache. She forgets her trauma. She cannot understand our counsel. Learning by doing is costly to all involved.

Karl and I have backed out of helping them and are requiring the following pieces if they want a relationship with us.

1. Counseling for their relationship
2. Both have a job
3. Both pay their bills.

Life is tough. Liz has a Treasury note coming due this week. She wants to manage all the money. It is the last of the money we saved for adult schooling. We have nothing left. I let go.

November 9, 2007
AUTUMN COLORS OF FETAL ALCOHOL

JODEE (Mother) – With the weather changing they wear fall colors in heaven ... a bright orange sweatshirt ... a pair of bright orange warm pants ... plodding in slipper - leaving behind laughing stupor with renewed acquaintances who come and go when it gets cold - warm food - clean sheets - a shower - for 72 hours a piece of heaven. They come inside safe for the first cold snap. Minnesota is hard on the homeless. Those who lost their battle to alcohol before they were born. I look at the faces - the placement of the eyes - once innocent filled with street pain. I look at the scars. Gashes and gnashes of white streaks on dark skin and dark streaks on white skin.

Scars have no mercy - they remain.

I ask for names to say hello. Most are older and many have children. How many children? It is easy to make a child when you are lonely. When you are scared. When you are hurt. It is easy to confuse sex with love. It is easy to hurt a child when you don't understand.

Understanding? I understand that my daughter is struggling with deep pain as she says hello to people she met three years ago. She is not afraid of these people. She greets them as old friends walking a common ground I walk with her in odd times and odd places. She recognizes a friendly face and says hello at a clinic or store. They wave to each other from a back alley of a church.

Had it really been three years since she came up the grey elevator to heaven? For some people life on earth is a hellish struggle. Here they laugh and smile. For a blink they are safe and warm and clean and the people who work here are good. Her birth father looks forward to the safety of this heaven. She talked to him again. Did she let him know she was his daughter? Not yet. Rejection would be too high of price to pay. Will he believe it is the daughter he gave away?

It matters less now. She knows and understands.

The hopeless pray to turn orange before the frozen truth is exposed. In three years his mind has gone. He is safe past the grey elevator. Hidden inside the tan building, surrounded by trees turning autumn orange.

Who dare explore this truth?

Are we smart enough to seek answers?

My daughter smiles her beautiful smile. I watch her. Did you come, as you say, to protect yourself from yourself, and the streets, and the bus ride home?

Or were you transported - like so many others, in a people shipment. Tomorrow some will leave. The state hospital awaits new guests with thin upper lips and ears not quite right, guests with beautiful smiles and innocent laughs, guests whose lives may end in this commitment, their souls buried behind walls, their gravestones numbered to hold a body without a name to prevent stigma of the dead. The walking dead.

My daughter is the youngest number. Tomorrow her social worker will pick her up. It will be time to go.

Where? Where, when you are lonely? Where, when you are scared. Where?

JODEE (Mother) – Karen – Liz is doing well clearing her head in County Detox. I asked Liz what happens when you go around the same tree over and over. In the wisdom of FASD she shared. "I fall down like a nut." I smile. I laugh. And I know there is hope. God, I love that kid.

She asked, "Do you think I could be a friend with some of the kids from camp. I bet they would be my real friends"

I promised to ask. She is writing again hoping to help other young adults. It seems writing is a family outlet. Perhaps our words can push this rope called FASD. I dream of a Liberty Ridge. I appreciate you caring about our family.

November 8, 2007

ANN MARIE (Job Coach) - Liz still does not have any funding. Yikes, this is going on too long. I have 1.5 hours a week to spend with her! That includes EVERYTHING that I do ... reports, applications, paper-work, phone calls, meetings, going out with her. She CAN use more funding, but her CADI wavier doesn't allow any more. We think it is a billing issue ... if it isn't her MA ... getting answers is difficult. It could be something that we have NO idea about. She was wearing LOTS of make-up yesterday. I will talk to her again, her face appears orange with black spots and streaks on it. I am sure she does not see how she looks, she tries so hard to be pretty. I just called and I told her that I was returning her phone call. It was quite apparent that she did not remember she called me. She was slurring.

November 11, 2007

JODEE (Mother) - She called me after she called you - she was very drunk. When she is drinking I have no clue if she is delusional or telling the truth. I probably won't see or hear from her again today. She said she has been drinking for 38 days straight.

She said she is scared of life. I guess all we can do is docu-ment. Ya know I don't have many rocks left to turn over and most of the trees in this FASD forest have ruts because I have been around too many times. She is falling fast. I feel it and let go. I no longer dance around her issues.

No swearing. I say, 'I love you too much to listen to you talk like that.' No purging. 'I take you home.' No calling me when drunk. I hang up after I say I love you. I take pictures when her makeup is too heavy. Hopefully by seeing she will understand.

December 16, 2007

ANN MARIE (Job Coach) - Liz did a great job at the interview with situational questions. She asked when she did not understand. She did not talk about drugs or alcohol. She was very patient when asking for an application at a restaurant (she usually isn't).

I am straight with her, but I have stepped back and stayed out of a lot of things ... money, drinking, drugs, her physical health, her eating ... to focus on employment. She does need to touch up on her appearance to look clean and professional for job interviews though she has improved since staying at her friends ... her clothes are clean now. They are her own, and tasteful, which helps.

Chapter 13
Bear in Mind

JODEE (Mother)

W hat didn't we do wrong?
So many things that others can point fingers to.
The train wreck moved so fast into areas of our life
we didn't understand.
We didn't have the skills or supports in place to stop it.

I don't think the hand of an abuser knows the pain and feeling of being on the other side. I didn't grow up in abuse, Mom yelled, and once she even slapped my face for swears, but I don't ever remember even being spanked by either of my parents, though they tell me they tried it once when I was two and I laughed and told them I liked it!

When Dad pushed me on the bed and I called it abuse I had no idea what abuse was. It was the strongest discipline he had used on me, usually we talked things out at the Truth Table or he yelled. The truth was I was so wrong, all I wanted to do was keep my CD I had JUST bought. He didn't even really push me, I tripped and fell on the bed. Then he broke my CD and I told him I'd call the police. He looked at me and said, "Fine, call the police." So I did. My parents were strict, but fair even though I know I was a tough kid at times.

I know Mom knew I was drinking again.

We had a four day speaking gig with her. It was me, my boyfriend, a friend with FASD and his service dog and Mom. My boyfriend was always sweet in front of my mom, when you are dirty in the background, it is a requirement. But I think after spending some days with us all she started figuring more things out. One night, at dinner Mom asked what kind of housing would work for persons with our kind of brain differences.

We had been staying in an AmericInn and our ideas built from that. We liked the layout and the place. We had made friends with the night guard. We shared all our ideas and one idea made another and another.

We would have small apartments a bit bigger than the hotel rooms. We would let men and women and married couples live there. We wanted it in a college town so people who would become police and social workers and doctors could live with us and get to know who we really are. Maybe they could have a special price and get credits. We would have the main room with the big screen TV, fireplace, games, computer and the kitchen breakfast area with make yourself breakfast and sandwiches and soups for lunches.

We want to be part of the regular community and be appreciated. We would have a heated swimming pool and share it with the hospital and old people and hurt people. We would have a craft room with classes for things that we really could use and learn to do to make our lives better and more interesting, not just pot holders. We would have three or four businesses on the main floor and the community would like to use them and buy things from us. We could have a tea, coffee, book shop and senior citizens could play cards or do puzzles there, a pizza, sandwich, subway, soup place and the prices would be good with special deals, a thrift store where people could donate their old stuff, a 24/7 fitness center with a health coach, a social service center or office for a counselor, a mailing center or copy center. It would be nice near a library or on a bus route. Maybe we would do dog training or have a little pet store. All those jobs we could do with other people who think they are normal.

We would have a guard at the desk to screen people so bad people would not get in and if we got bored or were awake in the middle of the night we could go visit him or her. We would have them all over the world so we could take vacations and be safe.

*

JODEE (Mother) - The bear is back in my mind, a grizzly wrizzly izzly bear, with a flurry of surly wurly feelings that want to grow, and growl, and snarl, but they can't because there is nothing and nowhere to place the snarly, warly baring teeth feelings so real. I have no fairy wand to wave to make life better - to change what has been done to 'tens of thousands' of children a year in this country. Under the hearts of those who may say they love them. I want to shout loud and clear that DRINKING while pregnant must stop! That the person you are growing matters. That this person matters to me and to the others who will love and care and hold the little he or she.

The bear is back in my mind as I remember when you came so small, with arms so thin and legs so small you were 'bearly' a nothing at all except a very big voice.

Bear in mind - A growling raging voice proclaiming your insidious beginning. An spindly infant who could project vomit into the air screaming in pain until we found special food for you to survive. And the mama bear in my mind went looking for answers to help you live and grow. And you did. And this mama bear asks, was I blind to not to see this as an eating disorder then, now mixed up with life.

Bear in mind - A growling raging voice proclaiming you could not be touched or held or cuddled and I wanted a snuggly wuggly buggly child who I could hold - and so the mama bear in me found ways to enjoy you and realize that you loved the best you could - until we learned about how your body worked. And you were thirteen with already interest in boys who lusted before you knew how to love. The bear in mind was there searching - but not finding - asking with no answers because I did not have the right questions. How could a mother not know? Or doctors or others so educated?

Bear in mind - A growling raging voice proclaiming that fun events were too intense and yet you, my child, were the most intense of all. I learned to calm and quiet all the grizzly voices in my mind and not add my energy to your world of chaos so you could learn, and grow, and go, and do like other children. And you grew into a giving, loving, forgiving child with a big heart woven into a mind we did not understand. Alien in a world of media and advertisement that undermined what we said. They knew. We didn't. We were not the TV family or glamour girls. We were happy in our little den with our close friends doing close friend things - while you my little cub needed to run and explore what you believed was pots of honey at ends of rainbows that did not exist except in the media of music and video. They were your truth. Where is their love for you today? Do the designers pick you up from the streets and hug you back to better in those little clothes? Do the rappers salve your knife slices from the gang? Do the producers repair your heart? The bear in my mind watched as you floated through your imagination of Truth with brain injury caused by alcohol to the unborn - 100% preventable – a simple choice of one. Oh, the bear in my mind wants to pound my chest and growl. Do bears roar?

Bear in mind – You grew, and you grew, and you grew away because we were not who you wanted to be - could be - would be. The bears in our minds no longer silent - pushing each other away with our snarls and growls and stares.

Bear in mind - I hope you have come to the end of yourself - your spirit intact to change the course. You, my child, are one of too many. Too many - 'tens of thousands' – a year too many. The bear in my mind wants to hibernate - to go away and sleep it off as a big bad dream. There is no time for hibernation. We, mother and father bears, must remain vigilant. We must embrace the voices of hundreds of thousands, voiceless participants in this charade. We must stand together with all the bears in our minds and change the course of time.

Sunday, December 9, 2007
A Gift from an Otter (a friend who understands)

CYNTHIA (Mother of Adult with FASD) - Poor old angry bear, torn and tattered, banged-up head, knocking on brick walls again. Rest, my bear friend, The otters are here, clinging, so you can float free for just a short while. Grab the hand of that small one fuzzy bear, The one you have hugged so often, hug her again, so she too can rest. We will hold you up, We will hold you both. -

JODEE (Mother) -

The Magic Cure ... The Silver Bullet ... The Garlic Around The Neck ... Prayer ... Roll up your sleeves hard work

There are caregivers in this generation of emerging young adults with FASD who have captured the dream of avoiding "secondary disabilities" handed down from the knowledge and hope of the previous generations. Yet, in spite of their best efforts to "make a difference" to avoid them, they discover between ages 18 -23 an ugly side of FASD. I reflect on the ugly side of FASD with Liz as a child before we knew what her disability was and how to help her. It is an interesting parallel to how the world reacts to her and how she responds today. History seems to repeat itself.

Our childhood success came with personal awareness of FASD, combined with supports for her developmental issues. It lasted through the moments she trusted us for guidance. Still, life readily collapsed with the change in seasons, new experiences, disorganization, wrong friends, unstructured activities, limited sleep, poor food, and/or stress. All of those are a very real part of everyday adult life. Today she has no guide to redirect, pick up or clean off. When and if I can it is for a glimmer. I expect the hurricane of her life may grow. People who know our kids understand what families live with, at least a bit.

Can we avoid the secondary disabilities or are they an inherent destiny? Perhaps, that depends upon the child, family and life experiences. Good advice has been written on avoiding secondary disabilities. The need for supervision, the opportunities for disaster and an inability to really protect are overwhelming. I believe the higher the IQ, the more they grieve attainment of skills, abilities and the lifestyle of peers, the more they are drawn to excitement, eroticism or violence, the more trouble you will have.

We live in the city, but I know families who have moved to the country to protect a child early in their life and had similar experiences after age sixteen. What may scare a normal person and twist their fate to change may introduce our children to "new friends" new ideas and more problems. When you mix their naiveté with jail or detox programs or institutions with criminally insane, you provide another window of opportunity to learn negative behaviors.

The FASD community still does not have the answers. It will take the children who have been sacrificed in jail, death, institutions of this generation, with parents from this coming generation to create the next steps. What we learn we must share for those who follow. I still dream of possibilities and I will always love Liz – Jodee

Chapter 14
Secrets
Behind closed doors

My man, my bootleg, my boyfriend, said I made him crazy. His excuse to pick me up by the neck and shake me. I'm lucky my head didn't fall off. I'd go limp, I couldn't fight back, because when someone is holding your neck and shaking you have no control. He held a knife to my face and threatened to cut me. He put peppermint oil in my eyes and I thought I was going blind. Thrown dishes were nothing, fry pans, phone cords, hands, tables, cooking utensils, frozen hamburger, teeth clamping down, video and cell phone slap, head butts to my face, shoestrings tied to hold me, a hammer against my back, mirrors shattered, pillows held against my face, my pant legs pulled off and tied around my neck and then pulled up, the balcony railing all became weapons. He told me if I broke up with him or left he would find me and I would be sorry. I kept knives in my doorjamb. I spent more time in the bathroom.

I drank. I drank more.

I threw up everything I ate.

I was filled with anxiety.

I yelled at my parents.

I told them how much I loved him. I tried not to yell at him. I lied. I lied and then I lied some more. I drank. I passed out. I threw up. Is it rape when you are passed out, from someone you tell everyone else you love? I wet the bed from drinking so much. Shakes. Shakes. Always shaking unless I poured vodka down my throat. All I could think about was getting a fix. I just cared about myself and was paranoid about being found out.

The laundry piled up high and I slipped and split open my chin. Later I had flashbacks of being tripped. Bruises were on both my cheeks – one from the hand of my man and one from passing out. What I did to myself drunk and what he did blurred together. He put ideas into my head to tell my parents.

We'd been together a long time.

I loved him. I loved my bottle.

I loved my animals. I didn't love myself anymore.

And I was scared of my parents finding out the truth ... so unless I really needed them I did life on my own ... Until ... I again woke up in the hospital ER. How many times had I woken up in ER wondering where I was and how I got there?

Most times they let me go once I sober up. This time they kept me and moved me to the double locked area where you can only write with crayons. They said I was a danger to myself and I got interviewed by a bunch of people asking me lots of questions. They said my blood alcohol was .434 when I was admitted. I told them I had fetal alcohol. I told them I used to drink every day but now I drink the whole day long.

The doctor asked me why I drink. Don't ask me why questions, I can't think through them so I answered I was depressed. I heard other people say that so I thought that was a normal thing and he would not think I was stupid. The real reason is I liked the feel I got from drinking alcohol and it let me fall asleep. The doctor said I made suicidal threats. I know better than that. You do that you end up someplace you don't want to be. I told him I can't sleep unless I drink, that is true. I told him I was looking for a job and that is true too.

*

I guess I had called my Mom drunk that day and then when she called back I didn't answer the phone because I fell asleep. My job coach tried to call me and I didn't answer so the police were called. My boyfriend wouldn't let the police in so he went to jail. I told them I was feeling down because he had a relationship with my girlfriend a while back, but that is over. I tell them how kind my boyfriend is to me, it is really wrong they put him in jail for not letting them in. The nurse said they had to come in or I might have died. Then what?

*

At first I didn't like the hospital, but as time went on I liked it more. I was safe. No one hurt me and people cared about me. The medicine they gave me let me sleep, but it took a while to get it right. One medicine made me see the world in triangles and my stomach exploded on a nurse. I felt bad I threw up on her, but there was no stopping it.

*

Mom brings the puppies up to see me one at a time. Limey will be a service dog so he needs a lot of hospital practice. I would like Lana to be my dog, she is a wild thing.

I like OT (Occupational Therapy) where we did projects. I liked playing games with the other people there. The people who came here, as patients, were all different, some were old, some were young. All had been hurt, over, and over, and over. We were allowed to talk and become friends. We shared our stories. I realized I was not alone in my pain. I liked the daily activities in the hospital.

My roommate was a real clean person and very or-ganized and she got me for her roommate – messy Liz. We laughed and helped each other become better people. She was like a big sister to me. I liked her and then she went home.

     *

At the hospital, my boyfriend seemed to care about me, but he got frustrated if I didn't save my food and give it to him. One nurse saw though him and told him 'no.' Then he got mad at me because he thought I told, but I wouldn't tell on him. I promised. We played cards and games. People liked him and we actually enjoyed each other again. We laughed together and I dreamed we could make our life work. I never shared that he hurt me. That would have been a betrayal of my love for him and he promised me he was committed to me forever. We would marry when I got home. I had hoped soon.

     *

Mom wouldn't drive my man to the hospital, but he fig-ured out how to come everyday on the bus. When Mom would visit me, he'd ask and she'd drive him home 'to take care of all my animals.' Then my parents had my brother move into my apartment and made my man move back to his Mom's.

HOSPITAL PSYCHOLOGICAL INTERVIEW - The psych test battery was left for her ... she didn't do any of it ... she is initially irritable ... she talks of her 'sentence' in a treatment center ... Her outlook is reasonably positive and she has plans for her life, she does not like the way she has been living and should prove a challenging client and hopefully rewarding as well.

*

A guy left a big package of tests for me to do, but one of the other patients told me that is how you get into a really bad place. Plus, he said, the tests take two weeks to examine them. I didn't want to stay for two more weeks. I didn't want to go to a really bad place. I didn't do the tests. It was weird, then this doctor guy just pops up. I never met him. I don't even know the dude and I am suppose to spit data about myself. Some of the case notes say I can't read so people believed that - things written on paper aren't always the real deal.

HOSPITAL PSYCHOLOGICAL INTERVIEW - As we are doing the psychological tests, she says she is a good reader. I had been informed earlier that she cannot read, but apparently that was incorrect. Shown the MMPI to check on her skills, she quickly states that while she is a good reader, she is a very slow reader and that it would take "months" for her to do these tests unless somebody reads the items to her. She then almost lawyer-like makes a case as to why such tests would be unnecessary, because she has already agreed to her 'sentence' and there is nothing else to know about her that she has not already disclosed.

The only people you really remember are the people who work there a lot and some of the patients. The ones with the longer letters behind there names jump in and out, spit game, write their little notes and disappear for the rest of your life. It's those little notes that can seriously get you into trouble.

Why do people think that because I have fetal alcohol spectrum disorder I am a retard. Why do they jump on that like I am unable to learn or comprehend what they are talking about. Some people slow down their whole presentation and draw out their words like sticky glue.

Don't talk to me like I am an alien.

Don't look at me like I have two heads.

Don't get mad when I check your sentence to under-stand better. Don't you know everything you say you don't mean?

*

By this time the County was sick of my games and I was committed to state mental health. Mom and Dad weren't involved because I was an adult and I was no longer my own person. I was under state control. My life was not my own. I didn't realize what all that meant at the time, but I was about to find out. They decided I needed adult foster care. Funny I came from foster care and now as an adult I was heading back. Something about that word made me sick to my stomach. The people movers came to deliver me to court - big and strong in case I fought. I didn't. I had been on the street long enough to know when you see BIG men, you don't fight back unless you want to wake up in a lot of pain. I cried inside. I didn't want them to know how scared I was.

Chapter 15

Shelved

My bad decision-making of getting drunk got me sent to the hospital with a .434 – that's almost dead! I am writing this in adult foster care. Can you believe it? I was independent. I had opportunity for my dreams and one by one I destroyed my dreams and myself. My boyfriend of three years lives at my place caring for my birds – 13 of them and 3 guinea pigs. What will happen to my birds? I am so mad. What do I have to do, to help me learn?

March 13, 2008

The impulsive part of me is always waiting to pounce like a cat. I go into stores having three things to buy and I come out of the store with a whole cart full. I see something fun or cool looking and just want it so bad I put it into the cart. I am realizing that things are expensive and you don't really need everything.

If you have your heart set on getting a particular thing you have to save up to get it. If it is not longer there, don't flip out. Just wait. The money you saved will add up to something you will find in the future.

I could get so twisted here, but I am not going to break my sobriety. When I go out to smoke a cigarette some of the guys at the college party house next door ask me to leave this place and come over. They'll take care of me. Where have I heard that? Yeah right. Probably wouldn't be here now if I stopped listening to those lines.

Thank God, I have medication, or I couldn't sleep because my room is in the upstairs attic and the party goes right into my window every night – almost every night. The drinking and partying keeps shouting for me to get out of here, go visit next door. But no! I won't let go of being sober. I worked hard at the hospital and this time I am committed. That's funny. I am committed by the State. Minnesota is a big piece of land. The real commitment is inside of me.

It would be so easy. They don't supervise the smoking when it's so cold outside and smoking is a big deal here. I've gone from two cigarettes a day to over thirteen. The only real free time we have is when we smoke – so all of us go out on the hour for our sucking five-minutes. It seems weird to me, but it is the one freedom I have – the privilege to fill my lungs with cancer sticks and listen to the guys next door cat calling, "Yo' girl why don't you come over here – we got beer – come chill and relax, forget those people, you can stay here. I think you're pretty."

I slap myself "No!" and come in to listen to staff talking on the phone to friends, feet on the chair and watching television. I ask to play a game - just cards, She's busy again, too busy for me. I ask to watch my show, but the staff's show is not over. I climb the steps to my attic room thinking, "Oh well better than listening to them talk about me."

*

I hope the time goes fast so I can go back to my man and animals. My animals and in my mind my man are the only things I have left. He tells me he loves me. He tells me he misses me. He wants me to get better. He cares about me. I am now his fiance, we talk of marriage.

*

March 30, 2008

I have a stay of commitment now and it is for six months. That means I will get back to my life on July 31, 2008. I understand I almost killed myself with my drinking and eating issues. I thought when I left the hospital that I would be going to a treatment program with lots of groups each day to learn to challenge myself. I have been sober now for over two months and I have been on my medication for one month. I am disappointed in this program. I feel like I am in day care. The staff expects so little of who I am, but expects behavior that is exactly what they want. Obedient. I am used to being obedient to my parents when I was little, but this is different. They seem to want me to be a less-than. Maybe less-thans are easier and do not challenge them. Curl my mind into myself and pretend to live, but not grow. I am finally sober. I can read. I don't understand this. No one believes me.

I know I am capable of independence without alcohol. I appreciate attending treatment and now that my head is clear and I can sleep with my medication, I never want to go back to how I was. I will work with a group therapist and a job coach. Now that my thirty days is over of watching me maybe I can get a job and become a part of the community. I am afraid the government is wasting their money putting me here – I am worried I may lose myself. People always expected me to rise to my challenges. Here I am expected to obey and sit and be kind. It may make me crazy. I am getting afraid. I hope soon I can talk to a nutritionist. I feel like they do not understand I really have a wheat allergy. I am not making it up. My wheat allergy is irritating them. I think I am beginning to irritate them. I hope that I meet with a therapist soon. I need to work on my eating – a professional will help them believe me. Maybe? I don't want to lose myself. My stomach hurts. Now I get a laxative to drink four times a day. I wake up and it's the first thing I drink, even before I brush my teeth. The watchers watch each pill go down. They watch me as I drink the whole little cup.

March 31, 2008

They promised things would change after 30 days. Thank God, that time is now over. I know I can build my brain back I can feel it changing. I can't loose what I have gained. I know if I go back to my parents for a while and work on Brain Builder and all those nuero exercises I did when I was a teen I can work to put the pieces back. I know I have to prove myself to everyone that I am going to stay sober and get healthy. I will need aftercare programming. Going to my parents will make me grow and put my brain back so I can teach and touch others with fetal alcohol (FASD) and hope to change their lives for the better and forever. Once I prove myself I will gain trust to go back to my independence of living in my own place. I will have the skills and structure to maintain my own life setting. I know I can do it. I feel strong again. If I keep believing I am capable. Now that thirty days of watching me is over, I look forward to getting on with the program!

April Fools Day

It is a new month and still nothing has changed. I need a better outlook on life and attitude. I can't expect a program to pursue my dreams. They said to move ahead I need no daily living crisis. I need to improve my daily living skills. I can work on my hobbies and read. I need to keep myself self-directed. I will try to get a "Chicken Soup" book from the library when we get to go. I need help with my jewelry. I wish we were allowed to be friends with the people who live in my house. I found out the other girl with an eating disorder was told to not let me influence her and best to stay away from me. It is hard. I also overheard staff talking about me – that hurts.

I have finally figured out I am considered an other. I have never been an 'other' before. I have just been Liz. I am beginning to feel like I am trapped in a box where no one understands. I don't get the things I need to help me grow to become a stronger person. I am living in an adult day care. My birth mother named me April. April Fools who I am becoming?

When you are in a program little things disappoint you that outside may not phase you at all. It is just that the day to day is so same-o – same-o. Staff tells they would bring in games to play with us and then they forgot one day and they forgot the next day too. There are so many disappointments. I feel caged, and wonder if prison wouldn't be better because at least you know you are behind bars. Maybe this seems worse because everything looks normal on the outside, but inside is so controlling ... medicine .... check .... schedule ... check ...

paperwork ... check ....check ... check ... write ... write ... write ... notes about April, not Liz.

Later, they say.

Later they never come.

It is getting later, and later, and later. They raise their voice and eventually I don't want to talk to them to make them mad at me. They look at me and roll their eyes. They huff and puff. I go to my room, I quit talking. They write more notes.

*

On the low, without the eyes of the watchers, I see the heads turn away as they tear up. More than one tells me, they wish they had a mom that cared like mine, a mom who sends presents and little notes of cheer. I ask what they mean. My heart hurts from the answers.

"I wish my mom still cared. Mom gave up on me."

"Mom is frozen when she talks to me I feel it."

"I don't think my Mom loves me anymore."

"My mom sounds like she is forced to talk to me."

"It is like I have vanished in her life."

I begin to think my mom might do that too. I worry she is not listening to me as much as she used to. When I talked to Mom last time she told me she was not a part of this program, I did this to myself. These people are trained professionals to help me grow and get well. I have not talked to Dad for a long time. I hope they don't give up on me to. God, please, please, please! My parents are my connection to hope and growth.

JODEE (Mother) - Karl and I don't want to be over protective. We want to follow the rules. We don't want to interfere. Social services is finally involved at a high level and we trust them. We are in new territory and they have far more experience than we have.

We ask, "What are the expectations of parenting or loving a child in residential care?" Social services tell us a ten minute phone call a week and two visits a year. We are shocked. We would never leave our elderly parents alone like that, why would we consider that with a young adult? We have worked with this kid for over twenty years, we believe we have some clues to help them work with her. We don't believe they understand that just because Liz can process once, does not mean she can process it again, even the same day. And just because she cannot process something does not mean she is a incapable of ever doing it. It simply means whatever she is learning needs to be broken down into smaller steps. A list to refer to as she is learning. We challenge Liz to become her own advocate and teach staff what they need to know. We begin to back off.

*

I watch a staff stuff her face with food the clients were suppose to be eating and then relock the cabinet. It is not time for the others to eat. I go to the store and ask for wheat free foods and they tell me it's too expensive. It's not our problem.

Can I get better?

One staff took me out to buy food and she even bought me a coffee. We talked like two regular people. I was normal and we laughed and we shared ideas and she made me feel like life had hope again. We went to a garage sale and she paid for a used CD I said I liked and gave it to me.

So many people are fakes. People can tell when a person cares about the job, but not the people they serve. There are a lot of people like that in the system and only a select few who put their hearts on the line for you. You just hope to find them. Those who actually care and are there for the individual client instead of just a place to go to spend time to get a paycheck. You see that a lot in how they act. I don't get why people have those jobs if they don't care. Maybe the money is OK.

People that care carry on a conversation. They check up on you to see how you are, talk to you about your day and experiences They don't judge what has happened. They seek solutions. I learned it was wrong that the one staff cared like that. What she did was wrong? I thought it was nice and caring. She lost her job and I felt like it was all my fault and now I was all alone. One guy who was a resident bought me coffee and little things. The staff took the little things he bought me – little fidgets nothing expensive– the staff took the knick knacks – no clients were allowed to give little things to each other. He gave me a nice smelling potpourri. All he did was care and was nice to me. At least when you are a "less-than" you are not as sexual to the staff. That's probably good to prevent abuse, but you are more than just a body. You are also a mind and not a nothing. I don't get it. These people are hired for low wages and being paid for bad attitudes. These staff are fakers and I am learning the differences. I am.

*

One time in two months we did my jewelry and for a two to one staff twenty four hours a day seven days a week they keep busy doing paperwork and talking on the phone to important people – like their friends. They are busy. I have learned that. Busy doing ... eating ... watching TV ... watching others ... looking good for supervisors.

April 3, 2008

I am sitting in my room just wishing I did not make such bad decisions. I got myself into a jam where people took all my freedoms away from me and I just want to scream. I'm so far away from my boyfriend and family. It is making me down and depressed. I can't believe I am in a house with 2:1 staff plus a supervisor and I can feel so alone. They said they were waiting for my honeymoon to be over, but that's not the case. I could have stayed upbeat if I was working on me – knowing I was getting smarter and better but I am losing myself here.

They say the honeymoon is over. I give up on myself. They don't realize I surrendered Liz at the hospital with my sentence and was ready to work on a new Liz.

I push my spirit down and stay in my room like I watch my roommates do.

*

I call Mom and beg her for help. She says to make the best of it, it will be only a short time. I begged my social work-er to send me to the state hospital. She said, "Liz, they won't even accept you, you are not mentally ill." I think the staff is thinking I am trouble and I think my social worker thinks that too. I need help. I want help. I need someone! When I know what works for me I am persistent!

*

I hope soon I can see the therapist. I am worried be-cause I wake up in the morning and am not hungry, my stom-ach hurts and my fingers and feet are so cold they curl up. My muscles are getting sore. I am getting down and depressed, I can feel that. I have never felt this way before. I am an up per-son. The doctor at the hospital believed me when I said I have depression. I didn't then. I think I do now.

The rules here are for babies. Everything is locked. The cupboards and the refrigerator are locked. I can't eat when I want to eat. I cannot go anywhere without a staff next to me. I have to get up at a certain time and I have a bedtime. I know I need help and I am worried this is not the place for me. I'm not getting anything from this program except kept. It is like a place to be watched 24/7 so I don't do anything bad.

Oh God, please help me!

April ? What was her name?

Staff offered to take me for a ride and I was excited thinking I was going to get a cup of coffee or have a friend kind of outing. But in the silence of her car without the hearing of any ears, I was told directly I belonged in adult foster care and it was a good place for me. Don't worry. Many clients stay ten years before they are ready to leave.

My mind wanted to turn her off. My heart turned into a ball of playdough and thumped into my feet. I hurt all over. I wanted to scream. I pushed all my feelings inside. I can't believe what she said is true. I wanted my Mom. I wanted my man. I felt scared.

How could six months – July 31st – turn into ten years? Keep me for ten years like the 'others.' How do I keep Liz? Where will she go? God, is it true they will keep me here for ten years? What did I do so wrong? My spirit is hiding in my big toe it is so little now.

I am crying on the inside. I don't cry.

*

This little house, on a street that looks like a place normal families live is a bookshelf for people who have file numbers. They provide five minutes of freedom every hour. My freedom is now a five minute smoke break. I had cut back to two cigarettes a day and none at the hospital - I was already smoke free - now I hit the stick every hour - thirteen times and I savor each puff. Each suck is freedom.

Funny how life works out.

My meds numb me, but they don't take away the pain in my heart and my mind. The pain grows bigger everyday and no one notices. They do not see. They promised me a therapist. At the hospital, meetings, projects, people to talk to, things I could do.

Mom sends boxes I put on the floor and line them up. They are filled with things I need to do with other people. 'Others' I am not suppose to talk to – one of the girls here was warned 'be careful of Liz.'

The loneliness is growing bigger every day.

I want to do things - a job, a project. Day activity is just that - it dumbs down my abilities.

Finally, I am sober and I am able to prove who I can be and my life is placed carefully into a little house with four girls and staff 24/7. The watchers watch me. That is their job. They do it well when they are not talking to boyfriends or girlfriends.

Luckily, my meds put me to sleep just like the alcohol did. I want to sleep like real people? The 'others' - the clients - the people staff calls 'the others' who give up themselves are part of the walking dead I am becoming.

My heart is gone. God help me.

April 6, 2008

I am all alone and lost. No one understands me here. Bits and pieces of me are dying each day. I am treated like a little baby and they seem to want it that way. I am wondering if everyone in the program has something seriously wrong with them that they don't want to change. I haven't learned anything new here. Everything I've practiced in my own life.

Some staff have told me this is the wrong setting for me.

I hate it here. Real hate is a new feeling for me. I protect myself with rudeness. I know it is wrong. I don't know what else to do. I need to be someplace where I am learning and practicing things I will use for the rest of my life.

Please, please God help that come true. I need to go for a walk. I need to get outside. I am not even allowed to walk alone. When I am stressed I walk. Here I walk back and forth again and again. I get fresh air walking to and from the car to day care. I get fresh air sucking smoke. That's funny!

*

One staff took me to the library. She was happy like a real person. She smiled when she was at the house sometimes – between the hours of 5-11 really sweet – have fun with you – make you laugh – She was just a real person. We did not have conversations but we did talk. Usually the time we go to the library we go in and get right out. It feels like only seconds. I am losing track of time. But I wanted a *Chicken Soup for the Soul* and there were so many different ones. The staff said "just take one, we have to go right now."

I can't take one, that's stealing. I would have to pick one out. Check it out. Going right now meant there was no time. I don't have time to choose. I took nothing with me. I so wanted to read again. They don't get it ... they go too fast, too slow.

The staff have started talking down to me like I am plastic and have no brain. One talks about 'the others' and I can hear them all the way up in my attic room. I heard I was a "real piece of crap." I was a "pain in the ass," "she talks really stupid, you know cuz she has fetal alcohol so she's just retarded." I never felt bad about my brain damage from fetal alcohol before. Mom and Dad accept people how they are, they tell me to go with the flow. Get used to it.

I am in a program to help me and I am getting smaller and smaller. None of us matter here. They 'the staff' are happy on payday. They 'the staff' laugh at us, not with us. With is a big word and with you are an equal. They 'the staff' do things for us and to us, not with us. They 'the staff' talk about what they will do with their money.

Secretly almost all the clients hate it, but have to be careful saying what they really feel. It is safer to learn to be an 'other' a nothing and keep your life on a shelf until you are done with your commitment. People – human beings – living human beings - who had been there for a longer time had learned to keep their mouths shut. They were committed and if they didn't like the way they are treated and wanted to go home they told me there was only one way out. "Play by the rules of the 'theys.'" Playing the game of the program is the only way. But I am so hard headed and stubborn and I don't know how to keep myself and play the game. I am not a blah. For my whole life I have been sparkles and filled with energy.

One person – then another person took me aside and they said things like "I've been here for seven years and I keep on trying to fight it but whenever I fight it I get more stuck here. The more you try to do what they tell you to do the less they bother you. I stay by myself – keep my mouth shut now – they think I'm doing better. If you try to fight it they will keep you longer. It has taken me seven years to learn to put up with their garbage. I finally learned not to care."

My heart burned. I am not a person who gives up anything easy. I stand out. How do I hide my Liz?

*

I can't believe it. I asked to stay for prayer and church and they rush us out. They say there is no time. I ask to go to Bible study. They say it is not in their program. I ask for a person to come to our house to talk to us, they say, "No, not allowed." My roommate reads her Bible. They take it away, because she has read it too long. Her Bible is with them now.

At least I can go to a Chemical Dependency program now in the community. I wonder how come it took so long?

*

My teeth hurt – they give me headaches, I hope I see a dentist soon. I hope I get a therapist for eating – I need help. I think I am losing weight. I am worried I can't eat until I take my nighttime meds. Then for about an hour I just want to stuff my face. It makes the staff crazy. I don't throw up here, but with the laxative four times I day, I don't have to because the food I eat never stays.

April ? Is going away.

I feel smaller and smaller. When I wake in the morning I am always cold. My hands are curled into mouse claws and my toes scrunched to stay warm. When I sit up my stomach hurts. I am never hungry during the day. Eating hurts. I am the steam in a teapot. Only I can't blow the whistle for help. Nothing I do matters here. I don't matter.

It is easier on staff if I take naps and stay in my room. They don't get mad at me or look nasty at me when I don't bother them. I try not to look at them, I put my head down when I walk to avoid looking. I am going to try to write today. It is getting harder and harder. They say I am very manipulative and my mom will do what I say. They say I don't have a wheat allergy, I am not affected by fluorescent lights. I do not react from chlorine. It is all in my head. They say I make it up. I have an eating disorder. The meds feel stronger, but that is okay because I can sleep more. I won't bother the staff. I won't be such a pain to everyone. It is harder to think. I know I need a place where I can grow. I am not growing. I am shrinking and I know I need help. But no one is listening.

I need relationship classes, and craft classes, and health care classes, and writing classes, and AA, and exercise. If only I had groups to work on these to give me stability to maintain a happy structured sober life with follow-up from aftercare and sober persons in my life. I can go into the community and see other normal people. God I hope to gain from programming of all the above and I believe the best thing for me is to go to a hospital. Yeah! We are going to go to the Y and go swimming.

I like that. It will be nice to be outside in the community. I miss community. That will be nice.

*

I think I need to go to the hospital. Maybe back to Methodist where I worked on my eating before. I might need a feeding tube. I am getting littler. I need to get better on my weight and then finish my stay of commitment at another treatment facility. I am wearing so many clothes and blankets and I can't stay warm. It doesn't matter where you send me, but I need to go someplace to change. God is what I believe will help me change and maintain my life for all the better for the rest of my life. This is adult day care. I am a nothing here.

Help me God.

I think I need a doctor.

*

Mom and Dad trust what is going on. They think I am in just another treatment program getting services like the smiling lady at the hospital told us. Mom and Dad don't visit.

They ... *(rest of handwriting is unreadable)*

*

I continue to get smaller and smaller. All the food is locked up so you have to ask permission to get it unlocked to get something. When I first asked they are busy.

Then they are still busy.

Then they say they were busy.

'Later' they said.

Eventually I quit asking.

I will not make waves; maybe if I keep to myself I can go home. Maybe I can get better, but I am getting smaller and smaller and I am scared. I start packing my life with candy to keep energy. I hide the candy and now I am hooked on it like the alcohol. Candy is my happy friend. We didn't have candy at home. I made it my new addiction.

I am now only hungry after I take my medication at night. I am med compliant. When the medication started taking effect my mouth gets the munchies and all I want to do is chew. I eat everything I can. I worry without those munchies I may go sleep with my three shirts and four pants and two pair of socks and mountain of blankets and not wake up. I am so cold. I am cold all the time. I feel I only have seconds when my brain is working. Then it goes off. Then on.

I hide candy to eat. . Candy turns my brain back on so I can talk and write.

*

I call my boyfriend and can't talk. I just sit there. I call my mom, I think I say things over and over. It is like a sentence echoes in my head and comes out my mouth to make sure I know I say it. I don't know anymore. I try to think. My head is like glue.

*

I went swimming and an old man said he had not seen anything like me since Germany. I wonder what he meant by that. Germany is a nice place where my sisters Susi and Rici live. It is pretty. I think I remember.

Then one night in our group program I fainted and a client gave me a candy bar to help my blood sugar get high enough to sit in a chair. He snuck it when no staff was paying attention. I was shaking and I couldn't stand up. It was really scary, but when I got to the hospital I felt safer. People seemed to care about me. They told the staff I was not drinking enough water. But, I was drinking water and everything I ate went right through me. Finally after six weeks I got to meet with the eating disorder counselor. Staff stayed in the room with me until the doctor asked her to leave for ten minutes. The doctor talked to me like I was a person. She was real and she tried to tell me I needed to get someplace else. But how?

*

They found my candy. It is gone.
I keep praying God, but even my prayers are smaller.

*

Finally I get to see Carolyn for my eating problems. Staff

told me she was a hard person and people didn't like her. She was the first REAL person I met. I like her. I like tough people. I even got to talk to her for a little bit by myself without staff. That was nice.

*

JODEE (Mother) - I arrived early to read a book while I waited in the corporate lobby. A well dressed young woman sat next to me with a cup of coffee and we began chatting and laughing over weather and simple things. Her eyes sparkled.

"We're leaving," gruffness snared her thoughts, and she looked at the person speaking, who added more snark. "Dump the coffee."

"May I finish it," the young woman asked politely.

"Absolutely not!" was the answer. "Get up."

I noted the shoulders fall with the woman's eyelids as she submissively poured the rest of her coffee into the sink. Her step plodded. The glint in her eyes silenced.

*

Surprise! Mom came up for the big meeting.

I was so glad to see her.

They asked me to begin the meeting and my brain was so foggy that I said I was sorry. I thought that was a good start. I didn't understand why I was here and my mom explained it was because my RISK was bigger than my life and if I wanted my life back I had to make my risk to myself smaller. The smaller my risk, the bigger my life could be. I remember that. Right now my RISK covers over my life. Mom asked me to tell the people in that meeting what I thought were my risks and then she asked me to tell everyone what I wanted in my life. Mom asked everyone if they wanted that too. Everyone did.

Mom got to visit my room and do nuero. I love nuero because her touch triggers my brain to work better. I felt her hands stop and gently put little circles on my arms. When Mom is massaging me, I can feel how she feels. If she is frustrated or angry I can feel that from her fingertips. I know when she realized how small I was. Bones wrapped in skin ...

I was 84 pounds. Mom's fingers felt mad. A staff told Mom she was getting headaches from wheat. She just learned she has a wheat allergy. Mom gave her good tasting ideas.

I don't know what happened after that, but pretty soon they told me I was moving to a hospital in far go in another state. Mom was speaking at a mental health conference and I had permission to speak too and then Mom could take me to the new hospital. I really did it this time, didn't I? Even in a place of safety I don't succeed. I am nothing. Less than. No purpose of living. Mom says, "Every life is worthy."

I am not smart. I am not good. I am less worth.

JODEE (Mother) - She walks frail and medicated desiring to speak to the audience she has been called to give a testimony to. Her mental processing is fogged with medication. She speaks slowly. I cringe.

"When you lose your hope, you are nothing. You lose your belief in living. There is no life when nothing is expected but to obey as an other."

JODEE (Mother) - The audience squirmed. When does helpless become hopeless? When does committed to safety become abandonment? How was hiding her from the storms of life a shelter?

We got to stop for french fries and malts. Mom said I could eat whatever I wanted and I ate for her. I got to spend a night in my old bed and eat all my favorite things. I didn't get sick. Mom videotaped my body and getting on the scale. The video camera recorded my weight – neither of us knew what it would be. It said 78 pounds. I had lost 6 pounds since last week. I was losing myself. By the time I left corporate adult foster care, my brain was so starved I don't remember much. Mom made my favorite dinners and gave me warm clothes.

Everything became a blur – the last week was like a never-ending black out and I only remember bits and pieces.

I remember calling Mom and telling her I was losing myself – I almost did myself in.

They say I did this to myself on purpose.

I have learned whatever is written on paperwork – never lies. People can write things about 'others' and it becomes your reality, even if there is more to it. Life always has more than one side and I know the difference between fake and real.

JODEE (Mother) - To my child I whisper, "I love you," and I pick her up and swing her tiny body around. I know in my heart there is very little left – of soul and spirit. A blithe body giving up on life. Together we flee for miles and hours, and hours and miles to Fargo, North Dakota.

I know to recover from anything such as drinking or any other disorder is a struggle and you have to decide what is hurting you. I have already been in treatment more times than I want to count. I know I am the only one who can change me.

I want to live to put my truth on paper.

I am alive.

Chapter 16
Wither I go?

"Mom, I am pieces broken,
and shattered, and empty.
Placed on a shelf for safety
… Lifeless."

JODEE (Mother) - Liz withered in the crucible as her last placement ate her sense of self to a wisp. Feelings slapped down. Growth pushed back. Her radiant smile folded into sullenness hiding feelings too painful. She laughs with a laugh that moves even the angels, a crooked smile, a drip of drool. A spirit festering to the surface. Scabs picked off.

Covered in warm clothing she sits in a chair with wheels – restricted to rebuild her strength with courage to allow the Master's hand to reform the broken pieces and rearrange them anew. And I "with her" will help her walk again. Stand tall again. Laugh with the angels, oh daughter of mine. We will march for the voiceless and be thankful we have been given the privilege to see the unjust. Lord, may this springtime bring new growth on old stems. Our water runs deep and our roots know their source - the source of re-creation for living.

I wanted people to know, I did not do this on purpose. There are many things I did when I was out of control and stupid acting. 78 pounds was not one of them. I did not choose to starve. Life happened. I feel stupid. I read stupid. I can't do math any more. I know I flunked all the tests they did. I can't think good. I ruined even my brain – I can't feel my stomach. I am on restriction. My activities are confined to a wheelchair and I must stay on the unit. My weight status must get higher to participate in stretching! They weigh my inputs and outputs, the doors are left open. All my meals and snacks are chosen for me. I am going to get well. I know it!

  *

  I was trouble at my last placement and I think my social worker thought that too. I needed help. I wanted help. I knew I needed to see someone. When I know what works for me I am very persistent. I think the nurses here figured that out right away. The nurses here don't make me do things alone, they try to work with me to help me understand things that are not right. Once I know it is not right and understand I move on. But I think they realize that making the new change is very hard for me. I had never been on medication before the first hospital, I am committed to take meds and I am committed. That is good I guess, at least the first commitment is. The second one was me being a hard head.

Fargo Hospital

  I have had to rise to a higher level here because I am around people at a higher level. They say I am fetal alcohol deficient. Do they realize I can change when I have the right supports? I know things even the professionals don't know because they are too busy to see.

May 8, 2008

  I am twisted with pain and worry. My body is on fire. In suffering, I lost of myself. I dream of being back with my man and my birds singing around me, at ease with no worries. I worry he is cheating on me. He came here to visit I smelled alcohol. Only an alcoholic to another cannot hide it. I worry, worry, worry. What if I lose him? I will have nothing. Who will take care of my animals?

I know I need to focus on the good things to be happy and I hope to be back soon as I work on my recovery and then I will have my life back. I need to learn about normal eating. They say that is when I eat when I am hungry. First I have to know when I am hungry. They say that is when I have to eat until I am satisfied. I need to learn that too. I need to learn to accept things they way they are and learn to start a plan to cope with it.

*

I like people who talk to me straight.
There are no games here!
Life is not fair.
"Get over it," they said.
They are real not fake.
I need a plan so I don't over react.

*

I try to listen to grow from almost death again. I always want my outside appearance to be perfect – my eyebrows have to be exactly the same – my hair perfect, my makeup perfect, my clothes perfect. I want my body to look just the way I want it. Want. Want. Want.

They tell me I am so sick I cannot see how I look.
Not yet, but someday I will.

They give me hope to change. I learned in the last place I lived that you can tell when people like you because they like to be with you. A lot of the nursing staff didn't understand me or like me.

I am a big job.

I am not easy.

*

When I first came to the hospital I couldn't smell any more. I didn't taste things right. My brain did not work. I was always freezing. My fingers and toes were hard to move. I had to have a lady do all my paper work for me. People had to explain things over and over. The words floated inside my head. I am doing those things my self now. I am growing. I've gained back my brain and am moving forward again because I am with smart adults that push me. I am probably functioning better now than I have in years. I don't want to lose this. I am proud how hard I have worked here.

When I am expected to be helpless I am hopeless and when I am hopeless it is a disaster like at the last place. I need steps and goals. I think if I could do neuro again and work with Toni maybe I could build my brain back.

One nurse acts more like my mom. She tries to figure out how to talk with me and help me understand. By caring she gave me hope. With her I am a person, not a patient. That is important to help me.

When she works I feel safe. She explains things. I try hard to listen to her and do what she says. I look forward to her work time. I do not feel alone when she is here.

*

I worry.

I worry all the time here.

I worry my body is not like it used to be.

It is growing and changing.
My body forgot how to live.

*

May 21, 2008 – How Far did I Go?

My body image is a struggle for me. I just want to be perfect so at times I am very worried about a change. My weight it going up and that means I am getting more healthy which I know is a good thing but it scares me sometimes. When I have urges to purge I try to think positive and of my loved ones saying, "You can do this! You can beat this."

The last place was taking care of me to keep me safe. I ask myself, how come when my papers said I had an eating disorder I didn't get to see an eating doctor for six weeks? That eating lady was nice. I think she cared about what was happening to me. If I am so stupid, then someone should have noticed that when I walked from the shower to my room. I wore a towel and not my millions of clothes.

*

Coping is hard.

For instance, at Steak Buffet I had to eat a hamburger. I have not had a hamburger in years. I just kept eating it and thought about the ice cream I could have next. As I have gotten healthier I have been able to communicate better because my brain is progressing because I am eating. I bet I really did those first tests bad because now my case manager and the county team want me to go back into foster care. They say I may never live on my own.

I may never be independent? I feel angry, scared and depressed over their idea. It feels like they want to throw me away. I am afraid it will be just like the last place and this whole mess will start all over.

Give me a chance. I can rise to any occasion, just give me a challenge, give me a goal in steps I can do.

*

I am worried if I go back to foster care I will go backwards real fast. It did not go good at that last place. First I tried real hard and then I felt more and more alone and like I was being kept like a pet. Not even a pet, a pet gets more attention and care, at least my pets had more caring. This worries me. I am not a thing. I am a person. It is important for me to grow and prove I can do things.

I learn it's okay to make mistakes. I sure made a lot of them. I learn other people are okay and I am okay too, I cannot control other people or change them I can only change me. I learn even if I don't like it, I can learn to live with it. There is no reason why I should have to like everything!

*

My wheat allergy doesn't make people mad here. They don't stomp and roll their eyes when I don't eat the same things as the other people. They don't leave me alone if they can't handle me, they get in my face in a fair way. I learned at the last place how much staff makes a difference. Staff can gang up on you. They can write anything they want on your papers. I was a job they had to do!

I have been taught to ask questions to keep out of trouble. I know what anxiety is now. I have a word for the feelings I have when I am overwhelmed or confused or frustrated or worried. It gets overwhelming here. I am worried. People don't understand how hard I've tried to beat this.

The County is in so much control of me. I had to come

here. It does help knowing I have people who will fight for the best place possible for me and I have to have faith that God's will will get done in this whole mess. I am really in the middle of the good and the bad, but trying to look at the positive side of things.

*

It worries me they think I cannot cook, because I ask questions. I really am able to do things. I don't think they know I want to be sure what I am doing. They think my questions are stupid. I feel it when they talk back to me. I just need to check if my idea is right. I am not stupid. Please God, don't let them think that everything I say is what I think. Sometimes I am just checking what I heard to understand. I don't want to make more mistakes. I am trying to be careful.

*

I don't know what I was thinking. I haven't been sober for this long since I was 18 years old. Adding alcohol to a brain already damaged by fetal alcohol sucks the rest of them out. I was a space cadet when I arrived here – I couldn't write or read anymore. I am writing again. Why do I have to live my new book? Will people read it? Will my dumb self teach others to help people with FASD?

*

I learned a lot of things about myself here. I still don't like washing my hair. It is horrible. It hurts and makes my skin crawl. I don't know why, it just does. It is kind of like the seams of my socks – I get shivers and my back sweats. I hate those feelings. A shower feels the same way and the hospital only has showers. At first I was so cold. If I get my hair wet I really will get cold and my body gets stiff from my shoulders to my ears. Maybe I need someone to wash my hair. Gently sometimes – my mom did that when I was little. On my own, I took very warm baths and I always use a hot washcloth. I do not like water splashing on my face, but I am trying to do that now. They say I must. I have never taken showers because I do not like the feeling of water falling on my skin. In the beginning I was cold all over. I have adapted and am also washing my clothes again.

The whole time I was in the last place I wore my Tweetie pants, they are very warm and soft fuzzy. I always wore two pair to stay warm, now even one pair of them feels too warm. My hands and feet were always cold and it feels good to finally be warm. When my body warmed up the staff started to tell me I smelled. I couldn't smell anything because I had a tube in my nose and I had not had to use deodorant for three years because I did not sweat. As I got warmer and my body worked better I started to heat up. I didn't need to wear three pair of pants and three shirts and two socks. I started wearing clothes more like other people. I also had to start to use deodorant.

*

The helplessness of being safe and maintained turned into hopelessness. I was so lonely I curled into a ball to sleep and medicated to unthinking. I tried so hard, but I could not. Reached a plateau they say. Metabolizing again, body working again. They want me to eat so much and I can't contain. I am afraid I will learn to eat too much and then do a big Liz again and stuff my face all the time. So today I surrender to a tube down my throat to feed me while I sleep so I get the extra calories without having to stuff my face. I worry.

I surrendered today. Mom, was that right?

Please pray, don't stop and please tell your friends.
I need everyone. I have given up all my old friends.

JODEE (Mother) - She got a feeding tube in her nose today - they tried to up her feedings from 30 to 35 units and it was too much so they will be feeding her at night through the tube and she will be eating normally during the day ... for our kids I think that is better - teaching her to eat too much is just WRONG protocol for kids with FASD. They expect she will be her at least eight weeks.

I know now that a tube has been placed in my nose for re-feeding. Starvation is more than just not having food but also not having family life – it starves my joy. It is NOT that I will not!. Sometime I cannot no matter how hard I tried to want to. Don't they understand. They tell me "jkljkuiouao-j8habnabkj" and expect me to do it. When I finally figure it out, I think, well why didn't you just say so. Too bad my brain is invisible to people who know everything.

JODEE (Mother) - Liz is making life miserable and confusing for everyone who is making her life miserable and confusing. I try to phone coach her thoughts and I look forward to the nights the special nurse of mom proportions is on duty so I can collaborate information and translate an understanding of Liz. She raises the standard of behavior for Liz in a way my daughter can understand. She is pulling Liz out of hiding.

The hardest thing in re-feeding was the tube. It hurt so much; I was in pain 24/7/365. The tube pushed on a nerve inside my head and the pain shot down my throat, and into my ear and gave me migraines and the food continued to flow into my stomach so that I could gain weight ... I think it is the nerve Mom rubs when I get headaches, I feel better when Mom comes and does neuro and uses the oils. I like the lavender and peace-and-calm the best. I will put up with the pain to gain weight and go home. I am determined.

*

How can a judge who doesn't know me decide what is best for me. Full commitment? Until where? Until what? Who am I to go before a judge with my new nose? I worry that sleep will never come - the tube - the feeling - the noise. They are trying meds, nothing works, then something works, then it doesn't work. They think I have trouble, they are having trouble figuring me out. The pills for sleeping start to take away my ... ask for prayers ... close in heart.

May 28, 2008

The most stressful thing for me now is the fact that I am in so much pain I just want to jump out of my skin. Another thing that is stressful is that my body is changing and I don't want my stomach to get fat, so I am praying for that not to happen. When I discharge I will still struggle with the eating disorder, but I will never let it put me down again. I will have a support team of people I can talk to. I will have a therapist and counselor. I will have things to occupy my mind so I don't have to let the eating disorder get me down. I will not be alone.

My body is something very special. Something that God created to be a part of this world. Over the years my body has been a big issue where it is too big and where it is too small. I have not been satisfied with it. I have hurt my body from the inside out from poor nutrition and then not eating at all. By doing that to my body it went into starvation mode and it is now causing me pain when I eat. I am not mad at my body. I am mad at my brain because if it did not think so distorted I would not be in this predicament.

I am now in a hospital getting fed all the time and even by a tube at night. The tube causes me so much pain – my throat, jaw, ears and head feels like knives are going through it. In and out. I don't think people understand or care about me so that makes me very mad at myself because if I did not put my body through all this junk I would be happy and healthy with my man enjoying my life. Why do I worry so much about my man? He is all I have left of my friends. My body does not deserve to starve. I have to go through this pain to get healthy and survive. I am a strong advocate for myself. I am a fighter.

The nurses and the doctors know that. I think some think I am a hard case. More physical strength gives me more thinking. Liz is coming back! I will survive.

June 15, 2008

I appreciate that I'm not having as many pains with my body. I am doing things. I am able to go out into the community with the energy from my body. My thinking ability has increased with all the nutrition I am giving to my body. I came here and sat in a wheel chair, with energy my body will be able to write music again and rap. I will be able to dance again. I've missed out on a lot of things because I did not feed my body. I have missed family vacations and pet training, playing sports with my man and more all because I didn't have the energy to do so. I have learned I don't have to be a certain way because of what has happened in my past. Everyday is a new day.

Things worth having are worth the effort. I might not be able to do everything, but I can do something. I can change.

JODEE (Mother) - Karl and I visited the recommended next placement. We will trust their decision, but wonder if they are making recommendations from the initial testing when Liz arrived in a state of starvation. Language always surprises me. The staff at the new placement assured us that a nurse visited regularly. For Liz, living in a hospital setting, she would assume the nurse would visit a couple times a day. I asked how often? The answer was once a month.

A RED FLAG to us in future communication issues.

How come I always have to over do until I lose big time? I am grateful I can walk and talk.

Normal eating is being able to eat when you are hungry and continue eating until you are satisfied. Three meals a day and some snacks. It is eating healthy and fun foods. It is eating with people and being able to eat alone. It is flexible and times and amounts can change. Sometimes I can be stuffed full and sometimes I can be still hungry and that is okay, It is leaving cookies on the plate for tomorrow or eating them all up because they taste so good. It is letting go of eating and food controlling my life and me controlling all my eating and food. It is believing I can change. I am learning to accept things the way they are and deal with things I see as problems and not overreact! Make a plan...It is learning to be patient with my body and my mind and my life.

I believe I am beautiful the way I am.

June 28, 2008

I breathe in all my problems in one big gulp of air and I try to hold them. They are too much for any person to keep and I slowly release them into the air – one long slow breath – one long slow breath.

I say to myself, "Self, you went way over board eating and drinking. Yo', self, you almost died for each one of them. Three BIG times people put you into treatment to help you. Self , where were your ears. You were not listening."

*

I am still controlling myself, but now I am doing it in a good way. The name recovery give me hope, it is not like the word placement. I'm in treatment and taking everything I can from it. This time I am serious.

The good things about me today:
– I so hate alcohol and what it has done to my life.
– I believe I can beat my eating disorder.
– I have faith in God and myself.
– My brain is working again. I can read and write.
– I have better relationships.
– I am able to advocate for myself in a good way.

*

To recover from anything such as drinking or any other disorder you have to decide what is hurting you and be strong enough to get some help. One of the first pieces of my recovery was to realize that the people I hung out with were taking advantage of me, so I decided to stop hanging out with almost every person I had called 'friend." I am friendless at this point and only have my family and my fiancé. It is better that way. I sometimes feel lonely, but I am no longer so hurt and pressed down or used. When I am strong enough to make new friends I will look for positive people who do not judge me or my past mistakes.

I only get one body and one life. I am not a lard. I am not a blah! I am finding my Liz inside. I need to learn to let go of my worry and my impulsiveness, especially when my man does things or other people do things I cannot control. I am afraid to let go of trying to control things because if I lose everything then I will be all-alone with nothing and nobody to comfort me. Also if I let go I might end up with someone else controlling me.

*

I know that I have done some good things already in my life, besides just messing up. I know I am a talented person and I have a reason to be in this world. I just need to weigh out the good and the bad and hopefully I will make better choices and succeed. People don't understand that when something finally gets into my head it sticks like glue.

*

Some good things I believe made a difference.

I wrote *"The Best I Can Be Living with Fetal Alcohol Syndrome"* and I have spoken to a lot of people about my life and my book. I change hearts and minds. My book is in the 7th printing and shipped all over the world. Mom said it will be in Russian someday too.

I have been on national TV talking about FASD and I changed people's lives and how they thought about FASD.

I made a CD with eleven songs and performed in a lot of places. I even went to Chicago to AMS and people talked about record deals.

I won the Tiger Woods "Start Something" Award.

*

I know that I can relapse if I start missing meals, or am under huge stress. Stress happens for me when there is a major change in plans, moving or if I have a weight change. I also get stressed out at large family gatherings and people not understanding. I get stressed when people don't understand that I don't understand and it becomes a big frustrating circle of not understanding each other. They end up thinking they are so smart and become condescending to me. Don't they know my thoughts are deep? Why is it right for people with different brains to believe they are superior and more able?

Also little stresses add to big stresses if they are all lined up in a row. Those things have stuck with me since childhood. Seams in my socks are still screaming inside my shoes if I don't flip them. I can't sleep with socks on my feet, even if it is blistering cold. I have to take them totally off or I go crazy.

*

I talk to Mom about my ideas to help people with FASD. What can they do? Where can they go when they have gotten themselves into really stupid trouble. Where can they learn the life skills they need to get strong and be successful so they can have a job and feel good about being a human being.

It will be important for me to find things to do to fill holes of my addictions. I like dancing and am good at it, but I need to be careful to find healthy places to have fun. I would like to make another CD – this time a single. It would be really nice to have a weekend with my fiancé to see a movie or go shopping. I would like to ride my bike around the lake, get my nails done, roller blade, get an ice cream cone, go to the mall and have coffee or simply lay out in the sun and soak up some rays. Laugh with real friends.

*

When I don't know the next step I worry. I need to know what's next, when and how I will get there. I made a list of my wants and needs. My needs have to come first. But I want my wants! Wants are what I like doing, feels good or looks good. Needs are what help me in my life and move me ahead on my Life Plan. I wrote down my list, the problem is that writing and knowing and doing and being are all different.

My List:

Wants	Needs
Family Support	Sobriety
Relationships	Healthy Food
Friends	Sleep
Fun Activities	Family Care About Me
Travel	Healthy Body
Do speaking	Healthy Exercise
Do crafts	Place to live where I am encouraged to be independent and not maintained
Job/Skills	Job/Money
Write on my book	Prove myself
Write more music	Challenges

*

I ask myself. "Self, can you handle your needs, so you can have your wants?" And when life happens ... I can grab a want first ... without thinking.

I have real concerns about my commitment and am

angry because I trusted people. Then when I finally read the information and was asked to sign the releases I felt betrayed. To find out lies made me really mad.

*

No one except my family come to see me here. No one except my family came to the foster care place. That will have to wait. Seeing friends – Ha! ha! What friends? I guess they taught me something. I learned I don't have friends!. Until I am uncommitted from the county and committed to myself in a healthy way 'new" friends will have to wait.

COMMITMENT ... Finding of Fact ...
2. Respondent is also diagnosed as suffering from major depressive disorder ... depressed, resulting in suicidal ideation.

When I am angry because I am worried or overwhelmed or frustrated or when I am drunk I say things I shouldn't. Mostly I don't mean them ... saying I wanted to end it and die was a real dumb move, but in another way it probably saved my life. Then I almost lost it again and now I am once again living. I cannot forget this experience. I learn by living and this is a big one!

*

SOS, Liz!
Slow Down. Orient (figure out) and Self Check. That means I stop, breath, relax and pay attention to my body. Then I look around and pay attention.
Who am I with?
What am I doing?
Where am I?

Then I see how I am doing.

Am I completely calm or really distressed?

Am I completely in control or totally out of control?

The big "M" is moderation!

*

Bouncing around screws with my mind. I hate change, moving, not knowing where I will go. Don't they realize I have to start from the beginning each time I am in someplace new. Don't they get it?

I believe Grandma's Place might be an option for me. I believe that, not because I want to get out of a lot of hard work, but because I want to work hard. Karen is a pain in the butt! She doesn't put up with anything and she wasn't there when I went the first time. She says it like it is. She cares. She doesn't put up with crap. Grandma's wouldn't be a walk in the park. I blew out there because it isn't a walk in the park. At nineteen I wasn't ready.

Do people know the good I was able to do since my last treatment and Grandma's Place blowout?

I kept my apartment for 1 1/2 years.

I did not have parties.

I did not invite friends over.

My landlord and manager still like me.

I shopped for my own groceries.

I cooked my own meals.

I had a job for a while.

Alcohol pulled me into a big hole and then the eating disorder held me back. I still need help with those. I wish I had not be so stupid to tell the doctor I was depressed because everyone else said that. Major depression is not who I am. I have seen people with it now and I know the difference. For me it was what I became with the wrong programming.

Give me a chance. I can do it.

Life will start again when I am less risk to myself – that's what Mom says. I will have to start my Life Plan in little pieces by first following my sobriety plan and setting up a meal plan with someone I know. I want to work on my relationship with my man and build our friendship stronger and deeper. I need a small job to gain skills, maybe a class. I want to become part of the community, a group, church or school. I look forward to cooking my own meals again and shopping for groceries. I need to learn to save my money and budget so I can have my own place again with my man.

*

Here in the hospital we do a lot of work on ourselves. I work on DBT skills. I learn to think before I react. At first it all didn't make sense. I call Mom to tell her what I learn and she talks me through it. Mom helps me understand better what they want me to understand. Sometimes she can be really funny and dramatic to bust into my head. She breaks things down to fit into my brain without me feeling stupid. Mom tells the nurse I like to tell me again.

I learned I couldn't see myself anymore and how I looked was very different from what others saw. I had to teach my eyes to see. I had to learn to look at all my problems that I was holding onto and slowly release them. I really went overboard with my eating and drinking. I almost died from each one. I've already been to treatment three times. I know I am still controlling myself, but this time I am working at doing it in a good way.

I am still in treatment and taking everything I can from it. This time I am serious. I may not get another chance. I need to let go of my impulsiveness, my worry, my actions, of my man, and know that I cannot control what other people do. It is enough for me to care for and about me.

To do so:

- Follow WISEMIND

    (from DBT-that's Dialectic Behavior Therapy)

    That means think before I do

    Camp said get three pieces of information

- Protect myself
- Tell my needs
- Fix my problems
- Speak up for others.

June 30, 2008

There is nothing I cannot do if I put my mind to it. I have grown here. My mind can think again and my body is stronger. I am able to read and write. I worried I lost those to starvation, but I didn't. How much of my brain did I hurt?

They say I have the ability to make wise, productive decisions. I am grateful that I am able to listen to my inner knowledge. I feel blessed to be alive. I am aware of the miraculous light that flows through my body to keep it alive. Today is the beginning of the rest of my life. It is a clean slate. I will begin totally refreshed and just live it.

Today I get to go home for the weekend.

I am now 100.4 pounds.

It has been a hard path.

I am such a hard head.

I have been sober for five months.

JODEE (Mother) - The treatment plan determined two additional placements would be necessary to keep Liz secured and sober for one year. Statistics say people with a year of sobriety have a better chance of recovering. They have stated her next placement will be at a chemical dependency program and after completion in a community housing mental health component.

Chapter 17

Next Stop
On to another treatment program

The hospital sent me home with a long list of prescription drugs. I believed the drugs would keep me together like the alcohol refused to. I hold on to my medication like a monkey with his hand in a cookie jar. I am going to do everything right! Finally I get to go home, even if it is just for a night. I sleep in my old room, in my old bed at Mom and Dad's.

*

The first night home I celebrated by staying up late – too late and I took my medication and stayed in the bathroom instead of going to bed like I was suppose too. I conked out on the bathroom floor and Mom thought I died. I didn't even wake up when she screamed! And she couldn't wake me up, my eyes were open and rolled back in my head. She was pretty freaked. My vegetable growing mother wasn't ready for my medication. My go-to-sleep med cocktail knocks me out and I hadn't learned how to manage it. It was what the hospital finally figured out would get me to sleep.

I think Mom called the hospital to find out what I could

have done. She was full of questions.

Did I take to much?

Did I do something?

I tried to explain to her it was the way they worked, I was wrong to not get into my bed. I goofed. My meds put me out like a light bulb and when they begin to work I look and sound drunk so it is best for me to get in bed. They also give me the munchies in a big way once I swallow them, so it is hard to not go into the kitchen and get major food.

*

It was only the beginning of learning to manage my pile of medication. How they all work and how to keep the refills and how to get meds when the insurance company said I had already used the quota. Like I can have my meds for 1/2 of the month, but more than that was not covered. It didn't make sense to me. You'd think if a hospital works on you like a lab rat for two months, they would know more than the insurance company!

*

I was scared going to a new treatment center, but Mom told me it was friendly. I had had six months of sobriety and I wasn't about to lose it. The hospital was so physically painful and the adult foster care emotionally painful. I didn't know what to expect here. The place was way out in the country with a long driveway. They usually put these kind of places way out somewhere probably to keep us there. At first I thought, wow, this place is a dump, but the longer I was the there I realized it wasn't the way a place looked, it was the people.

But, this place was for real!

I planned to bust loose from the hook of alcohol forever

and at this place I learned the first day how true that was.

My new roommate met me with a, "hey girl, ain't it stupid they don't want me drinking when I'm pregnant?"

Duh, look at me. I keep shut.

*

I am forced to look at myself here. I came with a clear head. Most of the people have less sober time than I do.

I work on myself. I try to remember that it's okay to make mistakes. I try to remember I don't have to control things.

*

I make a list of things I have to change in my life.

Change is not bad. I am capable. I can change.

I have to or I might not make it next time.

I have already died and been restarted twice!

Behavior	What can happen
Have sex	Could get virus/pregnant
Swear	Mom get mad
Be Disrespectful	It's a sin - do to others what you want them to do to you
Drink	Something bad always happens
Smoke	Cancer
Stay out all night	Get killed, stabbed, raped
Binging	Out of control, starvation

What happens in treatment stays in treatment – the stories, the relationships, the reality. *Two realities really – the clients have one and the staff have one.* Sometimes they meet and sometimes they don't. You have to wonder how people who have the education just don't get it that when they work an eight-to-five or whatever shift. Why do they think they know so much more about the people living there than the people living there? We see each other all day, every day. Maybe they can put pieces of us together because they watch us. Maybe they can find some of our puzzle pieces. Most of us have so many scrambled missing pieces only God can help us.

Keeping things inside treatment a secret keeps the truths of some realities from coming out. Only those of us who have lived behind these kinds of walls know what really goes on in our secret society. That's funny since alcoholics live in a secret world when they are hiding their booze from family and friends and even lie to themselves about it. That's funny when we are suppose to be getting well we hide stuff again for protection. It seems like it is just one big spinning secret circle I want to get out of.

It didn't take me long to figure out who were the fakers and who were real in the staff and in the people I lived with. The counselors don't really know what's going on in the day-to-day nitty-gritty. Everything that was to-too was kept on the low. Just like everyone had done in the street. You put a bunch of people who have spent a lifetime hiding the truth from everyone including themselves and you expect there not to be a bunch of crap going down inside? You got another thing coming. I tried my best to be kind and friendly and not make enemies. Street taught me that much.

Most of the staff knew pieces, but if they did they didn't care. They worked their job, smiled at us, didn't talk about us within our hearing and got their paychecks. Caring was too much work. It meant too many forms to file and paperwork.

I learned that the first night contraband came into my room. If you think a treatment facility is clean of contraband think again – you can get anything you want and there are always ways for it to come in. Every program I had ever been in and with every new addict or alcoholic new garbage happens and I didn't know the hidden rules.

*

There are ways to handle things to get them to work themselves out without reports – overlooking, nudging, checking, timed and announced room raids. It worked – some ran, some fought, some were discharged early and later died. We all die someday one way or another. So what I am saying is some important things were overlooked except by the sergeant. She called people on their stuff privately and held them accountable. She had done her own crazy stuff and had barely lived through it.

Most of us learned that if you wanted something handled you brought it to her and the problem would disappear without a week of staff complaining about paperwork. These women were strong. They walked out of garbage lives. I learned the most when we got to run our own groups. When others were willing to share stuff and get out of the hole I got myself into.

*

I learned my life could get worse.
Do I want that?
Once I am sober, you don't fool me.
The streets made me smart.
Too bad I was so drunk.

*

Staff worked with me when I got confused and frustrated. They made me deal with my anger. They made me deal with my messes. My meds were running out and the staff couldn't get them for me and the insurance said they would not let me have more. I can't sleep without my meds and it will mess up the whole schedule I have.

My stay of commitment says I must be med compliant. How can I be med compliant when I can't have my meds because they will not send them to the treatment program? I ended up getting an angry moment worksheet I had to do. I talked to my counselor and we talked about thinking before I act. My goal for expressing my anger is to be calm, cool and collected. My counselor says when I learn to do that life will work better for me. Anger has been a problem for me. Instead of letting it go I focused really hard on it and then do something crazy. When I do that, I make my life more difficult. This program makes me look at myself in an honest way. It is good for me.

I need to not pay attention to others' problems.
I have enough of my own problems.
I have to work on me.
*

I am a funny person and a good listener.
So many of the people who come into this program have no one to visit them. They have nothing, this place was not a castle, it was really basic with people who are at the end of the road. I looked at all the stuff I had and started to give my things away. The ladies were so appreciative to have nice clothes and hair things. Their eyes sparkled and their smiles were alive. They felt good looking good. I asked Mom to bring

all my clothes and a bunch of my other things. I had so much fun giving all my stuff away. I figured whatever was left would be enough for me. It went for a real good cause. After nine apartments and three placements, Mom was probably pretty sick of moving it all over the place anyway.

I think staff thought the idea was pretty crazy, but then they don't know all the stuff our family does.

*

I am grateful I have been able to speak nationally about fetal alcohol to adults and younger people. People here think I am easy to talk to and a good friend.

I am outgoing and welcome new people.

I am learning I am gifted and talented.

*

My faith in God is growing. He is here for me and God gives me peace. They let us be spiritual here, they don't judge anyone. People come with all kinds of beliefs and it's okay. Spiritual music calms me. When I pray I feel hopeful. I hope to live independently again and stay clean. My alcohol and behaviors took away my freedom and independence and made other people make decisions for me. I am now totally involved in social services. I learned it is easier for people to look at the bad stuff I do and not look at the positive things in my life. My behaviors are written down. My actions are written down. I think paperwork will follow me my whole life. I learn I have completed almost all the FASD secondary disability statistics.

- 94 % have Mental Health Problems (I did that) I can change. If I have the flu I get sick and well. I can do the same with my brain and crazy ideas. I am not a Mental Health Problem for life. I can heal!

- 80 % Dependent Living (I will again live on my own, I know I will do it!)
- 80 % Problems with Employment (did that)
- 70 % Females experienced substance abuse problems (oh duh!)
- 70 % have Disrupted School Experience - suspension or expulsion or drop out (didn't do that - I graduated!)
- 60 % Confinement - inpatient treatment for mental health, alcohol/drug problems, or incarceration for crime (doing that now)
- 45 % Inappropriate Sexual Behavior (I try hard not to get myself into those messes and sometimes I don't think)
- 42 % Trouble with the Law (I made the police crazy, but I didn't do any crimes!)

They say if you are diagnosed by six-years-old you do better. It would have been easier if teachers would have known how to teach me and I would have kept believing I was able to learn. It would have been easier if I had realized I had to work with my challenges instead of believing I was a "bad" person.

Kids need to know what is hard for them and why. Then they can move on. They can learn to ask for help and that can explain some weird behaviors. If they know how, they can work on changing behaviors people look at strange.

*

I know now I am a good persons with serious challenges I can work on the things I struggle with when I know what they are, but I have to know what they are.

It is not easy when you ask for another person to tell you ALL the things WRONG with you in THEIR eyes.

Too many things.

Overwhelming.

I shut down.

I need to work on one thing at a time.

*

I grew up in a stable home with parents who loved me. We always lived in the same house, that was good because I don't like change and to figure out my schooling I went to a total of nine schools. Some people can do okay with change, but what people don't get is when you change one thing for me, I may have to learn everything again. I have to learn over and over the same stuff in different place. Until I learned enough times, I feel not sure. Each major change in schools or jobs is overwhelming.

Mom and Dad protected me from violence pretty much until I was a teenager, then I went looking for it on my own. Somethings, you just can't keep your kids away from, I wish that was different. I have flashbacks of the things I have seen on television, movies, in my apartments and on the streets. I am good at over do.

Now, I need a do over.

I have ideas.

I would like to be a part of my future planning.

I would like to be in charge of my life and not have the state involved. At least here in treatment we are called by our names. The staff don't judge us as incompetent. Here and at the hospital I am becoming my person again.

*

I feel safe and cared about not for. There is a difference. When I am cared about I feel so much freer. Plus, alcohol no longer controls my life. I am maintaining my weight. I am stronger. Now I love being sober.

*

The people at the county say it will be back to Corporate Adult Foster Care for me – I hope I don't die there like I almost did before. How can I not worry about that? How do I show them I am good? I was in so much pain and lost myself and now I have worked so hard to grow and get healthy again it does not make sense they would make me go back where I started. They don't trust I will not be a RISK!

This whole time started because I didn't have a choice to be sober inside myself. I no longer like alcohol any more. I hate it. I don't even crave it.

I've been sober for six and a half months.

They say they want to keep me away from my life for a year! That's how long it takes to really get to the next place. I don't want the next place to be foster care. I really don't want to leave to begin life outside if I have to get flushed down the toilet again. Water savers don't do nothing if you have to flush two times.

*

At least in this treatment place I can be Liz. People laugh and goof around. Here, I have to look at my bad self and my good self! I know I still react without thinking. I worry what will happen in the future. I have high expectations of myself and I know it takes longer for me to recognize and learn things because of how my brain works. People with fetal alcohol brain damage have poor decision making skills and learn by experience. We also want to feel accepted and fit in to our communities. Sometimes my attention is short unless I am really interested.

*

When I became free from alcohol I was able to understand things better and I was not paranoid. I am able to have better relationships with people I love and conversations with clearer thoughts.. My mood is more stable and I am getting stuff done. I am cleaner and more organized. People say my eyes are brighter and I have clearer skin. I have more energy and more inspiration. I can read again. I passed the math tests here and scored higher than other people had in three years. I got a certificate.

I AM CAPABLE! My brain is coming back. I wish I could stay here. I am so worried about going backward again.

*

When I go back to the community it will be important I find friends who are trustworthy and do not steal from me. I don't want to have people manipulate me anymore. They have to be active. I don't sit around. I will have to look for people to share my interests and be honest with a sense of humor. I like caring compassionate people. One problem I may have in the community is that I am not afraid of taking risks because I don't think about what can happen next. I don't think people know how sensitive people with FASD really are and how easy we get hurt. We try to hide our hurt and when we push it down we end up self-medicating.

When we are scared we fake it to make it. I look forward to going someplace where I can work with animals or children with Fetal Alcohol. I liked being a PCA for those little girls and we had a very good time. I want to travel and see new things. I can see my hopes and dreams are back. I have faith in God and myself that I can make a better life this time.

*

I don't have low self-esteem now that I have been sober for over HALF year but when I did drink I was sneaky and not truthful. The more I drank the worse and worse I got. I tried to hide things because I thought people would think bad things about me. I was trying to be like other kids and my drinking lost me my freedom. The only people who have stayed by me are my loved ones. Many of the women here have lost the people who loved them. That is sad.

*

I have learned the most from the women here who lost big! I know that their life could become my life. It is for real. I don't want that.

I realize now that I am an intelligent person even though I have a brain injury. I want other people to continue to learn about fetal alcohol. Too many people are hurt and put away because of it. I know I am not alone. I have met people who when they know me figure out they have fetal alcohol too, and then they realize they are not bad.

*

God touches my life and I am not alone.

A human is someone you can touch with your body, but I can touch God with my heart and mind. I am God's creation, I am human and I am a grateful lovable person.

JODEE (Mother) - In speaking with Liz's counselor at treatment we discovered the new program wanted to meet with Liz alone and in following their request we planned to not attend the meeting but sent our requests. Karl and I would like to note the following:
1. Liz's medication is not adjusted without communication between her hospital doctor, Karl or myself.

2. A gluten free diet is followed so that Liz can maintain her weight and that she has access to food.

3. Her medications are provided for her per her doctors' prescription.

4. There is a treatment plan in place and that Karl and I are given a copy of the treatment plan.

5. Karl and I have opportunity to review the risk management plan.

6. Karl and I have the opportunity to meet staff and visit the facility.

7. If requested by Liz - she could have three way conference calls with her staff and parents.

8. There are goals in place with attainable steps so Liz can understand the progress she is making.

9. Programming began immediately and not wait for a 30 day observation period.

10. If staff sees a change in Liz that is listed as warning signs in the Vulnerable Adult Act, Karl and I are alerted.

11. Liz will be weighed at least weekly and Karl and I will be able to access that information

12. We are given information regarding policies and restrictions.

13. Liz's medical, dental and other health needs are taken care of.

We have been advised by her attorney that her County team and case manager are in agreement that this is the best option they have for her and if Liz furthers the issue, the court will defer to her county team and the outcome will remain the same.

CADI CASE MANAGER - Jodee - I checked the facility and they said their program is all about behavior modification and they have an excellent team of behavioral analysts. Out of the five years they have been in business they have only had to discharge two people due to the fact that they probably belonged in a prison or jail. They have a very good track record with the most difficult behaviors. Most of the people who leave there, when they leave, move back down to the cities into apartment complexes with ILS staff The team feels Liz would thrive the most in this placement.

JODEE (Mother) - They sold us on their program. I liked the staff, the program and the housing. They seemed competent. Karl and I willingly backed out and let go as we had tried to do at the previous program.

First they interviewed me at the treatment center. I had written a list of questions that were important to me and my future. I took my time to think about and write them. Some were simple things like schedules and groups, other things I know would make a difference in my success, like -

Do you have a thirty day policy of watching me before I get to participate in real programming?

How do I prove I am capable of living back in my community? What do you look for?

What particular skills is your program providing?

What are your rules? Are they written down?

Then they said I could go up and visit. My mom could go too. I went up there with a staff because I was still under program care and Mom followed in the car. I really didn't like the idea or the placement, and was not happy with Mom who seemed to go along with it. But I did pick out my room and put my name on the door.

ADULT FOSTER CARE PROGRAM - Jodee – After careful consideration and review of our meeting, your last e-mail and taking into account the needs of the clients that will be placed at our new site, we have decided that it would not be an appropriate placement for Liz. I will be notifying the county of our decision today. – Thank You

*

They denied me the program. They are afraid I am too much trouble. My time is up here. They need me out of this program to open another bed. Now the county had to decide WHAT to do with me. My sixty days are over.

*

I get to go home for the weekend!

Yeah! I get to be with my man, my fiance!

I hope I can do Grandma's Place. I know the people there. I know the staff there. I believe I could do a good job and make everyone proud of me. I wish that was where they would let me go. Karen would push me hard to be independent in a good way.

They told me my commitment will last to January 2009. So much for July 31! At least I am going to be close to home. I feel great. I am sober. I have maintained my weight!

My BMI (Body Mass Index) is in the normal range.

JODEE (Mother) - Heartache grew in my mother's heart. Today, there's swirling a twirling heartache knowing you are alone in your experience knowing you are too closed to open the next piece for help knowing that without the ability to reach out you won't reach safety.

God grant me the serenity for the things I cannot leave to chance but You can change. Stand alongside as she struggles. Help her remove the chunks in her life so that she may see a wholeness of spirit and loose the bondages created by herself. Protect me from interfering in her process of becoming who your have meant her to be. Teach me to stand stubbornly still, yet ready to embrace her when she returns, but not seek her as she runs toward the ruins to trust that you are there, knowing more than I will ever understand.

The County has a new plan for me. It is called an IRTC (Intensive Residential Treatment Center). At least the new place is near my family. I will not be all alone. Mom is coming to get me after she shuts down my apartment. My lease is finished. I can't go home and Mom and Dad said I couldn't live with them if my boyfriend was going to be involved unless he is working on himself and has a job or going to school. He is almost thirty years old.

*

Little did anyone know what my life outside had really been about? I had stuffed down so much hurt and pain and there was no way it was going to be shared. It was buried. My life was onto the next placement of commitment – an intensive treatment residential home for my mental health.

I was afraid if I shared what 'really all' happened to me they would keep me forever!

To get accepted into the new program I need medical release papers from current doctors. I don't have current doctors or a psychiatrist in town that know what I have been through. Mom needs to get them for the county in 48 hours. Mom said, sometimes psychiatry appointments take forever to get but somehow she did it!

We got the doctor appointment and Mom made it early in the next morning. Guess what my stupid self did. I stayed up late and took my meds late. SO, yes, you are right. I went to the doctor over medicated. I was only about five hours into my eight hour sleep cycle. At least I was awake when we saw the psychiatrist later in the day. I liked him. He didn't play. He was not a faker and because of that I didn't play games either. He tells it like it is, but he is fair, like Dad. I can see he won't put up with my crap.

*

JODEE (Mother) - The psychiatry report was the most accurate set of DSM Axis I-V Karl and I had read on Liz. It began with mood disorders due to Fetal Alcohol Syndrome, Alcohol Dependence, Eating Disorder, Dysomnia in Axis !. Celiac was listed in Axis III. It omitted severe depression and without that listing or another mental illness, Liz no longer qualified for the IRTC program. This placed her back into our home until a living solution could be found.

*

Once I was home with my parents and sober, I could see things differently. I had been working on Liz for almost a year, and my fiance had been hardly working on much of anything. In one way he still wanted the old Liz, or at least part of her and if any of the old Liz came back, the new Liz might go away. He was smoking and selling while I was locked away. He is always asking for things from me. One time in four years he took me to dinner. He paid $12.00 for dinner, then later he said, "well, now you owe me for a case of beer." Why can't he just do something nice, instead of requiring pay back. He didn't hold power over me anymore. I was not a nothing. I stayed in our relationship for two weeks, but everyday it was harder because I could see more things I was not happy about. We got into a fight and once he was out the door, I had Mom lock it. Our relationship was over!

It didn't take him long to find a new girl and get married. I soon learned I was right, he had been having a relationship with her on the side when I was in the hospital and treatment. He had been using while I was working on my sobriety and challenges.

My worry was right all along.

I knew it. I knew, I knew it!

I took back more of my life.

Mom and Dad supported me in my decision, but didn't

make a big deal about it. They didn't tell me to let go of him. I did it myself. All I could think of was all the pain and all the hard work and losing it!

JODEE (Mother) - The treatment center sent us home with med sheets and a boxful of medication. They warned me I would not like the way Liz looked on her night meds. I didn't, but a near comatose Liz was far better than Liz in an alcoholic stupor. At least now, I knew she was simply sleeping and not dead like the first experience. The complexity of timing, dosages and amounts of medication overwhelmed my Excel spread sheet, but with the help of the pharmacist, I think we will manage. I pass out her a.m. meds when she awakens and give her p.m. meds when I go to bed at 10:00 p.m.

I was never really into drugs of any kind so having to manage my pile of medication once I returned home was a big adventure. First Mom took care of everything, but eventually that felt too controlling because in order to manage the meds I had to live a day shift life like my parents who go to bed before 10:00 p.m. and get up to exercise at 6:00 a.m. I still like night-life, so that wasn't my style. I think because I have always had a hard time sleeping I was used to being a night person.

JODEE (Mother) - Karen – With Liz just released from eight months of institutional care and back at our home we needed structure and strategies to keep her moving forward. She quickly is settling in and wanting freedom in the community. She seems to be choosing safe friends. It is a all bit overwhelming to be working and managing a home and her care, but we have risen to challenges before. Let me know if these make sense.

Med Sheet – Structure of daily meds – Meds are kept in Karl's and my bedroom. We are using those little plastic envelopes. I hope to transition to a daily med box she can manage. Perhaps someday a weekly med box.

Approved Outside Activities – Church events, mental health community drop in center, AA Young Adult Meetings.

Meal Planning – Coupons, groceries, meal plans, recipes and shopping. Cooking wheatfree meals and managing eating without having structured program. She is on her own for breakfast, a.m. snack, lunch, and p.m. snack. We cook dinners together.

I am still hoping Grandma's Place will be an opportunity for her. I worry the longer she is in our family home, the less she will want to take this step. She is still looking forward to this and I think we will have a small window for cooperation and success. I hope we get meetings and approvals soon. Stay close to me on this one, I want the strategies we are using to transition easily to her next step.

I was denied access to the IRTC program because I do not have major depression, or any other mental illness that wouldn't fit into a check box for acceptance. My social worker was really frustrated. Mom asked me how the depression had gotten onto the paperwork long ago and I told her. She said there were times I was probably situationally depressed and that meant there were events that created it. But she had never seen me truly depressed except during my starvation time. She said she and Dad would stand by the diagnosis from the new psychiatrist and if that meant me living at home again for a while they would do that too.

Interdependent Care Plan
Provisional discharge – September 15, 2008
Chemical health relapse prevention:
YOU MUST REMAIN COMPLETELY SOBER & ILLICIT DRUG FREE

_____ Refrain from using ALL illicit drugs including alcohol, or utilizing ANY other substances not prescribed by a doctor over use or improper use of over the counter meds is NOT ALLOWED – for example hair spray, cough syrup, mouth wash, diet pills, nail remover, white out

_____ Avoid over the counter meds not prescribed including laxatives

_____ List others that could be triggers

_____ Remain in contact with sober and supportive peers.

_____ Attend two AA/NA or other support groups each week for one year

_____ Join the website www.womenforsobriety.org and visit the chat or bulletin boards

_____ Refrain from ALL individuals who are using illicit drugs

_____ Report to Treatment Center the first week of EACH MONTH (between the 1st and the 7th) to do a follow-up study, say how you are doing and share your accomplishments or concerns.

Recovery environment

_____ Keep your living environment safe, sober and constructive

Biomedical concerns / Physical issues
YOU MUST MAINTAIN A HEALTHY WEIGHT AND REST SCHEDULE

_____ Practice responsible medication management/psychiatric care

_____ Monthly visits to psychiatrist. You MUST attend all appointments on time

_____ Begin by Nov. appointment to secure your own medical transport to the clinic to prove your independence

_____ In October, make your own appointment for November and continue to do so for 12 months.

_____ Maintain a healthy weight – you cannot go below your BMI low - eat three well-balanced meals everyday.

_____ Continue to challenge yourself with new healthy foods – two each week at least

_____ Make and follow a meal plan

_____ Eat well – enjoy fun foods but balance healthy foods with times of fun to keep you body healthy include proteins, fats, carbohydrates with grain, fruits and vegetables daily

____ Healthy exercise – develop and follow a program you enjoy

____ Gain strength in your body

____ Maintain healthy sleep pattern to not affect your meds or next day activities.

____ Know how your medication affects your day and plan for it

____ Get adequate rest

____ Visit your general doctor yearly for a general physical

____ Learn when it is appropriate to visit when you are not feeling well

____ Make your own appointments and get your own transport

____ Visit your dentist to complete your dental care and follow up

____ Follow recommendations for your teeth

Emotional/behavioral/cognitive concern

____ Continue developing your self-awareness skills

____ Keep a journal for yourself to see your progress

____ Take a class or join a group to learn more about yourself

____ Avoid negative self-thought or messages

____ Realize you are an adult capable of adult behaviors. Remember you "teach" others how to treat you. If you make it a practice to treat others with respect, you teach them how to give respect.

____ Set and implement healthy boundaries with family and friends

____ Establish your own "personal space" to be able to remove yourself when you need to or want to refocus

____ Take time to pamper yourself, meditate, enjoy each moment of your sobriety.

____ Read <u>The Long Way To Simple</u> and then begin working Mr. Neafcy's program one step at a time.

Employment / education

____ Secure your financial independence by gaining employment skills

____ Volunteer if you find something that interests you – give back to your community

____ Prepare a budget/spending plan for yourself and stick with it without relying on others to help you if you overspend. You will learn to be responsible for your money.

    ____ Understand your spending patterns

    ____ Choose needs over wants

    ____ Plan your monthly expenses

    ____ Work with your rep payee to understand your finances and how to manage them

____ Begin a saving account, small and keep adding to it

____ Meet with your banker to learn about your accounts and how they work

____ Make a list of the things you need to learn

____ Secure a job/life coach to help transition to future independence

____ Increase your skills to return to a more independent lifestyle.

____ Complete your own laundry

____ Manage your breakfast, am snack, lunch, p.m. snack

____ Keep your living space organized

____ Pick up after yourself

____ Learn to make a new main meal recipe each week

Spiritual

____ Begin each day by stating what you are grateful for

____ Stay in touch with nature

____ Find a church and participate in an activity once a week

Recreational/Leisure

____ Get involved in sober activities

____ Participate in day programming when you are not working, volunteering or have appointments to further your health or independence

____ Take time out to relax and clear your mind

____ Read one book a month

____ Plan fun sober activities with family, sober friends, lifecoach one or two times a month

____ Become secure in eating at restaurant and managing celiac diet

____ Pay attention to your relapse warning signs – write them out and post them where you and others can see them

Guardianship concern

____ You will remain under legal guardianship of Jodee and Karl Kulp until October 2008, moving forward in your life as an adult toward a safe independence getting a job, volunteering, participating in community, taking classes for future independence

Reports to case manager

Report weekly via telephone, personal meeting, fax or e-mail
Share my daily debriefs so case manager can watch my progress.

I agreed to Mom and Dad's program with my social worker until they found a placement to accept me without the major depression diagnosis. We found some local AA meetings but most of them are for old people that do things different than I do. I wish I had sober friends, my sister Kat is sober and safe. Mom lets me spend time with her. Mom also lets me spend time with my sister Anna. My Grandpa is getting sicker.

I hate when we talk about money. It makes me so mad at her. She asked the County to get another person to be my Rep Payee. Even if she makes me mad I still want her to do it. I trust Mom. Time and money make us both crazy.

I am glad to be home, Mom and I talk at night about my day and I fill out the high points and the challenges. I have to provide three ideas to help with my day's challenge and write what I learned from the hard places. I have high expectations for myself. I know it takes me longer to recognize and learn things and I am more okay with that than other people are with me. I need to learn to think before I react. I worry about what will happen in the long term. I am still committed.

JODEE (Mother) - We slide into family life from institutional care. Each day we review the day and talk about next day. I have been trying to figure out how to help Liz manage money and I wonder if it possible. I have found it easier to discuss a spending plan and work to select needs over wants. My words trip us up, last time we went shopping, I told Liz she could only spend $10.00. She arrived at the cashier with a shopping cart FULL of items all under $10.00! I need to learn to be more clear. She has already been home over a month.

Karl and I have met with an attorney to research guardianship, conservatorship and power of attorney. As an adult, Liz has the power to fight for her independence and be privately interviewed. After this year under state commitment, she is wary of any type of legal control over her life. We let go of that piece, to maintain our forward motion.

Mom went up to spend a day with Grandpa and then let me spend the weekend at Anna's house because she had a book show in Atlanta to visit some lady with another dog and kid with FASD. Grandpa died when she was at the airport and she came home and headed up to Grandma's. No matter what I asked for, she said, 'No.' Plus, she wasn't answering her cell phone. She kept telling me this was her time with her Mom. My sister dropped me off at home, so I could go to the funeral. I couldn't get help from Dad because he was down in the basement with my brother making a box for Grandpa. It was a hard place to be, because I felt really alone and not used to death.

After the funeral, Mom wrote this poem.

Grandpa died on Friday and I really did my best.
My mom left home without me
        and my dad was put to the test
My father is a woodworker like my grandfather before
And my uncle asked my daddy
        to make the box for grandpa to soar
And so I went to my friend's house
        and had a really good time
I missed the mortuary so I wouldn't stand in line
I called upon my mother who was busy as can be
Writing up the remembrances and an obituary
I asked her to please come home and do my pretty hair
I wanted my sweet Grandpa to really know I cared.

"I'm sorry darling I can't come home tonight.
        I am sleeping with your Grandma.
        Go to bed, turn out the lights."
I went downstairs the best I could, it was time for meds
I could feel my hands shaking deciding not to go to bed
Instead I stayed up fixing and fixing my pretty hair
        And nothing seemed to be working
        As I thought of my grandpa a way way up there.
In a mighty fit of frustration I pulled out and then redid
Only to see in the morning bald spots on my head
I picked my clothes carefully something grandpa cared
A bright red shirt, blue jeans and barrettes for my hair
I worked til' almost morning the sun was about to rise
I took my medication and closed my pretty eyes

I didn't hear the alarm clock, Dad jumped me out of bed
We're leaving in five minutes was all I heard he said.
I grabbed the red shirt I'd chosen, I jumped into my jeans
This wasn't how I wanted it I hate being me.
I wanted to look pretty, I wanted to do my best
Instead I went overmedicated and looked a sorry mess
The red shirt I was wearing was a night club fright.
And the jeans I jumped into fit me really tight.
The medication was humming as we pulled quickly away
And I could tell inside myself it was a terrible day.
I did my best to be happy, I forgot my morning meds
I wanted to show everyone
         how hard I'd worked to be my very best.

We missed the visitation, we almost missed the church
I missed the long progression headed with the hearse
I missed the soldiers shooting.
I missed putting grandpa in his grave
I finally understood this was not a very good way
I wanted to hold my mother who was busy for her dad
I wanted to hug my family
         who seemed sometimes happy sometimes sad
I didn't eat a breakfast, and I forgot a snack
I even forgot the medication that I usually pack
I called Dad to say sorry, I tried really hard to be nice
But it got really obvious people were looking at me twice.

My Auntie told me about the rose
         that laid upon the stone
And I went to say goodbye to grandpa when I was alone.

I looked upon each stone and saw eagles, words and pain
Not one stone held the rose I felt I was insane
I went back home to tell them that it was no longer there
My Auntie said go back again and look down and stare
The rose will have Grandpa's name I know you care
I watched my feet a walking, the rose still had it's stick
But the stone they told me to find was actually a brick.
  "She's 22, I overhead." "She's able to behave."
  "She's doing drugs," another said.
My grandpa in the grave!
 I ran away to Grandpa who was watching way up high
And I marched around the little town trying not to cry
Lost and scared and empty my Auntie took me in
And we journeyed to the jail house to prove I didn't sin.

I looked into the mirror at my face when I can home.
And I soon discovered I was not alone.
My mother saw the bare spots upon my painful head.
And I went into the bedroom
    to get my pretty shirt of red.
I held it up before her and I looked into her eyes
And we held each other and together we finally cried.
I told her that I loved her and I said it was too bad
And I told her I love my daddy, who is my real dad
And I told her not to worry
    because I knew something to be true
That Grandpa saw me for who I was and that she did too.
She showed me the spent chamber
    they shot for Grandpa today
"Grandpa knows I'm a good girl," was all that I could say.

JODEE (Mother) - Karen – Liz has been home now for almost two months. She has been spending more time with her sisters, staying sober and maintaining her weight. I am hoping she can get into Grandma's Place, it would provide independence plus structure and still allow her to have an apartment.

I am afraid if she stays with us, we will come to odds and return to teen style rebellion. I don't want to be an accomplice to backsliding and it is a new experience to have an adult child at home in early remission. We are still adjusting to each other.

CADI CASE MANAGER - I am proposing a meeting for Tuesday October 21st at 1:30 at our office if possible. We need to all get together to develop a plan for Liz as she is home now and the clock is ticking... Jodee, bring Karl and Liz, of course. Her social worker, myself and my supervisor will be here too.

Mom and I visited Grandma's Place and it really didn't feel like I could make it happen. The apartment was nice. The people were nice. I like Karen, she is cool. She doesn't play. I also know she is Mom's friend.

I could really mess up big. I told her, "No, it wouldn't work." I think I could do in Mom's relationship with her and I don't want that. I want to succeed in a big way.

KAREN (Director Grandma's Place) -You need to know Jod, Liz was honest with me and she may have to fall again. I sure hope not.

CADI CASE MANAGER - Hello team: Liz toured Grandma's Place and is declining the apartment living services. We should set up another meeting to finish our conversation/plan. I will list a few days that I have open ... Thank you in advance!

JODEE (Mother) - It is the little things that make day-to-day life with Liz complex. Today we had a honey explosion in the kitchen. Liz squeezed my unopened plastic liter of honey until the lid flew off and the honey went everywhere in the kitchen. She tried to clean it up and the sticky has grown into other rooms of the house. We have honey on knobs and counters and stair rails and floors and cupboard doors.

You won't believe what I found when I sat on the toilet!

VICKI (parent of seven children with FASD) - Well she is a sweetie - After I told Karen, I didn't want to stay at her place, I stayed with my heart sister, Kat, at her apartment. She has a little baby boy and we did well together. I like to cook and play with the baby and that gives her a break. She doesn't drink and that gives me a sober friend. I work better when life is calm, so I calm her down. She works better when things are clean and organized so she makes the messy part of me clean up my act.

We met a producer who also worked in Adult Mental Health. He had been looking for a roommate and offered to let me rent from him. I really couldn't live with Mom after the honey - she freaked. Somehow my being there was stressing her out. I told Mom and Dad, it was Kat's cousin, even though he wasn't. I just didn't need drama.

CADI CASE MANGER - Meeting is November 14

Mom, Grandma and my aunt went on vacation to Washington and Dad stayed home to watch me like a baby. He told me, I could not call Mom, it was her time with her family. I am still really mad at mom's family from the funeral. They think I am still using and I am not. I have been sober. I am doing a good job. It is getting harder to live with Mom and Dad. They expect me to still be a child and I have a lot more life experience than that. Unless I stay with one of my sisters, I am expected to be a sitting duck and stay home.

At least they have a computer.

I am learning to type.

Chapter 18
Take Me Away My Space

Like I said before, I get really over addicted to anything I get my fingers into. If it is a good thing the whole world seems to benefit, if it's a bad thing I get really hurt. You'd think I'd learn, but every new thing is a very new experience for me and My Space was an open hunting season to get Liz. I had no idea I was a deer in the headlights.

Within in a couple days I made over four hundred "friends" and spent hours writing. I found old grade school and high school friends. I connected with my birth sister. I even found my best friend in high school and we got together. I was excited to see her again, meet her baby and spend the night. I took my meds and heard later we got into a big argument, before I went out comatose. The only thing I remember is someone was hitting me with a big stick. It hurt, but I couldn't wake up. I heard a man say, "She's on drugs." When I opened my eyes, it was the police. The next day, my back was black and blue. Mom was furious and she grabbed me and my <u>Best I Can</u>

<u>Be</u> book and headed to the police station. The problem was, when we got to the parking lot, I started shaking and dry heaving. I couldn't stop myself. I was so worried that the County would think I had been bad and put me away again. Mom said okay and left.

*

On the Internet I met a lot of new people. Some came off as photographers and movie producers. They wrote all the right things. They offered good money, all I had to do was model and I couldn't get a job. Then they sell your pictures and you have no idea where your photos go. So many girls were younger than me – thinking it all cool - thirteen, fourteen, fifteen. But I'd been around – knew the street – saw the agents as fakers. I made them pretty frustrated. Then it became not nice anymore.

They wanted things their way. It's their money. But the things they wanted from me were things a person can't live right with. The money talks loud. It buys food and a place to sleep, clothes for the baby. Eventually it buys self-medication to numb the pain of all the crap you have been put though at the hand of men degrading you.

I am not trying to live my life like the girls that I model with. It was so evil. They tell you when to pose, where to pose. Everything starts at one jump and then they move it up a level the clothing starts out cool and then it gets smaller and smaller until most of the girls are posing without anything. The money starts out good. Then the money gets less like the clothes. They say, 'Oh, we'll see what you get by the end of the night.'

I'm not going to have sex with someone just because I am pretty. A lot of girls with brain differences are call girls. It is the one way they can make money without having to go to school and prove to everyone how stupid they are again. The money is good at $150 a call and it only takes a week to pay your rent. Just seven men they tell me. Yeah right, seven opportunities to be hit, stabbed, and killed. It's also the reason the boyz with FASDs run errands or sell drugs for thugs.

I don't play that stuff. I don't get naked. I don't do favors. I don't have sex. I let people know that from the get go and they still sneak up. I don't get it. But then when they push, I push back with all the anger from all the times men hurt me. I am a wild animal and their mind is already pumped on some drugs or alcohol – they try to seem cool and are just stuffing down their own crap. My angry energy blows their mind.

Girls like me make really bad decisions. It's horrible and a lot of females break down and kill themselves. So many are dead or cutting away a pain they need to let out. When life has hurt you so badly and you don't feel anything, cutting means you are still alive. It is another bad decision but for some girls their lifeblood is boiling with such anger and hate from deep hurts and fears they have to let it out before they pop. It is a release of feeling, the shame, the puss of an infected life they hide inside. Hurting yourself gives a release of anger and frustration and pain. I'm not going to hurt myself by dying. I'm not done with this life yet! I've never been suicidal. I've said dumb stuff when I go on a rampage, but that's to get attention. It is a way to get out my pain and anger. I spout to get it out.

Dad always said that if anyone ever kidnapped me, they'd drop me off at the corner. Dad was right, I've been kicked to the curbed and left on more than one corner. FASD rampage. Whatever place. I pop off my brain. Don't make me angry. I become a tornado. I never remember what I say or do until later. When the evil comes on I start kicking and screaming. I've ripped a faucet off the sink to hit an attacker upside the head. I don't play with bad guys no more, but sometimes I don't know they are bad until it's too late.

I am not an evil person, but if you set me wrong you pull out a totally different Liz attacking for protection. Nothing will stop me until I am free. Even in the hospital I can be a wild cat. Don't touch me. It takes time to tame me and get my trust. You best bet if I'm protecting myself watch out. I can't even get a decent female medical exam anymore without kicking at someone's face, they will have to drug me – just don't get me scared. Fear moves to angry hatred for me to stay safe.

I care about my life way too much. I would rather hurt somebody else after I've been hurt. I've been hurt too many times, now I just react and I react fast.

*

These men, some barely men look cute in My Space. Sound cool in My Space. But the cuteness is not always going to be there, they have pretty ugly insides. It didn't take too many times to realize they played me and if a guy wants you to get you intoxicated so that your mind isn't working he wants to get you loose so your brain does not engage – These guys wanted my brain screws loose to use me and they sure did and tried ova and ova. And I learned that if they are asking you this and they barely know you then the guy wants to take advantage of you or have his boys do it or worse yet, everyone.

Party Liz – get drunk, act a fool, talk all I want to, go on my little page, dance all over the place, lose my clothes and lip lock with guys is the Liz I don't even know when I am sober.

Alcohol sucks the brains right out of me. I didn't think I was still vulnerable and the guys I met on My Space worked it to get me to come on board. I didn't know it, but I still wanted to drink if it was offered. Alcohol ... FREE ... whatever you want baby ... clubbing Liz. I was single and looking. I still wanted to be party girl cool Liz with a Hotstyle. The problem is when I drink, it can be non-stop and even after "all I went through,"

I wanted to party on, at least one more time. That night I made a hundred dollars, legit. I had done micro braids in a girl's hair and I got paid. Then this guy and I had texting for three weeks on My Space called and we decided to meet up.

He was cute and texted me a good line. I know I can't meet up with anyone at My Space any longer.

In less than four months I had been raped, kicked to the curb, drugged and in the hospital again.

Ain't no body selling me another one of their dreams – a bogus story I fall for. That's just to shorten it up.

In one night of hanging out with the wrong people I lost the money and my self-respect got kicked in the stomach.

November 18

CADI CASE MANAGER - It looks like the hospital will be working on another commitment. Liz just isn't safe in the community and needs more supervision than an ILS worker or job coach can give her. She is where she was last year on the mental health unit. The same social worker and MD are still there so they will be following her.

JODEE (Mother) - Karl called letting me know Liz was in the hospital, raped. He will be visiting her later and he assured me he will handle it. I am not to worry, she is safe. It is my job to love my family and take time for me. He said she met some guys from My Space. I will be glad when the County can get us at least a job coach or ILS worker, doing this whole thing alone is really tough. She is managing her meds better and we have moved from daily boxes to weekend boxes if she is visiting Kat or Anna.

There was a homeless man living on the bus – he had a job and his job – the bus – provided his housing. The bus was running and he was waiting for his next shift. He let me into the bus to warm up. A few others shared a couple seats and lay down low wrapped in jackets hiding to keep warm. I blacked out and someone called the police to pick me up. They took me to the hospital. I used an alias. I didn't get into trouble. You learn what to do.

I am back in the hospital where this whole thing started. I can't believe it, once you're finally sober you feel really ran through. A guy just totally runs through your stuff and takes advantage and not just your body. They probably stole my bus card, phone and whatever money I had. Here they are feeling all okie-doke while I feel soul stomped. I don't let them get the best of me, though. I suck up. If they think you show you're hurting they think it's hilarious. People who do ya dirty talk shit and point fingers to keep people from looking at them.

The street life is a loser life. Most of my old "friends" from early apartment days have been or are in jail. They live the same life they lived four years ago. I don't need that. They hold each other in a death grip to stay street. When you do dirty, you point to others dirt. I don't like the gangbanger stuff anymore. The guys I've met tell me I am still in the gang since I got sliced in. Two cuts across my stomach when I was nineteen. They say "You're a Ranger – always be a Mommie."

I tell them, "The only gang I follow is God's gang. No one came to visit me in treatment. No one wrote me a letter when I was in the hospital."

Sometimes my anger is pushed against so much anger that it bubbles to exploding. All my stuff and all my energy gets involved in all my skin. My skin feels stretched.

Now that I'm sober they put their hands out or want their hands on me. That's crap. I tell myself I learned my lesson and I better not do that again. Life sure has lessons.

I woke up with a catheter and all my clothes cut off. Again, I wasn't even sure where I was – oh, the County hospital, again! I kick at the exam, they use no lube in rape cases and you feel raped again by the doctors.

Mom was out of town with Grandma and my aunt. Dad said I had to give her a break. There was nothing she could do from so far away. I was not to call her! People I don't know try to talk to me, they hand me a bunch of papers of what to do next. Papers called "victim reports." I refuse to be a victim.

*

My friend got me out of the hospital before the County could do anything. I am pushing to stay at his place. He works in adult mental health. He said I can live in his basement. He also produces music and I can do recordings while I am there. It is close to Mom and Dad but not in their house. They will still be a big part of my life. I am waiting for an ILS worker to help me with my independent living skills. He said maybe he could find me an ILS worker or a job coach. I really want to get a job. He worked to put together a rental plan for room and board to help keep me safe. It isn't the typical rental deal but I am okay with it. Mom and Dad agreed it might work.

CADI CASE MANAGER - Hi team: I am writing to express some concerns and edits our agency think needs to be made on the rental agreement put together by property owner. – Jodee can you give a copy to property owner. We had spoken at the meeting last Friday that property owner would solely be a renter to Liz if she moves in with him.

I have attached a generic rental agreement that I would highly encourage property owner to use for his lease with Liz.

Now to highlight the areas of concern with the current rental agreement:

FUN section: there would not be a "fun" section in a rental agreement as the only thing being provided is housing

Kitchen section: "no cooking after midnight". In a rental agreement this shouldn't be in there as criteria. Liz should have access to her own kitchen 24 hours a day

Kitchen section: what is missing is any statement or agreement on food and meals' being provided as was discussed at the meeting on Friday along with being a part of the rent paid each month. There should be a statement saying something to the effect of "renter will provide three meals and two snacks daily for resident and food will be easily accessible"

House section: Instead of telling Liz in the agreement not to make a duplication of a key, a key should be made that has "do not duplicate" engraved on it.

Guests section: There shouldn't be any statement on visitors as property owners only role is to be the renter and renters typically do not deny access to guests of their residents.

Guests section: The criteria that visitors must pick Liz up away from the property is not appropriate in a rental agreement. This wouldn't be in a normal rental agreement ever.

Respect section: The criteria that Liz must have "time outs" if she has outburst or alcohol violations is inappropriate for a rental agreement also. Property owner, as the renter, does not have the capability to send Liz away for a period of time. This would be different than a clause that would state if she was past due on rent or causing significant disturbances to other residents she would be given a 30 day notice to move.

Time out section: It is recommended that this whole section be omitted as renters do not have the power to put their residents in a "time out". It's not their role.

Alcohol use: It is not the renter's role to mandate that their residents go to AA meetings or provide documentation of it. If ILS wishes to work out a contract or goals with Liz and THIS be one of them then I would find that more appropriate, but its not property owner's role as the renter to ask for this.

I hope this helps with some edits and possibly using the generic rental agreement.

My friend agrees to all the County choices. He agreed to rent the same as everyone else. But I was not a normal renter and he knew that from the get go and I still did not have ILS or a job coach. So regardless, he becomes what he was asked not to be. The more control, the more shelter, the more isolation the more I over react. I know now the more goals and responsibility for my issues the harder I try to meet those because I care. He gets on my nerves nitpicking me.

It is easy for me to neglect cleaning up my after-beings. Clean up your stuff! Nag. My messy hands. Nag, nag. December ... My bathroom. Nag, nag, nag. January ... The kitchen. Ahhhhhhhh ... when will they stop, when will I stop. I leave a trail behind me like pigpen. He hates it. I turn up the heat, he turns it down. He puts a cover over the thermostat. I turn the lights on, he turns them off. I lose the key. I can't get it copied. I yell. He makes a new one. He laughs. He yells. I laugh. We record songs. We wait for an Independent Skills Person or a Job

Coach to help me move forward.

One night, I call my social worker and tell her I love her and I thank her for helping me. My reaction on my meds even surprise me!

November 21, 2009

I am uncommitted! My roommate buys us a bottle of vodka to celebrate.

I had been sober for so long!

I get sloshed.

*

It didn't take long before Mom and Dad's radar went up big time. Sloppy, drunk Liz is not a pretty Liz, I started losing weight. I was angry and snapping. I didn't drink often, but when I did it was overboard and he could get his needs met and I got to record music.

JODEE (Mother) - In the beginning of Liz's young adult adventure our elderly neighbor's home was offered for sale. The tiny house has a footprint of just over 700 sq. ft. and is smaller than some of Liz's previous apartments. It needed repair, but we considered it a possibility as a cottage home for her future. In 2005, Karl and I made an offer and lost it. Four years later, in December a new For Sale sign was stuck in the snow. Foreclosed and offered at less than a half of the previous sale price. We made an offer of a third and laid down our personal life's savings. Good bye retirement. We're we crazy? Liz for a neighbor? I guess we couldn't get much crazier than we already were.

For the price we got it for it seemed like the best thing we could do. The neighbors are kind people. She would be close, but not in our home. We could watch over, but not hover over her

January 2009

CADI CASE MANAGER - Hi Jodee: I think the house could be a great idea. I think that Liz may need more transitioning before moving her to her own apartment and if she is OK with the house and you feel that you can still be mom & dad, go for it. She will have ILS staff that will help her in what it means to have her own house and if it becomes too much too soon I think we`can talk about it as it comes up.

JODEE (Mother) - We hope this interdependent life test in the little home settles her down and provides security. It will be up to her to be accountable for her adulthood. We can always rent it or resell it if this project does not work.

I made an appointment for Vocational Rehab for job counseling. I ask Liz to clean my house in trade for errands. It gives me the opportunity to stay in touch. Karl and I do not want to handicap her growth and hope she get ILS support soon. I observe her skills. I hope she is involved in a training program before we tell her about the little house.

VOCATIONAL REHAB REPORT 2/2009 - Liz indicates she would like to work in some capacity ... Liz reasons and problem solves in a concrete, literal, or one-dimensional fashion struggling on activities which require cognitive flexibility and abstract thinking ... subtests indicate profound deficits in short term auditory information processing ... when directions move from one step to two steps, three steps, or four steps she is going to be at a significant disadvantage ... mood instability, impulsivity, low frustration tolerance, etc., can have a profound impact upon her social and vocational adjustments ... impairment in verbal strategizing, pattern analysis, fluid problem solving and executive functions ... because of her cognitive impairment she may misinterpret the intentions of others resulting in her becoming defensive or upset ... Liz would certainly be susceptible to virtually all types of exploitation. I question her ability to live independently ina safe and healthy manner ... prognosis for competitive employment would have to be considered guarded

I didn't know it at the time when I was renting from my friend that Mom and Dad had other plans. They bought a tiny house. I wanted to show my girlfriend and Mom told us to wait until she checked it over for danger. She didn't want my friend's one-year-old to get hurt from something the contractor left out when we went to explore the house.

Mom found danger, she fell into the open crawlspace and fractured her back. Minnesota is cold in winter and they were putting in all new plumbing. The hole was open to let heat get under the house. The ambulance, and the police, and a firetruck hauled her out. She was in the hospital for four days and couldn't drive for two months. That meant she wasn't there to help me with the house. I was on my own even though I lived right next door. And I finally got an ILS worker.

I so appreciate Dad and Mom for taking this BIG risk on me. I can be a real pain at times. I had left all my old friends, so I felt I was safe. Without my old bad friends, how could I get into trouble? I invited my girlfriend over and we brought this guy in to help us. He seemed so nice. He offered to clean and haul things for me. At first I thought I had lost my phone, then I thought it was stolen, then there is was! Meanwhile he ordered a phone on my account and used it to download garbage. My case manager spent hours on the phone trying to untangle the mess he got me into. Some guys are pretty slick. I learned guys think having a girl with a house is cool. I learned "get out of those relationships quick." Thank God, I had insurance.

JODEE (Mother) - Karl went over to Liz's place to get his truck and the side garage door was kicked in. The kitchen door was locked. He checked the other doors. The laundry door was unlocked. The heat was turned up 80° F and Slick Vic was sleeping next to a medicated Liz. Karl evacuated the boy with his "clothes" he had come to wash and dry. Her medication stolen with her phone. She called 911 to file a restraining order and get the police to take pictures. Karl put a glass case over the thermostat set at 72° F. He replaced all the locks and rekeyed the entry. The police will do a Safety Training Visit with Liz. Perhaps, she has come to the end of herself and a realization she IS a vulnerable adult, not just to alcohol, but also to men. This "nice boys" rapsheet was pages long. Her ILS worker is busy with the realities of Liz's life.

So, I quit making new friends and went to find old friends. I thought old friends would keep their promises of paying rent and helping clean. I learned life happens and they don't always come through. Talk is way cheaper than actions. They ate my food. They gave me new ideas to clean by mixing bleach with other cleaners. I thought I was going to die from the fumes and kill my birds. Thank God, it was summer. I am so blessed to have a laundry room with a real washer and dryer. It makes my life so much easier. I never had enough quarters, or I didn't have soap, or I forgot what I was doing. Now I can keep my clothes nice all the time. And I love my kitchen. The sunshines into the big window.

JODEE (Mother) - The old Cadillac pulled up into the drive as I tried to pull weeds from my neglected gardens. "Where's Liz?" he shouted.

"She's working," I hollered back. My daughter's laughter with her heart sister is unmistakable. Without skipping a beat, the older man walked to the back yard.

"What are you doing here? Get out of here! You don't belong here. Go find a girl your own age! Leave my sister alone!" my street savvy Anna's voice raised as she moved vocal energy to the back of her throat to throttle a ghetto girl growl. My little dark eyed beauty charms the socks off the unsuspecting. Nothing misses her attention to keep herself safe. Cortisol filled since pre-birth, her ever ready instincts remain honed

    *

"Girls like your sister always come back. Fed enough liquor, she will eat out of my hand." He shouted.

    *

The weekend with my little sister made me remember being a happy kid in the warm weather. Goofing off with no stress. Laughing about childhood memories. Working hard with family and hardly working to eat Mom's ribs and potato salad.

Mom picked out the colors for the little house; I was still trying to build trust with her from all my messes and I hoped for a soft blue. She looked happy when she showed me the yellow. I wanted her to be happy so I kept my mouth shut. Mom says when the inside has been clean and organized for a long enough time, we can paint the rooms. I want soft beach colors … calm, peaceful colors, beige, blues, pinks. This warm, cozy little box is my safe space where I feel safe to grow and over time the cravings for alcohol decreased so long as I didn't put myself in vulnerable places. Healing takes time. My sobriety is precious. Relapse to me is if I start the whole process again and I almost did. I am getting stronger. I grew up in a Christian family that supported me and still somehow loves me even after all what I put them through. Sometimes they turned their back on me while I did my stupid stuff but they never used me. There are many parts of my life that will always be different from other people. I still feel like crawling out of my skin when I am overwhelmed and I amputate all the labels from my clothes. Sirens and horns are frustrating and when I jump it takes me time to recover. Beep beep beep or buzz buzz buzz makes me want to scream. I wear sunglasses to the dentist and if I am in a room with fluorescent lights for longer than an hour I need to take a break or I get violent headaches. I can't believe those kind of lights will be the new modern style when they make me feel so much pain. Leaning on me gets on my nerves and please don't touch my hair unless you are dooing it. No groping and too much touching is smothering. Don't grab me when I am mad or scared because you will still get a reaction. Those are sensory things I still work on. They are things I can manage much better now than when I was a child, but the underfeelings are still there simmering.

I have flashbacks of the things that have happened to me – the abuse at the hands of men remain in my pain. A flashback is like a dream. Dreams of running, and running, and never able to get away from all these guys coming to see me, telling me they love me? I don't know why they say they love me. I think they want to get into my pants and just use me for their pleasure. I've been on the street too long to believe them or respect someone like that.

The bus is a place of danger for me and Mom believes I need Metro Mobility to give me more independence. People joke about the "retards" on that bus. They laugh and think it is really funny. I don't think it is funny. It makes me sad.

So many times I put myself in places where it was just God and me. There is no other reason I survived.

A lapse is a mistake of people, places and things I need to avoid to stay sober. One time – after a long time – and it can lead me to relapse if I am not careful. I have been tripped up. Sobriety is a process for me and I have got caught up into thinking this situation is okay. Visiting a club, 'oh, I'll be okay.' Or 'one drink, it won't matter.' Or 'it's just a little party.' Each experience gets me closer to know how to protect my sobriety. Each time I fall I learn how precious getting up and living is.

*

JODEE (Mother) - Blood dripped down her nose and forehead. It dribbled down her eye as a red tear. Because of her fall another line created a cross on her brow. Her scalp needed stitching. Karl and I looked at each other without words both screaming silently, 'one more time!' We sacrificed another night of sleep to the ER room with one difference – this time we took videos and pictures. After the CT scans, vitals and a promised early morning call, we departed with her clothes. She slept in a hospital gown on white sheets with a heated blanket.

*

I wake up in Bed 43. Cold. I knew by the smell where I was. I knew by my orange clothes. The words "commitment" screamed inside my head. I called Mom.

"How many sleepers in orange on plastic mattresses drank their first drink before birth?" Mom asked.

I told her I bet 75% have FASD. We know each other in ways others do not see. Boy, is this a reality check. Walking in the place I used to think was so amazing. I am a little bit older now. Now I see that my birth mother's life could end up being my life as well. And that's something that makes me very scared. This is not something I want for myself.

Gary, the counselor, says I have grown, he can see the change. It took less alcohol to get me admitted. That is good. My body cannot now handle full liters. I shiver at the thought.

I leave with a 'To do idea list' – crisis hot line, get a sponsor, AA meetings in my area with people my age, Goodwill employment. But, I leave without the telephone number to the crisis hot line, without a sponsor, without a specific AA meeting time or place. I realize, this time as I leave I care. My sobriety and keeping safe really matters. I make my list – avoid parties, clubs, bus stops, old unsafe friends. 4 I have the gift of being alive. My choice ... my life ... It is not worth throwing my life away for some stupid drunk night. What can get me robbed or raped, hurt, locked up or even dead?

This was a lapse. A wake up call. It will not become a relapse. I am writing again, more pages for my book. I understand. It took this good slap across the face to figure it out. This time I left a life already safe. I am responsible for myself. I see that now. I will stay my three days and you will see, and you will know who I am. Not who I was, but who I will be. My mother's path is not my path. I surrender. I finally surrender. Bed 43 is not my name.

A regular 'in heaven,' an old man with a loving smile and missing teeth, who I have seen too many times, sticks up for me and protects me like a daughter he may no longer remember. When he leaves, he hugs me and tells me he never wants to see me again. I understand he words of kindness.

Chapter 19
Metro No-bility

KAREN (Director Grandma's Place)

To: Metro Mobility

This letter is in support for April Kulp or "Liz" as she prefers to be called. Liz is in need of metro mobility transportation due to intellectual disabilities and mental health issues. Please consider this information during your evaluation process.

Least restrictive environment — Currently Liz is living in a small home next to her parents and is learning to manage her adult life. For her to continue to be successful and as independent as possible access to Metro Mobility will provide her transportation to her work and allow her to be involved in positive community activities.

Employment Opportunity – The employment opportunity currently available is at the Goodwill Store in Maple Grove. It is a supervised learning environment and will move Liz into employment skills that may be possible in a more competitive environment. There is no public bus that goes to this area from her current housing location and her employment program does not provide transportation.

Memory Confusion – Public transportation relies on cognitive skills to understand connections, time management and ability to make changes in your environment. Liz is unable to get from point A and to point B due to her intellectual disability. If there are multiple transfers, bus location change or schedule difference she cannot follow those directions. Metro Mobility will provide direct point-to-point transportation for Liz – giving her the support she needs to be successful in her struggle to independence.

Safety — Due to Liz's lower intelligence and difficulty under-standing verbal and non-verbal forms of communication she has dif-ficulty understanding personal boundaries. She may mistake a polite conversation to mean a new best friend or boyfriend. She may read someone's not wanting to have a conversation to being angry and start a confrontation with them. She may get off at the wrong spot to continu-ing to have dialogue with a 'new friend' on the bus.

It is important that Liz be considered for metro mobility due to her vulnerabilities that make it difficult to use public transportation.

Feel free to contact me with any questions.

Sincerely,

Karen C. Johnson MA, CPRP,

Program Director Grandma's Place

I have an opportunity to work at the Goodwill store and at first I don't tell my friends because I didn't think it was something to brag about. Even though my friends are poor they are into wearing name brand gear they somehow get or buy new. I've found really nice clothes thriftshopping and I like a good value to make my money go farther.

The vocational rehab program has some really great people. You are not treated like you are less or unable. My case manager is a good person, she helped me get my work uni-forms and introduced me to the realtor. I asked, Mom, why did the realtor care so much about my makeup, hair and earrings? And Mom said,"What realtor? There was no realtor at that meeting." I couldn't believe Mom said that.

I had told this lady, who said she was a realtor, I thought I could work with older people and do a good job. She told me over and over, "I am a realtor, do you think you have too much makeup? I am a realtor, what do you think old people will think

about your earrings?" I kept thinking Grandma likes my earrings. Grandma's friend said, 'if she was young, she'd have a
row of earrings too.' Why would a realtor care? A realtor sells
houses. I finally quit listening to her after she told me she was
a realtor over ten times. I am not stupid.

Mom was quiet for a long time, then she said, "Liz, that
lady said, I am a realist. That is a person who believes they are
telling you the truth about what people will say or think about
you."

Yo, brain, you did it to me again!

VICKI (Parent to seven children with FASD) - Jodee – Because of Liz, I
have learned to teach my children the Rule of Seven since kindergarten.
I tell them if you have more than seven things on you have too much! I
want them to have their own identity, but I don't want their individuality
to cause discrimination. I've seen that with Liz. The "realtor" was paid
to not be discriminatory. And she did her job in trying to teach Liz.
Even she blew it. The rest of the world won't be as kind, they will write
our kids off when too much sparkle, too much personality is showing.
Two of my girls get it - my sparkle kid runs out of the box. I tell them, do
you want to look like a toddler playing with Mommy's jewelry?

Hair, Shoes, Outfit, Glitz and Glamour - rings, bracelets, necklace, earrings, purse, glitter on your face - all those count as one each.
With bare feet you might get an extra, and with a nice array of matching jewelry it might give you a free card. Underwear and socks don't
count because they don't show.

We focus on modesty in dress and behavior. Everyday we talk
about boundaries and safety. We use daily examples. They are going
into middle school and they are getting it.

I ask the tough questions you didn't get the opportunity to have
a good handle on while you were going through it. Jodee, you were
blind sided by life. You needed much more help than you got, you

didn't have anyone there for you to walk ahead in understanding with a really tough kid. You didn't have someone who spoke the language you lived. You share and what you say goes into my head, probably like when professionals have a language because of their education. One quick question - do eyebrows grow back? One of my girls just cut hers off!

It is an honor God allows us to even be parents as messed up as we all are. What the heck is he thinking? I keep saying you want us to what?

I hadn't seen my ILS worker for a long time. She was probably busy with other people and I hoped I hadn't been too much trouble. My house was maintained. I was taking care of my animals. I was managing my meds and meals and friend-ships. My CADI manager, Mom, my ILS worker and I all met for a yearend review. It was a nice summer day and we met out-side. If the meeting went well, I decided I would invite inside my home to see how well I was doing. It would depend upon their behavior towards me.

They shared their report on me with me and I had to use all my skills I learned in ALL my placements and from my parents to maintain. The first sentence of my background – my background! – had "my age wrong!" And that was just the first sentence! I was so angry. They had not seen me for a long time. It said my weight was 90 pounds and I was 103 pounds. I kept thinking do they have any idea what this differ-ence means. Thirteen pounds for me is HUGE!!! It is a HUGE accomplishment and it takes a lot of energy and work to main-tain and eat healthy and be healthy. 90 pounds is not even to my BMI - and I am required to stay at my BMI of 103 to get off commitment. That's what the people at the hospital said, and you best believe I have been doing everything I can to keep that weight.

The person who managed my case had never visited my home and I had lived there now four months and my life was finally becoming stable. They did not know how I was really doing. One more time, the paper was going to tell my story in a different way from the reality I understood.

I said inside my head, "Oh, no it won't."

Mom had to go to work. I told her, "don't worry I can handle this meeting, myself." Mom left to go do her job at the pet store. Mom is now a certified dog trainer. She went back to college for animal behavior. My "keepers" never got invited into my house.

When Mom got home from work she asked, "'How did the meeting go, Liz?"

I told her, "I fired Social Services"

July 29, 2009

ILS WORKER - Liz decided to end all services through her CADI Waiver. I suggested that she switch case management companies but she does not want a social worker involved.

Unfortunately, per DHS, case management has to be involved in order to be on a waivered program.

Mom trained one of the pups as a service dog for a friend of mine with FASD. Her dog, Limey, helped my friend grow independent and leave a group home where he was supervised 23 hours a day, seven days a week. Limey let him get independent enough to get a job and live in the community as a normal person. My friend is a good worker and has kept his job. Limey kept Ken safe and free from my horrible lifestyle with all its hurtful experiences. Limey is now retired from his service job and is living with a new family as a pet, he did his job – for my friend Limey was his ticket to transitioning. Ken and I have talked about what kind of transition living would work with persons living with FASD, we shared a lot of the same ideas. Someday I will write them down.

*

One hour = one TV show. Time gets me into trouble. I do life and I live from event to event. Time things can get out of control so Mom and Dad and I created boundaries for respect. I don't call them after 10:00 p.m. and they don't call me before 9:00 am. I don't pop into their house and they don't pop into mine. I call them when I wake in the morning to check in. Summer continued into fall as I worked in my home. I learn to can pickled beans. I cook and test recipes. I learn to live with my medication and I pack my breakfast and morning meds in a plastic bag so I don't make a big mess in the morning while they wear off. Mom's back got better. Dad and my relationship grew. He is my 100% real dad. I know now he has loved me since I first came to live with them.

Then a friend who has also struggled with sobriety called to celebrate her birthday. I figured safe - no alcohol. I figured - safe - girls group. We went to a nice place, a drinking place and I soon learned how much I still needed to grow.

Chapter 20
Self Care

October 2009

"Mom, guess what happened?"

It was embarrassing to end up in orange again - back in County Detox, facing Gary, my old counselor. My blood alcohol was just over .2. For some people, that's a lot but for good 'ol party Liz that told everyone past the grey elevator, I had been maintaining. Being back in this place I used to think was so amazing no longer appealed to me. I could finally see how the life of my mother could become my life as well. And that life is not something I want for myself. I have the gift of being alive. It is not worth throwing away for one lousy night of getting drunk - and robbed, raped, hurt, locked up or dead. It took a good slap across my face to figure it out. I have a safe home I love. I have a family who loves me. I am growing stronger, at least I thought I was, each day. God, help me be wiser. Help me see those things that can trip me up!

This last year of 'early remission' was tough and I discovered there are simply things I can't do or you best believe I can get tripped up. Birthday parties where there is drinking and clubbing are out, regardless if people say it will be okay. Yeah, okay for you. You have no clue what I've been through.

I have been tripped up with new learning. Friends come in all flavors and some of them are pretty bad. Even after all I went through, I was still drawn to people who could hurt me. It has taken a lot of trouble for me to be wise enough to see what friends can do to hurt my life.

I thought I could trust a 53 year old mother with my story until one night I discovered her drunken self calling my voice mail 28 times with vulgar and excruciating messages about my adoption, my mother's homicide, my birth and adoptive parents and myself. In a witch like voice, she snarked and screeched "puke, puke, little anorexia, alcoholic, fetal alcoholic. H1N1 get it, get it, get it. I hope you die." They got worse. Luckily I was sleeping and my phone had been off. I reported it to the police and changed my number.

Making friends with work mates is not always safe. Girls who seem like church-going sweathearts are not always what they appear. And because of my past experiences I get pointed out as the bad guy. And there are times in my past pointing at me would have been right. Remember what I said before - when you're doing dirty you point away from yourself.

My 'best' friend in high school stole my new cell phone. This guy and I had talked everyday from ages 13 to 17. He shared his girl war stories and I shared my battles with boys. I was so glad to see him again, after being hurt by so many men. After that, at least for a while I've left men behind. I am working on myself and my life and that is big enough. I almost don't believe there are any good men left. It took me a long time before I realized that men were going to lust me not love me. They were going to control me not protect me. Thoughts of themselves and their personal needs came first. I try to stay away from people who upset or stress me. People who do illegal stuff or use substances. I have learned one too many times that being friendly and trying to help these people help themselves, only gets me into big trouble. They stay free and I get set up to be caught.

A homeless friend runs out of gas and I used my check card to put $8.00 of gas in her tank, I tell mom my card is over by $3.28 and she meets with the banker and gives them $15.00 like in fifteen minutes from when I say. The banker says it is covered. Only it isn't. There is a "pending" charge Mom and the banker don't see. I forgot to tell her I share a $6.00 sandwich too. The pending cost me $35.00 and then another and another and another and another. I don't get it. I would go to jail for stealing like a bank does! For less than $15.00 for gas and a sandwich I gave the bank a $175.00!

My impulsiveness still sometimes captures my being and I spout off things I feel sorry for later. I don't intend to be disrespectful and rude. But I know I can be. I hate it when I yell out what I am feeling in the moment. Then I think about it and later I apologize. I also still struggle with my mouth when it exaggerates less than or more than is really happening. It happens most when I need to get something done or not done, then it is like my emotions get mixed up with my thinking and everything gets bigger. Once words are out you can't stuff them back into your mouth and treatment got my mind crazy into swears – they never said you couldn't swear so everyone did. In fact it was encouraged in groups to show out emotions. Swears were like big exclamation marks! Everyone swore except some of the staff. It was the culture and once I am into a habit it is hard for me to get out. I get addicted to everything. So swears was one of the new habits I picked up. It is like when I am with a group of people things rub off. At my job, with my family and in the community I am working really hard not to use the language of the street and in treatment. I see people look at me. I used to think that was attention. Now I know that all attention is not good attention.

I am a small person and if a man decided he wanted 'his' way with me, the only thing I had to fight with was my mouth. So now, before things even got started, I use it. No one is going to "get me drunk so they could have me!" THAT is over and word has changed on the street "Wow, she's beautiful." "You won't get anywhere with her. She'll make you feel small." "I gotta try." "Yeah, and you'll be jacking your balls off until their blue, don't even go there." Now THAT is funny!

When I was drinking I was sneaky and not truthful. And the more I was sneaky the worse it got. I was trying to hide things because I thought people would think bad things about me. And I was trying to be like other people who did not grow in a bath of alcohol before they were born. That bad thinking almost cost me a lifetime of freedom. I almost lost everything with other's making decisions for me. But from that experience, I realized my ideas were important to me, my thinking is deep and precious and I wanted to be a part of my future life planning. My LIFE would be way bigger than my risk. Somehow I would learn to cope with my challenges.

My medication has worked for me. I can sleep! I can eat and not hurt! I feel like a regular person and I am committed to taking it exactly like the doctor says. My moods are stable and I don't need to self-medicate. I just follow the doctor's orders. It's that simple. But, there is a new twist - the medication is expensive and the insurance company didn't always cover it. That means Mom and Dad have to fork over big dollars for little tiny pills to keep me stable. And once we get one of the meds covered in the correct amount of refills, another med is denied by insurance.

Don't they have a clue what I cost them in my OLD LIZ STYLE? Don't they have a clue that, that is a big tumble down stressor? The battle is never over with the medication ... as soon as we get one of them worked out and on a refill plan, the insurance says no to another. How do they expect me to remain stable when they aren't? Why can't they just keep me on what the hospital told me to take? And people think I have messed up thinking. Where is their head? Don't they have better battles to fight then this? I wonder what happens to people who don't have someone like my mom or who are not as pushy as I have to be to watch out for myself.

I finally got a job just before the flu epidemic hit. The job was great, getting the flu wasn't. Neither was the bronchitis that came after the flu. But worse than the flu and the cold was the severe stomach pains I got the third week of being sick. I thought I had the flu again and so did my parents. We visited the doctor and no one could figure out what I had. My symptoms didn't match up. Then Mom talked to the druggist and asked him about the OTC (that's over the counter) that I had to switch to for my stomach because the insurance said I used my supply for the year. That seemed crazy to me since I had already cut my dose down to once a day instead of two times like the year before. The druggist told my Mom that the OTC would take 14 days to begin working and my curl in a ball stomach aches came from stopping my prescribed meds. And they think I have a brain problem? I wish my body worked like other people, but it doesn't and I can't change that. My birth-mom chose my first alcoholic drink, I didn't! With my whole crazy past doctors don't always believe what I say, they think I overreact. I try not too. Here I am doing better. I am not drinking. I am staying safe. I am finally working a real job and I miss three weeks of work, first because I am contagious and then because of the insurance company. Go figure?

When I work I feel a bigger part of life, but even at work I soon learned there were two levels - those of us in "the program" and the regulars. The staff above us don't see the under feelings I think because they are doing good things for people. It is the comments from the regulars that hurt the people in the program. On the first day, people introduced themselves to me and said, "Hi, my name is ... " and all is good and gravy, then later they say "Oh, YOU'RE in the program, you don't look like YOU should be in the program." and they say it like it is something not good when we are all doing the same jobs - go figure. Some of the guys ride metro mobility and I overhear, "Oh, that retard bus is here." spoken quietly and then shouted, "Hey, ---- your bus is here." It hurts. I don't want to use this even though we fought so hard to get the transportation. I no longer ride the bus, it is too dangerous for me and even I finally realize that. So why the stigma? Another friend with FASD helps me see how valuable this can be to my independence and tells me to pay no mind to those who do not understand.

My old boyfriend, the bootleg, found out where I work and started to stop in and check if I was there. I say, "Liz, get over it, get on with your life." But when you have had every part of your being - soul, heart, mind, body, spirit - hurt by someone that reality doesn't go away and old memories start popping back into my skull! The nightmares scream in my head even under the medication. It makes me freeze up and I want to hide, then I want to fight back. I know first I have to get through the emotions and get stronger. Perhaps I need all this so I can get past it and on with my life. He may be on the prowl for a long time, most of his adult life he has been homeless or attached to a girl who will keep him warm and fed.

I try to do the right things - get vaccinated, have annual physicals, keep myself healthy. But one twist can spin me around. I make sure I take all my meds, as a shortcut, so I wouldn't forget morning meds, I chewed them so they were all dissolved and I took them all at night so I wouldn't forget. That mixed with the vaccination set me back three weeks with shaking and twitches. I thought I was going to die! I felt poisoned inside, the doctor thought I was making up my symptoms, but I wasn't. My arms tingled, my legs collapsed. I fell and hit my nose. The skin on my face peeled. I don't want to go to a hospital; I am scared they might keep me again!

Mom records my reactions and starts researching. She discovers it looks like an overdose reaction and emails the emergency 24-hour medical staff and my psychiatrist. She doesn't know I am taking the pills all at the same time. I pick up one days worth of meds. My shortcut is an overdose reaction and I wait it out! It is time to cut down my meds. I can be like an emergency room - first you have to stop the bleeding of my crisis. Then you have to be a detective to get to the bottom of the problem. I am trying hard to learn to manage myself. Sometimes when I try to help myself it only gets more confusing. When life gets out of control for me, I take others on my adventure. Usually it is Mom and I know it messes up her life too. I try to help when things are calm down again.

I keep working to get myself healthier. I eat well and my weight is in the normal range. It is always the little things that trip me up. I set a "safety weight" for myself. I can't afford to lose weight and if I get sick it could be dangerous. For a smaller person, having a little bit of extra is a good idea. My hair has returned. I make appointments and try hard to keep them. Time is still hard; my life runs on a process not on a clock. My home is quiet and I work to keep it clean. Soon I will paint my rooms in calm colors. I am responsible for what happens in my home, my parents don't help with my clothes or food or living.

Dad fixes things when they break, sometimes I help. We make chicken and dumplings. Mom helps me run errands; I try to give hours back. We make lasagna florentine. I learn over time that having roommates makes my life more complicated. My home is getting cleaner; I keep it as simple as possible. There are plenty of things to do to not get bored. My clothes are washed and folded. I cook meals from scratch that are healthy. I plan a garden with mom for next year. I get plenty of sleep. Old friends return from my past who disappeared with my ex, and I sort out the pieces of craziness. Truth cannot be hidden, it is alive and rises to the top. I play with children of my friends who have little child giggles and we attend child parties. Animals and children bring joy. My birds sing in the morning and through the day.

Life still happens to me and things can twist out of shape for a while. A baby dunks my cell phone in the orange juice or breaks something I have that is precious. The water heater breaks and I need to boil water for a bath. A bottle of cleaner hidden in the closet sprays out vodka. I dump it down the drain. That is so opposite from licking a floor filled with broken glass to not waste it. People I think I can trust hurt me. Old boyfriends try to regain a position in my life. My ex-man of four years is already divorced from his wife of two months. He is on the prowl for me and uses people from the 'old crew' to call my parent's phone and track me on the computer. I get nightmares from the previous abuse, thinking about him or worrying he will pop up creates hurt stress and I miss work opportunities. It really is sick! I've been over him for almost a year and have moved on with that piece of my life.

I appreciate the people on my braided cord. I appreciate Mom taking me to the doctor and listening to what they say so I understand better. I appreciate being dropped off and picked up at the store. I appreciate Mom and Dad coming over to check on me when I don't feel well. I appreciate Dad making me a cup of tea and saying hello. I appreciate Mom untangling the messes I can fall into with medicine refills or banking. I appreciate Dad fixing things, getting the snow out of my driveway and making sure my house is safe. I am happy with myself and who I have become. My little home comforts me. I am safe. I am warm. I have food and I can sleep safely. I know I have people who truly love me and sacrificed so I could grow.

A year ago my choices under setbacks would be to get a drink, lie and make excuses for my problems. I'd act crazy and simply make the problem more difficult. I don't need that any more. I don't have low self-esteem. I can do most of my life myself. Each month, I need less help. Each month, I realize how important helping each other is. I help Dad and Mom and they help me. I help my true friends I call my sisters and they help me. I believe in my abilities and I'm keeping my head high as I walk out of my tough times.

I get caught in the big picture if I am in the details and I get lost in the details if I am trying to figure out the big picture. The two don't come together and that is a BIG problem. I get so mad shopping - looking for the best deals, reading the labels, knowing I did well and then realizing my WHOLE cart is full. I didn't over spend on anything just because of everything! I try to work with my money issues and Mom is helping me face reality here and deal with what money is and what it means and how to manage it. She turns ideas upside down to help me learn. We call it a spending plan instead of a budget. That makes more sense in my head. Learning things I can't touch takes small steps. I believe if I work hard I will handle it.

A job provides a schedule to keep my life structured. It works best with four workdays for four hours. Then I don't get overwhelmed. I can still maintain my home, care for my animals, prepare my meals and keep myself healthy. I have learned it is important for me to keep stress out of my life and live simply. If I am with friends who act crazy, it is easy for me to get sucked into their crazy behavior. I need to be cautious. For four years I held on to an unhealthy relationship because of the pull alcohol has in my life. I excused the abuses done to me and the abuses I did to myself. Today I realize I am worth more than all of that and if I get pulled under by a spirit of alcohol I can lose everything. Knowing is my beginning to wise up. I don't need a relationship now as I grow and get stronger.

Sometimes I miss my thoughts. These are my moments of not understanding or not knowing. I am in emptiness with no way to figure something out. The problem with those empty places is you never know where they are going to come into your life and you can feel really inadequate because of them. The empty place can be so simple and this Christmas I stood in front of my present not able to figure out how to open it. I have opened presents for over twenty years! It used to infuriate me to raging. Now, I say inside my head, 'oh well" and ask someone to share in the fun of opening. No one else knew I asked for help because at 'that' moment I didn't know how. Finally, I can look at a mess and say, "show me how" and it's okay. I need to get stronger and learn to plan for the simple things that don't bother other people. These can turn my life upside down and I need to be ready. I am an intelligent person, even though I have a brain injury. I happen to experience fetal alcohol spectrum disorders due to no actions of my own. That does not mean I don't take responsibility for my behaviors, I do. FASD is not an excuse, but it sure makes life a struggle. As I go to press, the dentist calls and says I no longer have insurance - I lost my filling - it is March 1, 2010 - my battle journey continues - they will hold my appointment until 4:00 pm today.

From the beginning I am a survivor. With self-determination to stay safe, continuing to learn self-control, medication, family and true friends I will reach high. I'd like to go to college for criminology. I think I'd be good at it. I most certainly have lived many parts of it. I think I could add knowledge to a case. Or maybe child development. I love preschoolers, but I am not ready to have my own. If I am going to work or try for college I need to keep my life simple and calm.

If I can leave alcohol behind, I believe there is hope for others.The first time I was drunk, I hadn't taken my first breath. I hadn't eaten solid food. No one had hugged or kissed me yet. I hadn't seen the sun or the stars or experience life beyond the bath of alcohol in my mother's womb. I guess that those times were between God and me. I can't touch God like I can touch a human being, but I know in my heart and mind that God touched me. He never left my side, even in my darkest times. He carried me when I couldn't walk. When I prayed in my darkness, I was given hope as a member of God's creation. Hope gave me the path of where I wished to go instead of where I was stuck. I am grateful, loved and lovable.

My spirit grows stronger. My name is Liz, not Bed 43 or tombstone 4989723. I am a talented, intelligent and creative adult woman and my life is about my abilities, not my challenges. Communication, high expectations and consistency I can rely on create space for my success. I will not become another number because another human being does not understand me. I am just one of hundreds of thousands of people whose lives are louder, softer, harder, scratchier, noisier, shakier, slippery and more chaotic than most of you who have just read my story. And for those of you who were not pickled before birth, who believe you are wiser than I am, I ask you to take my thoughts and use your brains to make a difference.

As my little sister of my heart, Anna, says,

"I dare you, no, I double dare you!"

My grandpa said, "never say can't" and my dad always told me, "Liz, you can do hard things."

Life is hard, but I'm not going to quit.

And I believe, you best believe, I truly believe!

God is good and I am strongly living life.

A. Elizabeth M. Kulp

P.S. I wonder what will happen to "the others."

Prologue

JODEE (Mother) KARL (father) - Children with brain trauma (injury or damage) often require a longer period of sheltered living and a stronger support system to develop the skills of adaptive living. Birth, adoptive and kinship families bear most of this initial task. When Liz was a child, I believed our parenting path was the hardest. Then when our daughter became a teen, she was a windblown tumbleweed pushed along by a media culture. Her outward expression and beliefs shouted at the world. Today, weathered by the secondary disability pieces of beginning adulthood, I honor the strength of my daughter to shine on the other side. Over the process of growing and learning together we have handed Liz 'her life' with its strengths and challenges. We could not save her until she wanted to save herself ... until we learned to brain coach instead of parent. We offer ideas and options, walking along side, not stepping upon. Liz does her meal planning and shopping, orders her medications and manages them, makes her dentist and doctor appointments, cleans her home and does her laundry. Each growth step has had it's share of failures. Guidance versus judgment was the key. We no longer stomp on her mistakes, but challenge her to discover solutions. Some of her ideas work and some don't. Isn't that true for all of us? With life experience and maturity, the storms have quelled and she is managing her life at a level higher than we ever expected. The school of life's challenges has tamed my wild one and her experiences have made her wiser.

We weep. We pray. We learn. We celebrate.

There remain many unanswered ifs.

If we had allowed more failure as a young teen, would it have made a difference? If we had prepared transitional services and had a program ready before onset of adulthood would we have never ridden the tsunami? Hindsight is 20/20, yet if we had been given a map of our future we may have evacuated and Liz may never have reached this beginning level of competence. Life for her is still a process in the making and we did not do this transition with Liz alone. We had help from two public school transition programs, ten different police departments, medical personnel, social services, five different hospitals, three court systems, three different treatment programs, psychologists, psychiatrists, four DBT programs, two detox centers, and a handful of counselors. Exhausted.

Each human being with FASD will be affected differently. Many end up on our streets, in hospitals, in our welfare systems and penal institutions. They budget out of services. Readers must remember that Liz is 'only one voice' of many persons.

The cost of inaction is escalating.

Tens of thousands of these children are born each year and we need to be wiser. A night in jail runs between $150 - $300. A month in an emergency shelter costs between $500 and $700. Two meals a day at soup kitchens cost $2.66. Meals for 200 days cost $532. A night at detox runs $150-$200. Emergency room visits average a $1,000. Homeless individuals average two visits per year at $2,000 per visit. One hospital stay averages $29,921. Residential care costs range from $1500 to over $13,000 a month. The average cost per state or federal prisoner: in 2001 was $22,650, or $62.05 per day; among facilities operated by the Federal Bureau of Prisons, it was $22,632 per inmate, or $62.01 per day. Check the costs yourself and then decide if this white elephant is a worthy cause for humanity. We are now in 2010! How long must this 100% preventable disability continue?

We deplete our budgets. The cycle continues. Liz's machete trail to independence is too costly. Over the process of writing her book, our daughter, used almost 1/2 million dollars of services, along with our savings, our business, and our hearts. It almost cost her life. Liz's greatest challenge to overcome was the lack of understanding and management of her symptoms of FASD, the impact of FASD on her life and the community.

The last year of navigating independence within the context of an on site cottage provided safety with independence for our daughter. This strategy allowed her to climb another rung of independence and manage more of her life, much like the Grandma's Place model in Minnesota. Still if a number of things fall out of place, stress creates chaos. Liz's sensory issues remain and they affect day-to-day living. For those of us who live in other skins, it can be complex to understand.

Liz offered her life and the life of our family to open the window of adult transition. Our whirlwind child has matured and softened with the wisdom from her journey. We hope by opening this window, new questions arise from the hearts and minds of persons in graduate studies in epidemiology, psychology, education and law. We need evidence based scientific study that allows for enhancement of the lives of this population with scientific research. We need repeatable steps to help us dependably predict future results.

Kristine Haertl, PhD, OTR/L, is associate professor in the Department of Occupational Science and Occupational Therapy at the College of St. Catherine in St. Paul, Minnesota, and chairperson of the Board of Directors for Tasks Unlimited, a large Fairweather-model mental health program. Her 10-year study of outcomes at Tasks Unlimited (peer supported living) showed a 95% reduction in the rate of psychiatric hospitalization, with less than 1% of client time spent in psychiatric hospitalization. It is an evidence-based research place to start.

We need affordable worldwide training academies for our young people where they can attend leadership and skill building camps from ages 14-17 learning to manage their neuro diversity.

Grandma's Place, Life Colleges, Opportunity Partners, Rise, College Living Experience, The Fairweather Lodge Model (evidence-based peer supported communities like Tasks Unlimited), Goodwill and Job Corp models need research and expansion for persons moving on to more independence. There are life education models coming from the autism and attention deficit community. Additional ideas arise from the Alzheimer and traumatic brain injury community. More strategies are developed to help persons with Downs Syndrome and Cerebral Palsy.

> We need to get accurate answers to these questions:
> How many persons with FASDs are 'really' incarcerated?
> How many persons with FASDs parental rights are terminated?
> How many children with FASD fill our foster care system?
> How many support families are crushed in the chaos?

We need young and older professionals willing to train, coach and mentor as a community. When we work to braid a human being into our lives we create strength. When we reach out to braid others we can create a safety net to cushion the falls of learning. Together we can learn to teach through failures. We can all celebrate success.

When persons with FASD live in a safe place where their needs are met in a wholistic way, they thrive being safe and secure. When they have employment or a volunteer position sharing their passion they have purpose and are happy. They excel in safety and purpose.

Don't we all?

Join our international Liberty Ridge team.
Karl and Jodee Kulp
www.libertyridge.net

SOME IDEAS FOR A
12 STRAND BRAIDED CORD

The transition to adulthood is a challenge for many people and it seems especially hard for people who begin a life with prenatal brain injury and sensory integration issues. We hope the ideas of the many who have walked with us on this journey will help 'able' healthy differences for adolescents and young adults with FASD in development of living skills.

Additional ideas can be found in Stephen Neafcy's *The Long Way To Simple Fetal Alcohol Spectrum Disorders.* He has lived with FASD for over fifty years, now that's a LONG time!

Areas addressed include:
1. Family
2. Public Awareness
3. Community/Recreation
4. Friends
5. Judicial
6. Housing
7. Finance
8. Safety
9. Medical
10. Outreach
11. Education
12. Employment

1. Families

★ Create a Life Action Plan to help reach a goal:

1. Write down two goals (dreams you have)

>> Idea is: small goal - learn to make spaghetti

> big goal - buy a new television

2. Break it down into steps you can do.

3. Ask people you trust to help you with steps

>> if you need that. Be truthful with yourself about what you CAN and cannot do.

4. List resources and/or people to help,

5. Set a time line for each step.

★ Please tell me clearly what you need me to do. For example, if you are carrying heavy bags and need help. Tell me, "I need you to take a bag to help me." I am glad to help when I know you need something. Do not talk to me like I am a child or a pet. I may not process everything you say, but if you communicate with me by checking what I said or you said we will get to better understanding.

★ Stay connected to healthy family members. These are people you can talk to, get advice, and enjoy time together.

Notes from family members

★ **Eva Carner (Mother of adult with FASD)** – Many challenges people with FASD experience arrive because of short term memory and mood. They may forget moment-by-moment what they are doing. Help create task lists, a day planner or program appointments. Place information into phone, computer and white boards as reminders.

★ **GUARDIANSHIP OR CONSERVATORSHIP** is renewed every year and can be item specific. It will only be in effect until the person develops the necessary skills to take care of themselves.

2. Public Awareness

✯ Educate yourself about your challenges so you can educate others and tell them what you need to be successful. Keep a notebook of your ideas so you can look back on them. If something works write it down and share it.

✯ Sometimes my brain shuts down to process the information I am hearing. When my brain is filled up, it's full. When I hear too many words I have to turn down the conversation and noise.

✯ FASD brain injury does not give me an excuse to be rude to people. It is not an excuse to not learn and obey rules to keep me safe. I may have a different brain and it may be an explanation of why I act without thinking or do and say some of the things I do. It is my responsibility to try to pre-vent those behaviors and if my ugly shows it is my respon-sibility to learn to deal kindly with the results.

Notes from friends

✯ **Lois Bickford, (Lifecoach for persons with FASD)** – When my friend learns something new it takes full attention and focus. I liken this to when a person first learns to drive a car. Each step must be thought through carefully to perform the action and yet over a period of time the process becomes automatic. Our young people with differing neurobiology may not get to or may take ten times longer to arrive at this place. During the phase of learning, prodding, interrupting, criticizing, doing for them or judging will shut down the opportunity to acquire the new skill. This process takes a zen-like patience from the teacher to honor the learning of the student. Even when they possess a skill, distraction may cease the ability to utilize it.

3. Community/Recreation

★ Find a community group you feel a real part of. A place where you can share your passion - it may be a church, a sport team, training animals.

★ The less distractions I have the better I can learn and understand. If I am learning something very new I need a step by step approach, but don't TREAT me like a baby!

★ Ask permission to give me advice. Say, "Can I give you some advice." If I say, 'yes', then I am prepared to listen, but please keep it short or you will lose my focus, I don't do lectures.

★ The hardest, most complicated system to deal with is the government agencies that provide services, get a person you trust to help you through all the papers and requirements or you will lose any services you may have.

★ Some people are afraid of FASD or fetal alcohol, so I just say I have a brain injury that happened before I was born, so I have to work really hard to cope with some things. If I ask for help, maybe you will help me.

★ Find hobbies you like to and are able to do alone and find activities you like to do with other people. Make a list of the people share this activity.

Notes from the community
★ Support your friend in transportation to community events.
★ Involve person in preparing for community and/or family events - reunions, holiday gatherings, picnics.

4. Friends

★ Create a circle of friends you can trust that will be honest with you and are not a negative influence on your life.

★ "True" Friends are people who help you accomplish good things in your life and do NOT hold you back. You help each other and you are nice to each other. You enjoy spending time together.

★ Fill your free time with things you love and surround yourself with healthy people.

★ Take a community class with a friends. Adult education is not the same as your childhood school experiences.

★ Find a hobby you can share.

★ Learn a card game or board game together.

★ Make meals together.

★ Be appreciative and thank people who help you.

★ Positive people who do not pull you into their chaos.

★ Understand that if the day has been stressful or I am tired, hungry or overwhelmed, I may overreact.

★ Tell you what you can do to improve but do not take away your goodness or feeling capable.

★ If we go out, I am usually more comfortable in an aisle seat or front or middle.

★ Surround yourself with 'friends' who understand and accept your challenges, but also don't let you get by with being rude or disrespectful to them.

Notes from friends

★ Making crafts, doing hobbies or working together on a project while talking about tough subjects reduces stress and anxiety.

5. Judicial

★ Judges determine your sentencing if you get into trouble and legal people who understand FASD have more willingness to provide appropriate sentencing that will benefit instead of hurt you.

★ If you are involved in the legal system, find an advocate who understands FASD.

★ Carry a medical alert card that states you have a disability and hand it to legal professional when stopped. Do not talk until you have an advocate present.

Notes from the judicial community

★ **COURT** – Advise court of friends medical diagnosis of FASD and supply appropriate paperwork as proof. Attend court proceedings to supply advocacy and understanding of process.

★ **POLICE - GUARDS** – Avoid grabbing the person unexpectedly. Break down the steps you need person to perform one at a time, then when person complies, (lie on the floor) add the next step.

★ **SUSAN CARLSON, JD**

— Inability to resist impulses can lead to shoplifting, not being able to think of consequences, and sexual offences.

— Poor memory retention and retrieval leads to probation violations, missed court appearances, false confessions, difficulty anticipating consequences of actions.

— Inability to function like their peers leads to depression, mental health problems, use of drug or alcohol, school problems, trouble with the law.

— Poor judgement and desire to please lead to aiding others in offences, being a patsy for others, or participation in gangs.

— Learning difficulties lead to not understanding the legal process.

— Communication difficulties lead to relationship problems.

6. Housing

★ Check out the neighborhood BEFORE you move in or sign any papers. Check with the police department if the area is safe.

★ Take time in the morning or before you go to bed to organize the day.

★ Solve one problem at a time.

★ Put reminder cards on things you may forget to turn off like outside light, stove, water.

★ Get a timer that dings when something is ready and get used to setting it.

★ Write your schedule on a white board in your home. Test out HOW LONG the important things you do takes so you have plenty of time to get to appointments or work.

> For example:
>> Getting ready in morning -
>> — Eat breakfast _____how long,
>> — Fix hair and make up _____how long
>> — Get dressed _____how long

★ Use yellow or orange night lights to help you find your way in the dark, the color yellow allows you to not fully wake.

★ I clean and organize when I am angry.

Notes from the housing community

★ Create successful situations.

★ Make a list of friend's favorite meals, simplify the recipes and teach how to cook them.

★ Teach to set alarm clocks and check they are operating

★ Access www.mycalls.net for scheduling and memory support

7. Finance

☆ Allow someone who can manage money to help you like a Rep Payee. If money or time is a challenge for you it is good to ask for support. Be involved as much as you are able to understand.

☆ Make a list of all the things you NEED TO PAY FOR and take care of them before you get FUN MONEY.

☆ When you provide me with information, that does not mean I understand it. If I don't understand it goes into a pile. Involve me, show me and make me a participant. Let me do the last part and finish, then add earlier pieces next time.

☆ Make my meeting space friendly, hang a "Do not disturb" sign on the door. Interruptions can erase everything we already covered.

☆ Learn to use money saving ideas - coupons, thriftstores, store sales.

☆ When you owe a bill that is bigger than you have money for you can work out a payment plan and you have to stick to it. Don't just use numbers to explain this to me, use actually money pictures and a calendar so I know how much and when.

Notes from the finance community

☆ Realize that money management involves many small steps and it is difficult to take in more than one step at a time.

8. Safety

★ Learn to cook with a crockpot, microwave, and rice cooker.

★ Invite a safety inspection into your home, these are community service police you can check that your locks work and let you know what you can do to keep the place you live safe. They also tell you things you can do to stay safe.

★ Be truthful with yourself about HOW you put yourself in unsafe situations. Get another stable and healthy person to help you role play and develop a plan.

★ Memorize important phone numbers and/or program them into your phone.

★ Stand tall when you walk. Don't walk in dark areas.

★ Ask for help when you cannot do something or when you don't understand.

★ Ask for help when you think something bad might happen to you.

★ Make a list of 10 things in your house that could be danger – mark them with a red dot of sticker. This means before you use them you must stop and think.

★ Everyone is NOT your friend. Just because someone is nice to you DOES NOT mean they are a friend. They can be people who want to hurt you or set you up.

Notes from community safety

★ Trust takes time to build. If you are a coach or social worker agree to do something before the next meeting and then do it before the meeting. Call the person or show them when it is completed.

9. Medical

★ Please have the "heat on" when it is too cold, I can't think as well and I also am not as cooperative.

★ Pick one clinic you can visit with a doctor or nurse you trust. Keep all your medical records in that one place.

★ Try to get appointments on the same time of day and on the same day of the week to keep your schedule.

★ Bring another person with you to the doctor so you understand what is being said or expected of you.

★ Check at the end of the appointment what was talked about today and write or draw what I need to do. Keep it short.

★ Take the medication prescribed by your doctor and work with your doctor if you believe it needs to be changed.

★ If you know your mother drank while she was pregnant with you, do not be afraid to get a diagnosis.

★ Take time to learn how your brain and body work differently so you can face your challenges.

★ Avoid addictions or self-medicating with alcohol, drugs, tobacco. Tell your doctor if have a problem and get help NOW!!!! Find someone to help you get into recovery if you end up in trouble.

Notes from the medical community

★ Assist in paperwork and transportation services.

★ Follow-up on any connections or meetings you set up.

★ Consider providing fidget toys in the office or an aquarium or waterfall style object.

10. Outreach

★ Make a 3 Ring Life Binder that includes addresses and phone number and how to get to (bus, metro mobility) contacts, (add photos in addition of doctor, dentist, mental health supports, social worker) and important information (fire, ambulance) .

★ Schedule your appointments with me on the same days and at the same times. I prefer afternoons if possible.

★ When you come to my house, if I only see you once a month, call before you leave your office and introduce yourself. "Hi, Liz, this is Sue, we have a meeting today at 2:00 p.m. and I am just leaving my office. I will be there in about 15 minutes." Then when you get to my home, "Please tell ask me how things are going and if there is anything I need to do, tell me what we did last time we met. Notice what I HAVE accomplished and give me a copy of your notes.

★ Don't leave a pile of papers in my hands to fill out. If they need to be completed help me understand and complete them or help me find someone who can help me.

★ When you change the piece of a routine you have created an entirely new routine for me.

Notes from the persons in outreach

★ Help find long-term mentors and life coaches. Families burn out.

★ Keep meetings relaxed and calm. Do not switch topics. Too many issues will only frustrate or freeze person.

★ **Deb Evenson** – Most difficulties come from taking in new information, integrating new information with previous learning and being able to use that information.

11. Education

* Tell people to use less words and wait longer for responses. Don't expect immediate response. I need time to think.
* The less distractions I have the better I can understand.
* If I am learning something very new I need a step by step approach, but don't TREAT me like a baby!
* If you don't understand something ask to have it explained another way. Do NOT step closer to me or speak louder to help me understand better. This is overwhelming and makes things more confusing.
* Realize that people with FASD may share common behaviors, but each of us is an individual human pieces with different hopes, desires, beliefs, skills and challenges.
* Learn what I care about and help me learn through things that interest me.
* Try to understand that each of us with FASD is different and that you need a range of understanding in how we each learn. When I feel dumb it makes it more difficult to learn something new.
* Not everyone understands everything being taught. Don't single me out. Offer an opportunity to everyone to get more understanding. The first time, ten to fifteen people went into the back room to get help. A lot of "normal" people needed help and got. Finally it was accepted that it was okay to ask for help when you didn't understand.

Notes from transition school staff
* Expect students to take ownership for their accomplishments, behavior, learning and future. Create community connections.

12. Employment

★ It is important I do not sound angry with a customer or peer. I need a list of what my jobs are so I can cross off where I am so I do not forget where I left off. The list empowers me to perform well even when I am interrupted. It allows me freedom to move into something else in my job if I need to help someone.

★ A visor cuts down on the glare of fluorescent lights and helps prevents the headaches I get working under them.

★ Do the same things every day, in the same order. Break the things you need to do into little steps to not forget details.

★ If things get too rough at work and you leave before you say or do something you will be sorry for later ... ask the supervisor for a 'cool down' job or place to regroup respectfully.

Notes from life coaches

★ **Lois Bickford, (Lifecoach for persons with FASD)** – My friend may be really good at her job and at any moment she can loose her abilities. Getting a stressful phone call or dealing with a complex life issue from the night before. It is important that these employees are giving healthy break times (five minutes of quiet, journaling, drawing) or periods of non-stressful jobs to them (fronting shelves, wrapping product, fetching carts). My friend has learned that because her brain works differently, she needs to be aware of "what causes her stress", take a break doing something simple or get fresh air. She keeps an employer approved task list and flips the colored laminated card over to signal her supervisor she was being proactive in supporting her team members, doing a good job at work and keeping her boss happy. She checks off one of three tasks she is heading to complete.

Words you need to understand CLEARLY!

Circle of Support. A circle of support is a group of people who help you reach your personal goals.

Goals are things you hope for in your life. Goals can be made in very small steps so they are possible. Make a chart of your goal so you can see your progress. Also you can change goals if you decide it is not what you want any longer.

Guardianship. Laws consider a parent your natural guardian until you reach the age of 18. Once you reach 18 years old, a parent or sibling (or other potential guardian) must petition (write on a form) the court to grant guardianship status over an adult with disabilities.

Person-Centered Planning are service options that are based on your choices, strengths, and needs. If person-centered planning is going to work for you "YOU" need to be really honest with yourself and the people who are helping you with your plan.

Rep Payee. A person who manages your money so you do not manage it poorly. This person helps you pay your bills.

Residential Placement. There are many kinds of places to live happily as an adult - some are with support of other adults (your family, adult foster care, group homes), some are peer supported (lodges), some are more or less independent (apartment or home with roommate or other caregiver). Be truthful with yourself about your abilities. It is better to start with support and have a life action plan to grow to the next step. If you live with what you think are huge supports that does not mean you have to remain there forever. Visit different kinds of residential opportunities to discover what fits your needs.

Here are some explanations of living styles:

Supervised group home Three to six individuals live together in an agency-run home where trained staff assists you the things you need help. There are usually organized activities outside the home every day.

Adult foster care Live with a family other than your primary family to help you learn living skills, medication management and budgeting your finances. There are adult family and corporate adult foster care homes.

Supervised apartment living This provides you some assistance in a larger apartment complex with other persons who need supports. Usually, there is a service provider on site to respond to emergencies and offer limited assistance based on your needs.

Supported living You live in your own place or in your home. Needed services and supports are brought to the home instead of the person going out for them.

Independent living This is an apartment or house rented or owned by you. Outside training and support can still be available and provided to help you learn to become independent.

Self-Advocacy. Parents or family are most often your best advocate. However, it is very important for adults who are able to learn how to advocate and become self-advocates. Learning to speak up for yourself is a process.

Self-Determination. Is your right to make choices about your life, to have the same rights and responsibilities as everyone else, and to speak and advocate for yourself. Most people are not ready for this WHEN YOU TURN 18. It takes hard work and it means you have to:

1. Know more about yourself.
   a. What are your strengths?
   b. How you can use your strengths to help you?
   c. What are your challenges?
   d. Who can help you?
   e. How can you get help to learn to overcome of
   to manage them.
2. How does your brain work?
   a. Can you read? When? How much?
   b. Can you write? When? How much?
   c. Can you fill out forms?
3. What is your behavior when you are:
   a. Angry
   b. Rushed
   c. Confused
   d. Worried
   e. Hurt
4. Dreams and goals you are working toward.
5. Have choices in your life areas

Social Security Benefits or SSI is a USA program that pays monthly checks to the elderly and people with disabilities who don't own much or who don't have much income. If you get SSI, you usually get food stamps and Medicaid, too. Medicaid helps pay doctor and hospital bills. You can also have a small job and that makes life more valuable because it gives you a purpose and by working you contribute to the whole community instead of just getting services.

Common Misinterpretations of Normal Responses in Adults with FASD

Behavior	Misinterpretation	Accurate Interpretation
Noncompliance	Wilful misconduct Attention seeking Stubborn	Difficulty translating verbal directions into action Doesn't understand
Repeatedly making the same mistakes	Wilful misconduct Manipulative	Cannot link cause to effect Cannot see similarities Difficulty generalizing
Often late	Lazy, slow Poor parenting Wilful misconduct	Cannot understand the abstract concept of time Needs assistance organizing
Not sitting still	Seeking attention Bothering others Wilful misconduct	Neurologically based need to move while learning Sensory overload
Poor social judgment	Poor parenting Wilful misconduct Abused child	Not able to interpret social cues from peers Does not know what to do
Overly physical	Wilful misconduct Deviancy	Hyper or hypo-sensitive to touch Does not understand social cues regarding boundaries
Does not work independently	Wilful misconduct Poor parenting	Chronic health problems Cannot translate verbal directions into action

1994, Debra L. Evenson, MA; Reproduced with permission

About the Author

Liz Kulp, was diagnosed with fetal alcohol spectrum disorders (FASD) as a young teen. Knowing her challenges and understanding her strengths helped her graduate from public high school and strive to move on to independent adulthood like her peers. But, she soon learned that life within the context of a family that understood and helped her gain the desire for independence had not prepared her to live in a world filled with predators and abstract thinking. Liz unashamedly lets readers inside the hidden world of adult transition for many of our young people with FASD.

It is a story you will not soon forget.

For speaking, workshops or wholesale books contact:
www.betterending.org

Braided cord : tough times in and out

31290094148632 BH

LaVergne, TN USA
24 October 2010

202031LV00004B/161/P